P9-BYY-420

NATURAL MICHIGAN

A NATURE LOVER'S GUIDE TO 228 ATTRACTIONS

by

Tom Powers

Friede Publications

Natural Michigan
Revised Edition

Copyright, 1995, by Tom Powers

This book may not be reproduced in whole or part
by mimeograph or any other means without permission.

Friede Publications
2239 Venezia Drive
Davison, Michigan 48423

Printed in the United States of America

ISBN 0-923756-13-2

OTHER GUIDEBOOKS BY FRIEDE PUBLICATIONS

Michigan State and National Parks: A Complete Guide

A Guide to 199 Michigan Waterfalls

Canoeing Michigan Rivers

A Traveler's Guide to 116 Michigan Lighthouses

A Traveler's Guide to 100 Eastern Great Lakes Lighthouses

A Traveler's Guide to 116 Western Great Lakes Lighthouses

Ultimate Michigan Adventures

Fish Michigan — 50 Rivers

Fish Michigan — 100 Southern Michigan Lakes

Fish Michigan — 100 Northern Michigan Lakes

Fish Michigan — 100 Upper Peninsula Lakes

CONTENTS

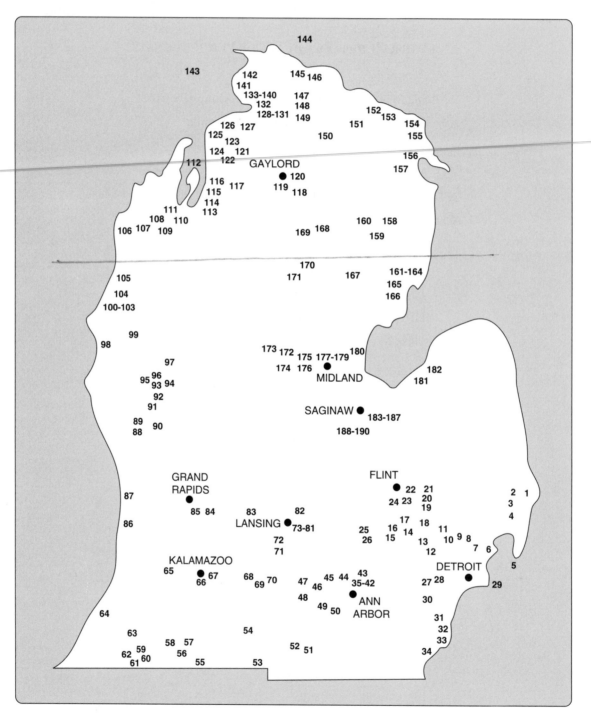

144

143

142
141
133-140
132
128-131

145 146

147
148
149

126 127
125
123
124 121
122

112

GAYLORD
● 120
119 118

152 153
154
155

151

150

156
157

116 117
115
114
113

111
108 110
106 107 109

160 158
169 168 159

105
104
100-103

170
171 167

161-164
165
166

98

99

97

173 172 175 177-179 180
174 176
MIDLAND ●

95 96
93 94
92
91

SAGINAW ●
183-187
188-190

182
181

89 90
88

GRAND
RAPIDS
●
85 84

FLINT

87

2 1
3
4

86

83 82
LANSING ●
73-81
72
71

● 22 21
20
24 23 19

17 18
16 14
25 15
26 13
12

11
10 9 8
7 6

5

KALAMAZOO
65 ●
66 67

68 70
69

43
47 35-42
46
48 ANN
49 50 ARBOR

45 44
●

DETROIT
27 28 ●
30

29

64

31
32
33

54

63
58 57
56
62 59
61 60
55

52 51
53

34

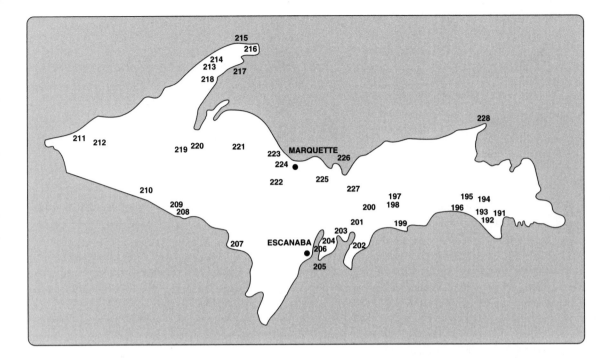

For Barb; Chris, Joane, Zachary and Samantha; and Stephanie, Timm and Bonny

ACKNOWLEDGMENTS

A book is never possible without the encouragement and expert assistance of an editor, publisher, layout artist, publicist, and creative consultant, all of which Gary Barf-knecht of Friede Publications does with the ease of changing hats.

Thanks also to long-time friends Dick Derenzy and Dennis Banks, who rode shotgun on my many forays. Dick said he was just along for the ride, but without his help I would still be floundering around on some nameless two-track. And Dennis made the long drives seem short and always knew north from south and east from west but rarely left from right.

And a special appreciative thank you to the Nature Conservancy, the Little Traverse Conservancy, the Michigan Nature Association, the Michigan Audubon Society, and other organizations that continue their fight to save our natural heritage.

Maps by Gary W. Barfknecht
All photos are by Tom Powers and Barb Powers unless otherwise noted.
Front cover photo: Jordan River Pathway (p. 129)
Photo, p. 246: Point Betsie Dunes Preserve (p. 112)
Back cover photo: Agate Beach Trail (p. 225)

SYMBOLS

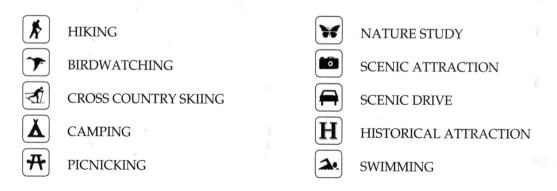

HIKING	NATURE STUDY
BIRDWATCHING	SCENIC ATTRACTION
CROSS COUNTRY SKIING	SCENIC DRIVE
CAMPING	HISTORICAL ATTRACTION
PICNICKING	SWIMMING

INTRODUCTION

In 1987 when *Natural Michigan* was first published, I wrote in the introduction that the book was written for people who needed "to escape the daily rigors, tensions and hassles of modern life by taking an hour's walk through a quiet, peaceful woods; by leaving civilization behind on a several-day-long backpacking expedition; or by birdwatching, beachcombing or simply enjoying a Sunday picnic in a beautiful setting."

It was gratifying to discover that there were a lot of people out there who, like me, enjoyed the solace, inspiration and peace of the natural world. *Natural Michigan* was so well-received that five years later *More Natural Michigan* was published. Between the two books, more than 300 natural areas, wildlife sanctuaries, nature centers, hiking trails and wilderness areas were identified, described and located. The first book also included selected state and national parks.

But things change (even natural areas) in eight years. Both books needed updating so that when using the books, you wouldn't encounter the very hassles you were seeking solace from.

This new, expanded edition of *Natural Michigan* is a combination of both books with some very important changes. First, you will not find any state or national parks in this new edition. You can find complete, in-depth descriptions of all of Michigan's state and national parks in my book, *Michigan State and National Parks: A Complete Guide*, which makes an excellent companion to this newly expanded *Natural Michigan*.

Second, information about the natural areas included is as current as possible. I contacted all the agencies and organizations — private and governmental — that manage the various areas and requested corrections and updates.

As a result, some attractions included in the earlier books were dropped because, for instance, trails are no longer maintained or sites are closed.

And third, I added several new natural areas. These new sites range from a spectacularly beautiful park at the tip of the Old Mission Peninsula near Traverse City to hiking trails through a wooded area on the Lansing outskirts that gives the appearance of being unchanged for the last hundred years.

In preparing this new edition I was once again struck by the amazing number and variety of Michigan's natural attractions. From vest-pocket parks to a wilderness tract of over 10,000 acres, Michigan offers outdoor lovers an almost unmatched opportunity to enjoy nature and marvel at its splendors.

If you used and reused the earlier books until they were held together with rubber bands and scotch tape, you will find this new edition equally indispensible for any trip through our great state. If you're picking up an edition of this book for the very first time, I trust it will guide you to hours, days and years of adventure and enjoyment discovering the wonders of natural Michigan.

Tom Powers
Flint Michigan

ST. CLAIR WOODS NATURE SANCTUARY 1

The Detroit Audubon Society and the Michigan Nature Association have combined four parcels of land, ranging in size from 7.5 to 75 acres, to create this 141-acre shelter for plants and animals, plus a place of peace, quiet and beauty for people. Maple, oak and birch — plus impressive stands of hemlock scattered throughout the south-central part — covers the property. The area also hosts ferns, shrubs and wildflowers, including three different types of trilliums (white, red and painted), cardinal flowers, Indian pipes and Michigan lily. Warblers, vireos, flycatchers, owls and Wood Ducks are among the many birds that nest in the sanctuary.

Though no formal trails run through the 41-acre Elmer P. Jasper Woods, a section owned by the M.N.A., guests are encouraged to leave a sand road that runs along the area's eastern edge and wander into the woods. Abutting Jasper Woods on its eastern edge is a 75-acre parcel owned by the Detroit Audubon Society. There, a 1.5-mile trail, which begins on the sand road, gradually heads south through imposing hemlock groves to a small stream.

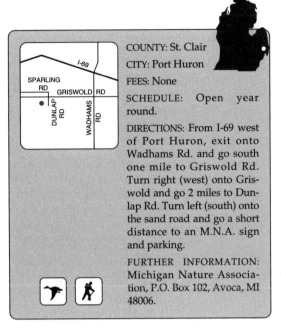

COUNTY: St. Clair

CITY: Port Huron

FEES: None

SCHEDULE: Open year round.

DIRECTIONS: From I-69 west of Port Huron, exit onto Wadhams Rd. and go south one mile to Griswold Rd. Turn right (west) onto Griswold and go 2 miles to Dunlap Rd. Turn left (south) onto the sand road and go a short distance to an M.N.A. sign and parking.

FURTHER INFORMATION: Michigan Nature Association, P.O. Box 102, Avoca, MI 48006.

2 PINE RIVER NATURE SANCTUARY

Soon after it had acquired this 17.5-acre parcel in 1963, the Michigan Nature Association conducted a 24-hour bird count and found 65 species within their tiny preserve. Ruffled Grouse Whip-poor-wills, Wood Ducks and Great Horned Owls, for example, regularly nest in the sanctuary, and warblers and songbirds are regular visitors along the river, especially in the spring.

Plant life, too, thrives in this peaceful, secluded section of central St. Clair County. A beech/maple/hemlock forest — with a scattering of white pine, black cherry, chickory, cottonwood and witch hazel — cover a varied terrain made up of rolling hills, riverbanks, flood plain and low ravines. Several interesting species of fern as well as a profusion of spring wildflowers make annual appearances within the sanctuary.

A mile-long trail, which begins at the rear of the parking area in the northwest corner of the property, meanders across the upland forest, dips into a ravine, then officially ends at the banks of the Pine River. During normal water levels, however, hikers can ford the stream if they wish and explore a small area of the park on the opposite bank.

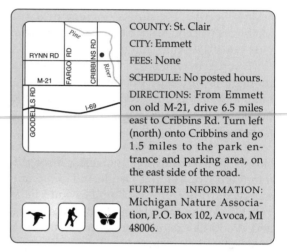

COUNTY: St. Clair

CITY: Emmett

FEES: None

SCHEDULE: No posted hours.

DIRECTIONS: From Emmett on old M-21, drive 6.5 miles east to Cribbins Rd. Turn left (north) onto Cribbins and go 1.5 miles to the park entrance and parking area, on the east side of the road.

FURTHER INFORMATION: Michigan Nature Association, P.O. Box 102, Avoca, MI 48006.

BRENNAN NATURE SANCTUARY 3

If you could attribute human characteristics to nature areas, you'd call Brennan Nature Sanctuary "bashful." This 118-acre Michigan Nature Association parcel is surrounded by the unremarkable, tabletop-flat farmland of central St. Clair County; its existence is marked only by a small, simple and unobtrusive sign; and you have to walk at least a hundred yards into the preserve before it begins to reveal its unpretentious beauty. But once there, you'll fall in love with Brennan's untrampled and varied landscape, the wide variety of flora and fauna, and the peace and solitude.

A hundred yards east of Bricker Road, a glass-covered display case briefly describes the area's natural features, and from there a two-mile-long trail plunges into an impressive stand of red pine called Inspiration Grove. The tightly spaced, mature trees have softened the trail with a thick carpet of fallen needles. The narrow path emerges from the cool, quiet glade into an open meadow dotted with Bluebird boxes, and if you pause for only a few minutes, you'll usually be rewarded with the sighting of one of the delightful, beautiful birds. From the meadow the trail descends to the flood plain of the Pine River.

It's along the Pine, which can't seem to run in a straight line for more than a dozen yards before breaking into S curves, that the preserve is at its prettiest. Thick woods crowd the low banks and create a vaulted ceiling over the slow-moving water. In many places, ferns cover the forest floor and add a lacy accent to the scene. Where the trees thin out, cattail marshes and swamps border the river.

You can walk the trail in under an hour, but you can also easily spend half a day seeking out and closely observing the profusion of plant and animal life. Michigan lilies, jewel-

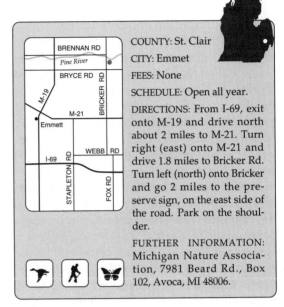

COUNTY: St. Clair

CITY: Emmet

FEES: None

SCHEDULE: Open all year.

DIRECTIONS: From I-69, exit onto M-19 and drive north about 2 miles to M-21. Turn right (east) onto M-21 and drive 1.8 miles to Bricker Rd. Turn left (north) onto Bricker and go 2 miles to the preserve sign, on the east side of the road. Park on the shoulder.

FURTHER INFORMATION: Michigan Nature Association, 7981 Beard Rd., Box 102, Avoca, MI 48006.

weed, wild iris and numerous other wildflowers thrive in the sanctuary, and eastern hemlock, white spruce, white pine, balsam fir, beech and maple are among the many trees you'll find here.

Thirty-seven species make up the list of birds that have nested in the 118 acres. Warbling Vireos, Bob-o-links, Acadian Flycatchers, Red-eyed Vireos, Yellow Warblers and Northern Yellow-throat Warblers, in addition to Bluebirds, all raise young on the preserve. Those and the other nesting species, plus birds you might see during migration seasons, add up to some prime birdwatching opportunities.

4 TRILLIUM TRAIL NATURE PRESERVE

From the entrance to this Michigan Nature Association sanctuary, an easily walked, quarter-mile trail takes you to a secluded, undisturbed 21-acre pocket of unique natural beauty. The lightly used path descends to a valley, where brush that crowds the trail and imposing hardwoods draped with hanging vines effectively cut you off from sight and sound of the surrounding farms, homes and highways. On the valley floor the trail crosses a small stream on a narrow footbridge, then begins to rise up the opposite side. Just before the trail climbs completely out of the valley and enters a meadow, a narrow footpath breaks off to the right and etches the edge of the steep hillside.

It is there that this preserve lives up to its name. Large-flowered white trillium — fairly rare now in Michigan because of the disappearance of woodland where it thrives — blanket the hill. During the first three weeks of May when the trillium bloom, you can be treated to a magnificent display of white flowers cascading down the hillside. May apples, violets and numerous other flowers also splash color onto the scene. From the trail the view of the long-undisturbed valley floor — filled with fallen trees, towering hardwoods and numerous shrubs — is equally impressive.

As evidenced by the nearly continuous symphony of singing and loud calling, birds especially like the shrubs and forest understory in the valley. It does, however, take both binoculars and patience to find them flitting around in the thick vegetation.

You can walk the entire preserve in 30 minutes, but don't be surprised if you end up spending hours searching for and identifying wildflowers or sitting on the hillside contemplating the beautiful lushness of the scenery.

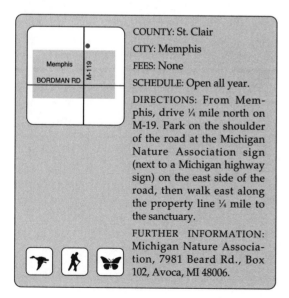

COUNTY: St. Clair

CITY: Memphis

FEES: None

SCHEDULE: Open all year.

DIRECTIONS: From Memphis, drive ¼ mile north on M-19. Park on the shoulder of the road at the Michigan Nature Association sign (next to a Michigan highway sign) on the east side of the road, then walk east along the property line ¼ mile to the sanctuary.

FURTHER INFORMATION: Michigan Nature Association, 7981 Beard Rd., Box 102, Avoca, MI 48006.

Whether you're touring the area or just studying it on a map, Harsens Island looks like it's 2,000 miles out of place. No one speaks Cajun here, you won't find Creole cooking, and there are no stilt houses. But the levees, dikes, mud flats, sometimes-indeterminate shoreline, open water, and wide expanse of grass-filled marshes seem like they should be part of the Mississippi Delta rather than Michigan's Lake St. Clair.

Harsens Island is, in fact, a part of a delta, but one formed by the St. Clair River and named the St. Clair Flats. For thousands of years, the river has taken in countless tons of sediment from the upper Great Lakes, carried it, then dropped its load when it emptied into Lake St. Clair. Those deposits of mud, sand, gravel and silt created a group of more than a dozen islands with convoluted shorelines that fit together as snugly as a jigsaw puzzle. The land is so low that in many places you can barely keep your feet dry. This complex and fascinating system of land, water, and areas that can't make up their mind which they are, is the largest delta in the Great Lakes.

Easiest to get to and easiest to see and see from is Harsen's Island. Its sheltered waters, sparse population and abundant wildlife make it a favored, no-frills recreation area for nature lovers.

Birdwatchers, including several Audubon clubs that make annual pilgrimages, are drawn to Harsens in spring and fall to enjoy the large number and variety of waterfowl that call here on their way north and south. Birders don't have to work hard here. Roads that skirt the numerous marshes and border the many bays and inlets make excellent observation platforms. Swans, ducks, gallinules, terns, gulls and grebes dot the open water and, in many cases, paddle about

their business only yards away from slowly moving cars. And if you're patient and careful, a search of the interior and along dense marshes that border many of the roads will turn up a wide assortment of marsh birds.

Harsens is also a great place to simply take a pleasant drive amid some of nature's most unique handiwork The island's most-striking and unusual physical feature is at its southern end. There, two long, low and narrow strips of land, separated by Little Muscamoot Bay, look like a pair of tails extending far out into Lake St. Clair.

A narrow gravel road traces the spine of each tail, and the roadbeds are, in many instances, the only high and dry land in a broad expanse of marsh and open water. Along the Middle Channel Drive, on the west tail, you come as close to boating on four wheels as it's possible to do without leaving a wake. Also, in places along that drive, the tail broadens to permit turnouts and at times even fattens enough to allow houses and cottages to be built on land virtually surrounded by water.

Other roads border the St. Clair Flats

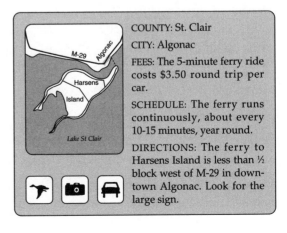

COUNTY: St. Clair

CITY: Algonac

FEES: The 5-minute ferry ride costs $3.50 round trip per car.

SCHEDULE: The ferry runs continuously, about every 10-15 minutes, year round.

DIRECTIONS: The ferry to Harsens Island is less than ½ block west of M-29 in downtown Algonac. Look for the large sign.

Wildlife Area, which covers almost half the island.

Not surprisingly, boaters and fishermen delight in the playground of bays, channels and sheltered backwaters. Twelve-foot bruised and battered aluminum fishing boats share the waterways with luxury motor yachts, sailboats of every description, and 600-foot-plus Great Lakes freighters and ocean-going ships.

The best views of the constant parade in the main shipping channel come from South Channel Drive, which follows the island's east shore.

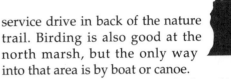

What's a park that's located on the fringes of the state's largest metropolitan area, whose 3,000-foot-long stretch of sand — the world's largest manmade beach — attracts a staggering number of swimmers and sunbathers on sizzling summer days, and whose parking lot is larger than many other Michigan parks doing in a book titled *Natural Michigan*?

Because in spite of the crowds, commotion and acres of asphalt, the park, located on the shores of Lake St. Clair, is one of the two or three best birding spots in the state. Extensive marshes, open water and woods away from the manmade attractions, plus the park's location on a major bird migration route are reasons that 260 species — some in large concentrations and 80 of which have nested here — have been spotted in Metro Beach Metropark.

The park is equally good for both waterfowl and shorebirds and is one of the best places in the state to see warblers during their spring migration. A short list of the diverse and interesting species you might spot here includes: Red-throated Loon, Red-necked Grebe, Tundra Swan, Snowy Owl, Oldsquaw Duck, Ruddy Duck, Osprey, Water Pipit, Loggerhead Shrike, Prothonotory Warbler, Northern Parula Warbler, Cerulean Warbler, Lapland Longspur, Virginia Rail, Yellow-billed Cuckoo, and Glaucous, California, Iceland and Franklin gulls.

For such a relatively short walk, a 0.75-mile nature trail that circles south along the western edge of the parking lot through woods, thickets and marsh and by a pond always holds great potential for seeing a large number of birds. Other prime areas for birdwatching include the park's two boat basins, a picnic area on Huron Point, the entrance drive that cuts through the south marsh, and the

service drive in back of the nature trail. Birding is also good at the north marsh, but the only way into that area is by boat or canoe.

Helpful literature — including lists of birds, fish, plants, wildflowers and wildlife common to the park and a flyer describing the ecosystem of the marsh — are available at park headquarters, at the southern edge of the huge parking area. The park's staff also conducts a wide range of nature programs throughout the year. For topics and schedules, write the address listed in Further Information.

Other attractions include a grass-covered, tree-shaded picnic area that extends into Lake St. Clair on a small picturesque peninsula. You can work off your lunch, if need be, on a fitness hiking trail that circles the grounds. Shorefishermen congregate on the eastern tip of this peninsula, and sailboarders cruise along the western side. You can get to the

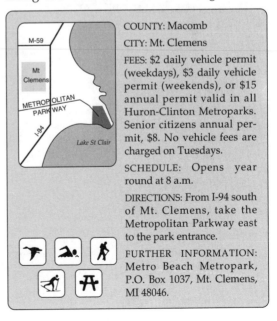

COUNTY: Macomb

CITY: Mt. Clemens

FEES: $2 daily vehicle permit (weekdays), $3 daily vehicle permit (weekends), or $15 annual permit valid in all Huron-Clinton Metroparks. Senior citizens annual permit, $8. No vehicle fees are charged on Tuesdays.

SCHEDULE: Opens year round at 8 a.m.

DIRECTIONS: From I-94 south of Mt. Clemens, take the Metropolitan Parkway east to the park entrance.

FURTHER INFORMATION: Metro Beach Metropark, P.O. Box 1037, Mt. Clemens, MI 48046.

peninsula's point either by walking or by taking a trackless train from the parking lot.

Unique to Metro beach is the Voyageur Canoe, an exact replica of the type of canoes early fur traders and explorers used to journey throughout the Great Lakes area. The 34-foot-long craft, which is available for group charters, makes hour-long trips from the North Marina into the 213-acre north marsh section of the park.

Other diverse Metro Beach Metropark facil-ities, services and activities — not all of which are usually associated with the Huron-Clinton Metro Parks system or any state or local parks, for that matter — include three marinas, a putt-putt golf course, a tot lot, a huge swimming pool, a bath house, an 18-hole par-three golf course, basketball courts, a dance area, and tennis courts.

Winter visitors can cross country ski, ice skate and ice fish.

STERLING HEIGHTS NATURE CENTER 7

The Sterling Heights Nature Center proves you don't always have to be in the out-of-doors to enjoy or appreciate nature. The focus on nature here is in a cozy brick building that overlooks a large, grassy meadow on the Clinton River.

In one small exhibit wing, stuffed wildlife — including a fox, an opossum, owls and hawks — perch on the rafters, climb the walls, and sit on tables waiting stoically to be examined. Environmental education exhibits and displays help fill the room, and children will especially like a hands-on nature exhibit.

In another wing a wide variety of science and nature programs are regularly presented in a comfortable auditorium. Nature films feature National Geographic and Disney releases, and a lecture series covers nature topics from around the globe, such as hikers who visited the Galapagos Islands and a naturalist's tour of Shenandoah National Park. Close-to-home nature study isn't overlooked, and sometimes the lectures move into a more natural setting outside.

A footbridge near the nature center crosses the river and provides access to more than 400 acres of parkland and five miles of paved trails. White-tail deer, red fox, horned owls and soft-shell turtles are occasionally spotted along the routes.

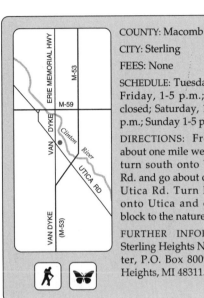

COUNTY: Macomb

CITY: Sterling

FEES: None

SCHEDULE: Tuesday through Friday, 1-5 p.m.; Monday, closed; Saturday, 10 a.m. - 5 p.m.; Sunday 1-5 p.m.

DIRECTIONS: From M-59 about one mile west of M-53, turn south onto Van Dyke Rd. and go about one mile to Utica Rd. Turn left (east) onto Utica and drive one block to the nature center.

FURTHER INFORMATION: Sterling Heights Nature Center, P.O. Box 8009, Sterling Heights, MI 48311.

8 WILCOX-WARNES NATURE SANCTUARY

The Wilcox-Warnes Memorial Nature Sanctuary proves that nature, if left to its own devices, is more than capable of producing an arboretum the equal of any planned or nurtured by humans. More than 365 plant species grow at this 45-acre Michigan Nature Association preserve, and they're divided between two unequal and contrasting sections.

The northern 18 acres is a farm field that last felt a plow in 1957. Nature took over, and the old field is now undergoing plant succession. Small trees and shrubs crowd most of the acreage and compete for dominance.

The southern 27 acres has never been plowed or even grazed and, as a result, is covered by an impressive stand of old-growth hardwoods. Beech, red maple, white ash, oak, basswood, cherry, walnut, shagbark hickory and more than 400 tuliptrees grow in this part of the preserve. A small stream cuts across the southwest corner of the old woods, and a vernal pond fosters aquatic life in the spring.

Trillium, monkeyflower, bittersweet, Mayapple and Jack-in-the-pulpit help make up an impressive collection of wildflowers. And the long list of shrubs and small trees includes sassafras, willow, prickly ash, serviceberry and flowering dogwood.

Bring a field guide to fully appreciate the amazing variety of plant life here. But you don't have to identify a single specimen to enjoy the abundant overall natural beauty that, because of the predominance of hardwoods, is especially memorable during fall color.

Narrow, easily walked trails crisscross the entire preserve, and the dense woods and underbrush shelter Woodcock, Ruffed Grouse, owls, hawks and songbirds. Deer tracks indent almost every piece of bare earth.

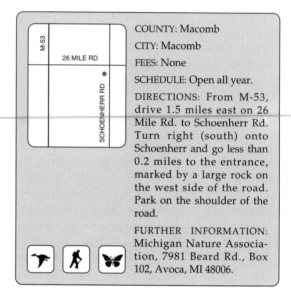

COUNTY: Macomb

CITY: Macomb

FEES: None

SCHEDULE: Open all year.

DIRECTIONS: From M-53, drive 1.5 miles east on 26 Mile Rd. to Schoenherr Rd. Turn right (south) onto Schoenherr and go less than 0.2 miles to the entrance, marked by a large rock on the west side of the road. Park on the shoulder of the road.

FURTHER INFORMATION: Michigan Nature Association, 7981 Beard Rd., Box 102, Avoca, MI 48006.

STONY CREEK METROPARK 9

Centered by a manmade lake, 4,461-acre Stony Creek Metropark is an excellent place to study nature and enjoy the out-of-doors.

The focal point for natural activities is a Nature Center, located in the northern part of the park. Maps to three self-guided nature trails, totaling 4.25 miles and ranging in length from 0.5 to 2.5 miles, are available at the Nature Center building. These paths wind alongside Stony Creek (which flows south to Stony Creek Lake), climb morainal hills, and pass through hardwood forests, open fields and marshes. Interpretive signs mark points of interest. A wildflower checklist, also available at the building, numbers an impressive 180 varieties, and a similar list of bird species numbers 170. The Nature Center building houses exhibits and displays, including a bird-feeding station. Nature programs and workshops are also held at the Center.

South of the natural area, a variety of facilities and attractions — including eight picnic areas, two swimming beaches, a boat-launching site (south shore), a boat-rental concession (north shore) and an 18-hole golf course (west shore) — encircle Stony Creek Lake, created by the damming of the creek from which it gets its name. All are connected by a scenic (especially during fall color) 10-mile paved road that circles the lake. A 6.2-mile-long paved hiking/bike trail also follows the lakeshore.

Fishing is good in Stony Creek Lake for pike walleyes, smallmouth bass and panfish. Shorefishing is permitted except north of 28 Mile Road, which separates the nature-study area from the other facilities.

Cross country skiers, ice fishermen and sledders can enjoy the park in the winter.

COUNTY: Macomb

CITY: Romeo /Washington

FEES: $2 daily vehicle permit (weekdays), $3 daily vehicle permit on Saturdays, Sundays and holidays, $15 annual permit valid in all Metroparks. Senior citizen annual permit, $8. Free entry on Tuesdays.

SCHEDULE: The park is open year round, 7 a.m. - 10 p.m. Nature trails are open May through September, 6 a.m. - 10 p.m. and October through April, 8 a.m. - 8 p.m. The Nature Center Building is open during the summer months, Monday through Friday, 10 a.m. - 5 p.m.; during the school year, Monday through Friday, 1 p.m. - 5 p.m.; and weekends year round, 10 a.m. - 5 p.m.

DIRECTIONS: To reach the Nature Center, take M-53 north of Utica to 26 Mile Rd. Turn west onto 26 Mile and go approximately 1.5 miles to Mound Rd. Turn right (north) onto Mound and go approximately 3.5 miles to Inwood Rd. Turn left (west) onto Inwood and drive ½ mile to the entrance.

To reach the picnic and beach area, take M-53 6 miles north of Utica to 26 Mile Rd. Go west on 26 Mile 1.5 miles to the entrance.

FURTHER INFORMATION: Stony Creek Metropark, 4300 Main Park Rd., Shelby Township, MI 48316.

10 DINOSAUR HILL NATURE CENTER

Though diminutive at 16 acres, Dinosaur Hill Nature Center is supercharged with natural programs and activities. Guided nature walks for groups of all ages, school programs, slide shows, plus outreach and regularly scheduled classes on nature study for preschoolers through senior citizens make this center the Rochester area's headquarters for nature education.

The center, named after a hill that local children believed looked like a sleeping dinosaur, is also a quiet, beautiful place to walk or bicycle. Three self-guided nature trails, totaling two miles, wind through the grounds: seven acres of woodland, open fields, a small swamp and wetlands, all bordered by Paint Creek.

The trails are open for cross country skiing in winter.

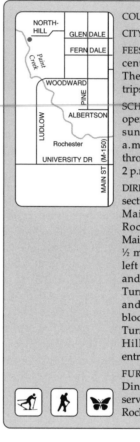

COUNTY: Oakland

CITY: Rochester

FEES: No charge to visit the center and walk the trails. There is a charge for field trips and programs.

SCHEDULE: The preserve is open year round, sunrise to sunset. Office hours are 9 a.m. - 5 p.m., Monday through Friday, and 10 a.m. - 2 p.m.on Saturdays.

DIRECTIONS: From the intersection of University Dr. and Main St. in downtown Rochester, drive north on Main (M-150) approximately ½ mile to Woodward. Turn left (west) onto Woodward and go 2 blocks to Oak St. Turn right (north) onto Oak and go approximately 6 blocks to North Hill Circle. Turn left (west) onto North Hill and drive to the entrance.

FURTHER INFORMATION: Dinosaur Hill Nature Preserve, 333 North Hill Circle, Rochester, MI 48307.

ADDISON OAKS COUNTY PARK 11

Don't think of this 794-acre outdoor playground as just a county park, but rather as a full-service resort. Whether for a day trip or week-long camping vacation, there's something at Addison Oaks — with its spring-fed lakes, hiking and biking trails, campground and much more — to keep just about everyone busy. Or if busy doesn't fit into your definition of vacation, there's plenty of opportunity for solitude and do-nothing relaxation amid striking natural beauty.

Near the park entrance, an immense picnic area spreads over a lush lawn the envy of most homeowners. You can pick from both sunny and shady sites, and many of the tables and grills cozy up to two spring-fed lakes that flank the area. Other facilities at the huge outdoor dining area include pavilions and a large playground.

The crystal-clear waters of Buhl Lake make an inviting swimming hole, especially from a sandy area fronting the east side of the picnic grounds. There's no public launch onto Buhl and the park's other lake, pond-size Adams Lake, but fishermen and boaters can coast across its quiet waters in rental rowboats, pedal boats and canoes.

Etching the park's eastern half are four hiking trails, totaling over four miles in length, that follow the shore of Buhl Lake, cross open meadows, pass small wetlands and roll over countryside studded with stands of pine, sugar maple, willow and oak.

For some real exercise, bring your mountain bike and cruise five miles of mountain bike trails that furrow the western half of the park. Four main trails and their connecting loops make it possible for peddlers to complete a circuit of less than a mile or bull their way through the full five-mile route through the rolling countryside. Rental mountain bikes are available.

Near the back of the park, 93 modern, semimodern and primitive campsites snuggle in the woods away from most of the day-use activities. Modern sites are grass-carpeted with concrete slips and electricity and water hookups. All are close to a modern restroom/shower building. Primitive sites are laid out in deep shade next to the largest tract of undisturbed woodland in the park.

Fun doesn't stop when the snow falls. Twelve miles of groomed cross country ski trails snake through the park, and skaters and fishermen dot the two lakes when they freeze over. A lighted, 1.5-mile ski trail is open on Friday and Saturday nights. Special events and learn-to-ski schools are popular winter festivities.

A bountiful variety of Michigan flora grows in the park, and birdwatching opportunities are excellent.

COUNTY: Oakland

CITY: Leonard

FEES: A daily vehicle permit is $3.50 for Oakland County residents and $7 for non-residents on weekdays, and $4.50 for residents and $8 for non-residents on weekends and holidays. Annual vehicle permits are $22 for residents, $44 for non-residents and $15 for resident senior citizens. Seniors pay $1 on weekdays and the regular rate on weekends/holidays.

SCHEDULE: 8 a.m. - dusk.

DIRECTIONS: From Rochester drive 9 miles north on Rochester Rd. to Romeo Rd. Turn left (west) onto Romeo and drive 2 miles to the park entrance.

FURTHER INFORMATION: Addison Oaks County Park, 1480 W. Romeo Rd., Leonard, MI 48367-3706.

12 CRANBROOK GARDENS

The view of the grounds from the west terrace of the Cranbrook Estate leaves no room for doubt that you are overlooking one of the great formal gardens in the Midwest.

George Booth and his wife, Ellen Scripts Booth, built a huge English country manor on rolling Oakland County farmland in 1908. In keeping with the beautiful mansion, they designed and built formal gardens on the west side of the house. In 1934 the Booths donated the gardens to Cranbrook Institute, which not only maintained their original beauty, but also made them available for all of us to enjoy.

Within the 12-foot-high fieldstone walls that frame the garden area, 5,000 annuals fill your eyes with a kaleidoscope of color and beauty, which reaches its peak of magnificence in late summer. Red brick walkways, gravel paths, sculptures, fountains and pools add to the enchantment of the scene, and because different flowers are planted each year, the show changes from summer to summer.

Dazzling landscaping isn't confined to the formal garden. At the back of the house, a spacious lawn sweeps down to a manmade lake, and you can find countless specimen trees throughout the grounds. An oriental garden, a Greek theater, a natural-looking grove of pine trees, a field sprinkled every spring with over a thousand daffodils, a rock garden, redbud and dogwood trees, massed plantings of perennials, and ornamental shrubs all ensure an ever-changing show from spring to fall.

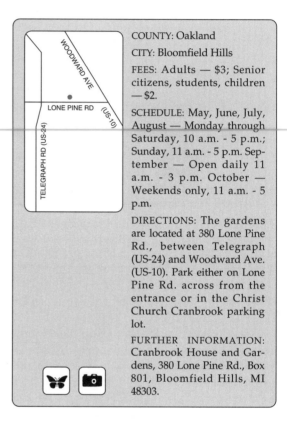

COUNTY: Oakland

CITY: Bloomfield Hills

FEES: Adults — $3; Senior citizens, students, children — $2.

SCHEDULE: May, June, July, August — Monday through Saturday, 10 a.m. - 5 p.m.; Sunday, 11 a.m. - 5 p.m. September — Open daily 11 a.m. - 3 p.m. October — Weekends only, 11 a.m. - 5 p.m.

DIRECTIONS: The gardens are located at 380 Lone Pine Rd., between Telegraph (US-24) and Woodward Ave. (US-10). Park either on Lone Pine Rd. across from the entrance or in the Christ Church Cranbrook parking lot.

FURTHER INFORMATION: Cranbrook House and Gardens, 380 Lone Pine Rd., Box 801, Bloomfield Hills, MI 48303.

E.L. JOHNSON NATURE CENTER 13

Surrounded by highways and the hustle and bustle of a busy suburban community, the E.L. Johnson Nature Center gives refuge to fox, deer, a woodchuck, raccoons, squirrels, and a host of other wildlife.

Owned and operated by the Bloomfield Hills School District, the 32-acre center is a "special outdoor learning area set aside to develop and encourage outdoor/environmental/ecological education and activities for students and community." To that end the nature center's educational programs are an integral part of the school district's curriculum from kindergarten through high school. Year-round programming for adults includes ecology walks, bird-banding demonstrations, and maple sugar making.

Or you can skip the formal programs and just take a quiet, peaceful walk along any of five nature trails that wind through the preserve's acreage, which is almost equally divided between woodland and open fields. The mile and a half's worth of paths cut through an impressive stand of pine, border a large tree-lined pond, pass a maple sugar shack, and edge pleasant meadows. A small stream, native wildflowers, and the rocky debris from glaciers that passed this way thousands of years ago add interest to any walk. Many of the trees and shrubs along the routes are labeled, so even an informal outing can turn into an educational experience.

The wide diversity of habitat, good cover and several feeding stations encourage numerous birds to set up housekeeping here, so bring binoculars and a bird identification book.

Children will be especially delighted with close-up views of penned owls, hawks and two deer so tame they walk up to the fence and almost ask to be petted.

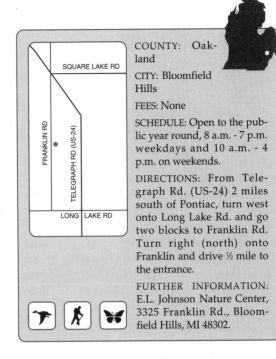

COUNTY: Oakland

CITY: Bloomfield Hills

FEES: None

SCHEDULE: Open to the public year round, 8 a.m. - 7 p.m. weekdays and 10 a.m. - 4 p.m. on weekends.

DIRECTIONS: From Telegraph Rd. (US-24) 2 miles south of Pontiac, turn west onto Long Lake Rd. and go two blocks to Franklin Rd. Turn right (north) onto Franklin and drive ½ mile to the entrance.

FURTHER INFORMATION: E.L. Johnson Nature Center, 3325 Franklin Rd., Bloomfield Hills, MI 48302.

14 DRAYTON PLAINS NATURE CENTER

Wildflower walks, bird and tree identification, maple sugaring and general tours are among the variety of programs the 137-acre Drayton Plains Nature Center conducts year round to introduce nature to the general public.

Eight nature trails, including two that are self-guiding, wind for 7.25 miles through the private, non-profit organization's grounds, which include woodlands, open fields, 10 acres of marsh, and ponds, all located on the banks of the Clinton River. A waterfowl wildlife refuge and nesting area is also within the sanctuary's boundaries.

One trail is open in the winter for cross country skiing.

COUNTY: Oakland

CITY: Waterford

FEES: None

SCHEDULE: The grounds are open daily 8 a.m. - 8 p.m. The Interpretive Center is open Tuesday through Friday, 11 a.m. - 2 p.m.; Saturday 10 a.m. - 4 p.m.; and Sunday, 12 - 4 p.m.

DIRECTIONS: Two miles north of the Pontiac city limits on US-24, turn west onto Hatchery Rd. and go ½ mile to Edmore Rd. Turn left (south) onto Edmore and to go Denby Dr. Bear right, onto Denby, and follow it to the entrance.

FURTHER INFORMATION: Drayton Plains Nature Center, 2125 Denby Rd., Waterford, MI 48329.

INDIAN SPRINGS METROPARK 15

Michigan maps of the early 1800s usually had two words printed across most of the Lower Peninsula: *interminable swamp.* In the southeastern part of the state, one of the dominant natural features that contributed to that label was the great Huron Swamp. Today, one of the last vestiges of that unique physical landmark remains at Indian Springs Metropark.

But there's much more to this, one of the newest Huron-Clinton Metroparks (opened 1982), than just a look at the "interminable swamp." Open fields, hardwood forests, a pond and the headwaters of the Huron River also make up its 2,000 acres, and the area is rich in plant and animal life. The park's bird checklist, for example, numbers more than 140 species. More than 200 wildflowers are native to the area, and especially beautiful in the spring are abundant marsh marigolds in the wetlands.

The best way to explore and enjoy the area is on nearly six miles of nature trails. The Woodland Trail — four loops of 0.75, 1.25, 2 and 3.5 miles respectively — heads through marshy lowlands and deep woods. The paths also cross and recross the Huron River where here, at its headwaters, it is almost small enough to jump. The Woodland Trail is especially enjoyable for spring wildflowers and fall color.

Best for summer wildflowers is the Farmland Trail, a 1.5-mile round trip along forest edges and open fields. As its name suggests, the short, paved Pondside Trail circles the park's pond. And as in most Huron-Clinton metroparks, a five-mile biking, hiking and jogging trail roams through the far reaches of the park. This paved path begins at the large Meadow Lark Picnic Area.

At the end of the entrance road in the solar-

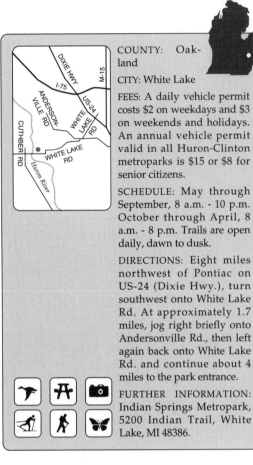

COUNTY: Oakland

CITY: White Lake

FEES: A daily vehicle permit costs $2 on weekdays and $3 on weekends and holidays. An annual vehicle permit valid in all Huron-Clinton metroparks is $15 or $8 for senior citizens.

SCHEDULE: May through September, 8 a.m. - 10 p.m. October through April, 8 a.m. - 8 p.m. Trails are open daily, dawn to dusk.

DIRECTIONS: Eight miles northwest of Pontiac on US-24 (Dixie Hwy.), turn southwest onto White Lake Rd. At approximately 1.7 miles, jog right briefly onto Andersonville Rd., then left again back onto White Lake Rd. and continue about 4 miles to the park entrance.

FURTHER INFORMATION: Indian Springs Metropark, 5200 Indian Trail, White Lake, MI 48386.

heated nature center, displays and exhibits explain the history and natural significance of the area, plus nature walks and workshops are conducted year round.

All trails are open for cross country skiing in the winter.

16 TIMBERLAND SWAMP

Scattered across the lower part of the state, sometimes surprisingly close to major metropolitan areas, are remnants of the great wilderness that formed in Michigan as the last glaciers retreated. No matter how large or small, these last precious outposts of prehistoric Michigan inspire a feeling of awe and a unique appreciation of nature within all who see them. The Timberland Swamp Nature Sanctuary is one such area.

Just minutes from Pontiac and Detroit, yet virtually untouched by man except for a brief stint of hardwood logging, Timberland Swamp is not only a quiet, secluded retreat from the modern world but also a showcase of nature. This 245-acre preserve and Indian Springs Metropark, which almost surrounds

it, together form an 800-acre swamp that gives birth to three magnificent rivers: the Huron, the Shiawassee and a branch of the Clinton.

A path that penetrates the swamp and woodlands from the end of Ware Road is a good place to enjoy a natural theater, beginning with a spectacular wildflower show every spring. Trillium literally carpets the forest floor in early May, and hundreds of other wildflowers add diversity and color throughout spring. The swamp also nurtures a wide variety of trees, including maples, beech and a few virgin oaks. Fox, deer, opossum, mink, woodchuck, snakes, turtles, salamanders and frogs find shelter in the swamp.

Waterthrushes, flycatchers, owls and grouse are among the many birds that inhabit the area. Thirteen species of warblers — including the beautiful blue, black and white-painted Cerulian Warbler — nest in the sanctuary. Birdwatchers also have a fair chance of seeing such relatively rare species as Cooper's Hawk and Pileated Woodpecker.

The preservation of this magnificent remnant of what was Michigan before settlers drained and tilled the soil, is an outstanding example of the work of the Michigan Nature association. The organization, dedicated to preserving natural areas in Michigan, persevered for 11 years to acquire the land in this sanctuary.

Though the sanctuary is open to the public, please remember that this is private land and that you are the guest of the M.N.A.

COUNTY: Oakland

CITY: Clarkston

FEES: None

SCHEDULE: No posted hours.

DIRECTIONS: From I-75 west of Clarkston, take exit 92 and drive south on Dixie Highway approximately 1.6 miles to White Lake Rd. Turn right (south) onto White Lake and drive about 2 miles to Andersonville Rd. Turn right (west) onto Andersonville and follow it northwest 3 miles to Big Lake Rd. Turn left (west) onto Big Lake and go for a short distance to Ware Rd. Turn left (south) onto Ware and proceed to the sanctuary entrance.

FURTHER INFORMATION: Michigan Nature Association, P.O. Box 102, Avoca, MI 48006.

INDEPENDENCE OAKS COUNTY PARK 17

Scenic views, a wide variety of plant and animal life, and good birdwatching come from 10 miles of hiking and nature trails that wind through valleys, over forested hills, across creeks and marshes, and around Crooked Lake at this 1,088-acre Oakland County Park.

Crooked Lake, which runs north and south, divides the park into nearly equal halves. Beaches, boat ramps, playgrounds, picnic areas and a ball field line the east shoreline. The headwaters of the Clinton River also pass through this section of the park in a low marsh area.

Across the lake, which acts as a barrier to the noisier day-use activities, a Nature Center is the starting point for the quiet and peace of the hiking trails, which vary in length from 0.4 to 3 miles. Trail maps are available at the 4,000-square-foot building, which overlooks a picturesque creek, and a variety of education nature programs are also conducted there.

All facilities at the park are barrier-free. In addition, the All Visitors Trail — a short, paved trail beginning on the east side of the lake near the boathouse — is specifically designed for the handicapped.

All of the trails are not only open, but also groomed in the winter for cross country skiers. Other winter facilities for skiers include a warming house, a concession stand and restrooms. For snow conditions call (810) 625-0877 or (810) 625-6473.

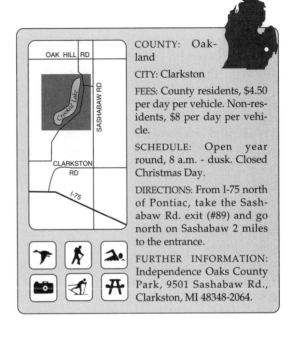

COUNTY: Oakland

CITY: Clarkston

FEES: County residents, $4.50 per day per vehicle. Non-residents, $8 per day per vehicle.

SCHEDULE: Open year round, 8 a.m. - dusk. Closed Christmas Day.

DIRECTIONS: From I-75 north of Pontiac, take the Sashabaw Rd. exit (#89) and go north on Sashabaw 2 miles to the entrance.

FURTHER INFORMATION: Independence Oaks County Park, 9501 Sashabaw Rd., Clarkston, MI 48348-2064.

18 ORION OAKS COUNTY PARK

Most people will look at this 927-acre tract of Oakland County land and think about what a nice park it will be, once developed. Nature lovers will see a lush, wild tract of land that suits them just fine as is.

Future plans may include facilities for activites such as camping, boating fishing, nature study and winter recreation. What you get until the park's master plan is finalized is a land of open meadows, stands of dense woods, wetlands and — a true rarity for Oakland County — a 90-acre lake devoid of development.

Marked trails from parking lots on Clarkston, Baldwin and Joslyn roads lead through and past the park's natural features, including Lake Sixteen. Broad wetlands border much of the lake's irregular shoreline, and numerous ducks, geese, swans, herons and other shorebirds find refuge in the narrow inlets and marshy edges. If you come equipped with a spotting scope or binoculars, even the parking lot is a good vantage point for picking out waterfowl during spring migration.

For more-wide-open spaces and good chances for spotting even more birds, squeeze through a gap in the fence at the park's service entrance, a half mile west of Joslyn Road on Clarkston Road. After a short walk south, you'll reach a high, open meadow ringed by distant woods and dotted with shrubby vegetation. No trails crease the fields, but you're free to look where you want for woodland birds and species that favor open spaces.

A fishing pier is located on Lake Sixteen with access from the Joslyn Road lot. No gas motors are permitted.

COUNTY: Oakland

CITY: Orion Township

FEES: An annual vehicle permit is required to park in the lots. The sticker is $22 for Oakland County residents; non-residents pay $44.

SCHEDULE: None posted.

DIRECTIONS: From I-75 take the Joslyn Rd. exit (#83) and go approximately 3 miles north on Joslyn Rd.

FURTHER INFORMATION: Oakland County Parks, Administrative Office, 2800 Watkins Lake Rd., Waterford, MI 48328-1917.

JONATHON WOODS 19

The last glacial age in Michigan left much evidence of its passage at Jonathon Woods. The sharply rising, heavily forested hills, steep valleys, potholes, lowland swamps, ponds and bogs in this 144 acres owned by the Nature Conservancy make up a classic morainal landscape. This great diversity in habitat accounts for the 330 species of plants and equally impressive variety of other wildlife found at Jonathon Woods. Approximately three miles of trails pass by ponds and bogs and through stands of maple, oak, aspen, ash, white pine, box elder, elm, ironwood, basswood, beech, willow and black cherry. Many of the hardwoods have reached imposing size, and the trails that pass beneath them offer peace, solitude and beauty. There is some evidence of old fence lines and attempts to clear some areas of glacial rock, but for the most part, Jonathon Woods shows little disturbance from the hands of man.

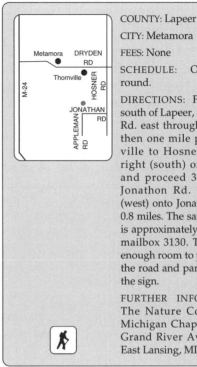

COUNTY: Lapeer

CITY: Metamora

FEES: None

SCHEDULE: Open year round.

DIRECTIONS: From M-24 south of Lapeer, take Dryden Rd. east through Metamora then one mile past Thornville to Hosner Rd. Turn right (south) onto Hosner and proceed 3.5 miles to Jonathon Rd. Turn right (west) onto Jonathon and go 0.8 miles. The sanctuary sign is approximately 40 feet past mailbox 3130. There is just enough room to pull a car off the road and park in front of the sign.

FURTHER INFORMATION: The Nature Conservancy Michigan Chapter, 2840 E. Grand River Ave., Suite 5, East Lansing, MI 48823.

20 SEVEN PONDS NATURE CENTER

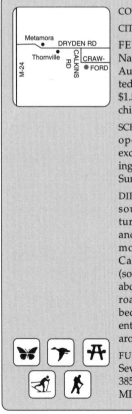

You can't help but learn about nature in this 273-acre outdoor classroom owned and managed by the Michigan Audubon Society. Close-up study or just plain enjoyment of the widely divergent landscape and habitat — including glacial lakes, cedar swamps, cattail marshes, open fields and woodland — come from boardwalks, bridges, observation platforms and 7.5 miles of trails. Maps and self-guiding pamphlets, available at the interpretive building, help explain the natural setting and important features of the area. What questions the booklets don't answer, the naturalist on duty will.

Areas of special interest include a woodland wildflower garden, a butterfuly garden, a waterfowl feeding area, an herb garden and a prairie reconstruction project featuring many rare and unusual grasses and flowers.

The variety of displays and educational exhibits at the interpretive building includes a Michigan bird display (with more than 100 mounted specimens), a "touch table" for children, a natural history collection, a beaver exhibit and a working beehive. Printed matter at both the bookstore and the extensive library in the building focuses on environmental education and natural history.

Seven Ponds also offers an impressive number of formal educational opportunities. More than 12,000 school children participate in programs each year, including the Natural History Field School, a week-long, in-depth summer study of living things and their habitats. Naturalist-training workshops are available for those who assist with the center's programs and also those who supervise nature programs, at camps for example. Adults can also enroll in a wide variety of activities ranging from natural history classes to field trips.

Other facilities here include a small picnic area. The center is open in the winter for snowshoeing and cross country skiing.

COUNTY: Lapeer

CITY: Dryden

FEES: Members of the Nature Center and Michigan Audubon Society are admitted free. Non-members pay $1.50 per adult and $.75 per child or $5 per family.

SCHEDULE: The grounds are open year round, daily except Mondays. The building is open Tuesday through Sunday, 9 a.m. - 5 p.m.

DIRECTIONS: Twelve miles south of Lapeer on M-24, turn east onto Dryden Rd. and go through both Metamora and Thornville to Calkins Rd. Turn right (south) onto Calkins and go about one mile to where the road bends to the left and becomes Crawford Rd. The entrance to the center is just around that bend.

FURTHER INFORMATION: Seven Ponds Nature Center, 3854 Crawford Rd., Dryden, MI 48428.

LAPEER STATE GAME AREA 21

The Lapeer State Game Area lies scattered across Lapeer County like discarded jigsaw puzzle pieces. The irregular tracts of land and many small lakes attract plenty of hunters and fishermen, but this is also a prime area for birdwatchers and nature enthusiasts.

To enjoy nature here, focus your attention on the area immediately surrounding Long Lake.The lake lies in the middle of a wildlife refuge, and although entrance is restricted most of the year, it's well worth a trip when the area is open. Wildlife habitat biologist, Jon Royer of the Shiawassee District of the DNR reports that you might spot Caspian terns over the lake and that a pair of Ospreys regularly fish the waters. The refuge includes an Osprey nesting tower, but so far the birds only visit the lake to fish and haven't yet set up housekeeping.

The refuge is open to birdwatchers and fishermen from July 1 through October 1. A visit in late September when early wildfowl migrants begin arriving offers the chance to see the most birds. During one recent trip, rafts of Canada Geese, cormorants, coots and a scattering of widgeons dotted the lake, and all were easily spotted from the entrance road that ends at a boat launching ramp.

The public, including fishermen, is also welcome from ice-in to ice-out during the winter months. The refuge is closed the rest of the year so that nesting birds are not disturbed in the spring and are not flushed out toward waiting hunters during the fall.

Birds may be the main attraction, but there's more here for nature lovers. Long Lake, which was created by the damming of a small creek, is fringed by marshes, flooded wetlands and dense woods. You can hike around the lake, and the habitat promises good opportunities for scoping a wide variety of birds.

The area is worth a visit even when the refuge is closed. Brief glimpses of the lake and the wetlands come from Five Lakes Road, Vernor Road, and Long Lake Road. Vernor Road in particular is a pleasure to drive. The narrow gravel route follows the top of a ridge, from which you are treated to views of glacially sculpted hills with small lakes, floodings and wetlands resting at the bottoms of the depressions. The land north of Verner and directly opposite Long Lake is open to hunters and hikers year round. From a small parking area on the north side of Verner Road approximately a mile and a half east of Five Lakes Road you can walk along an old two-track path that leads between two floodings and another promising area for birdwatching.

COUNTY: Lapeer

CITY: Lapeer

FEES: None

SCHEDULE: See text.

DIRECTIONS: From I-69 east of Lapeer, take the Wilder Rd. exit (#159) and drive north 2.5 miles to M-21. Turn right (east) onto M-21 and go one mile to Five Lakes Rd. Turn left (north) and drive 3.5 miles to the refuge entrance, which is almost directly across from a parking lot of a field dog trial area. Verner Rd. is another ¾ mile north.

FURTHER INFORMATION: Michigan Dept. of Natural Resources, District 11 Headquarters, 10650 S. Bennett Dr., Morrice, MI 48857.

22 FOR-MAR NATURE PRESERVE AND ARBORETUM

Nearly 400 acres of woodland, open fields, restored prairie, marshes, five ponds and Kearsley Creek make up the For-Mar Nature Preserve and Arboretum, located just a few blocks outside the limits of Flint, Michigan's "Vehicle City."

Like most Michigan nature preserves, For-Mar is dedicated to the study and enjoyment of nature, and an enjoyable learning experience here is almost guaranteed by eight nature trails. Some of the nearly seven miles of well-trodden paths follow the creek. Others circle small ponds, cross open meadows or meander through woods. All provide excellent opportunities for birdwatching, searching for wildflowers, or full exploration of the variety of habitats where nearly 475 species of flora and fauna flourish.

Two trails, both of which begin at the DeWaters Education Center, are specially designed for the handicapped. A wire-guided trail designed for the visually handicapped, for example, circles through a small woods. And the Woodlot Trail, a 0.2-mile paved self-guided trail through the same woods, is accessible by wheelchair.

The DeWaters Education Center, which houses a variety of nature displays and exhibits, is the focal point of educational programs for all ages. Guided field trips — including wildflower walks and a spring birdwatching class — and other programs are offered throughout the year.

Other attractions at For-Mar include a 113-acre arboretumthat, though still under development in the southwest corner of the grounds, already features many interesting specimens. And the Foote Bird Museum, near the entrance, displays 600 mounted birds.

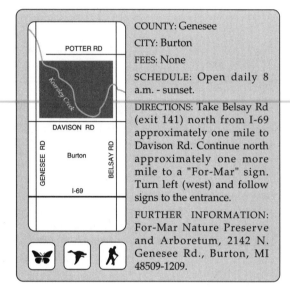

COUNTY: Genesee

CITY: Burton

FEES: None

SCHEDULE: Open daily 8 a.m. - sunset.

DIRECTIONS: Take Belsay Rd (exit 141) north from I-69 approximately one mile to Davison Rd. Continue north approximately one more mile to a "For-Mar" sign. Turn left (west) and follow signs to the entrance.

FURTHER INFORMATION: For-Mar Nature Preserve and Arboretum, 2142 N. Genesee Rd., Burton, MI 48509-1209.

BURR MEMORIAL PLANT PRESERVE 23

This five-acre pie-shaped piece of land, squeezed between a marshy stream and a section of Grand Trunk Railroad tracks, shelters a precious slice of Michigan real estate. Except for the possibility of some gravel removal from a small hill, this Michigan Nature Association-owned parcel is a piece of the less than one-quarter of one percent of Oakland County's original land cover that remains untouched by humans.

It's a living biological museum that shows what this section of our state looked like before it was drained, plowed, leveled and subdivided. Packed within the little triangle of land, you'll find both a wet and a dry prairie, a small creek narrow enough to step across, a fen, a bog, a marsh, and a gravel ridge that runs down its middle parallel to the railroad tracks.

From a short trail that creases the top of the gravelly ridge, you get some good views east, where the land slips down to the picturesque creek, which winds through a marshy wetlands. Tamaracks edge the far side of the fast-moving stream, and rising hills blanketed in hardwoods frame the scene.

The preserve's importance as a refuge for Michigan flora surpasses its scenic beauty. The striking diversity of landscape nurtures an amazing 289 different species of native Michigan plants, some of which bear equally amazing names such as golden alexanders, bastard toadflax, pussy toes, cotton grass, New Jersey tea and hoary puccoon. From mid-May through mid-September, eye-catching wildflowers are everywhere underfoot. You don't have to carry a wildflower identification guide to enjoy a visit, but it does add to richness of the experience.

Bluebird boxes dot the preserve, and the marsh, creek, and surrounding wooded area present fair opportunities for birdwatching.

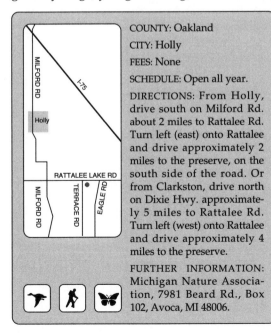

COUNTY: Oakland

CITY: Holly

FEES: None

SCHEDULE: Open all year.

DIRECTIONS: From Holly, drive south on Milford Rd. about 2 miles to Rattalee Rd. Turn left (east) onto Rattalee and drive approximately 2 miles to the preserve, on the south side of the road. Or from Clarkston, drive north on Dixie Hwy. approximately 5 miles to Rattalee Rd. Turn left (west) onto Rattalee and drive approximately 4 miles to the preserve.

FURTHER INFORMATION: Michigan Nature Association, 7981 Beard Rd., Box 102, Avoca, MI 48006.

24 SHANNON NATURE SANCTUARY

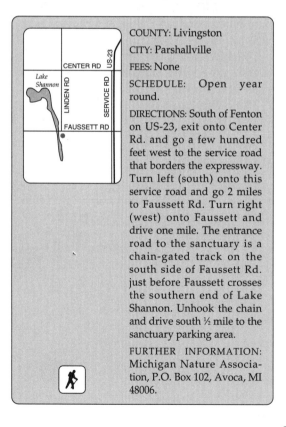

Quiet and peaceful, easy to get to but off the beaten track, and small but packed with varied habitats and scenic beauty, the Shannon Nature Sanctuary is both a treat and retreat for nature lovers. Here, you can spend an hour roaming one of several short trails or spend half a day in seclusion amidst the beautiful surroundings.

A surprising number of habitats — including a hardwood forest, a cattail marsh, a flood plain, a pond, a pine plantation, two streams, an old field giving way to young trees, and the shore of Lake Shannon — make up the relatively small 19.2-acre sanctuary. The forest floor is lush with ferns, vines, shrubs and other low-growing plants. Wildflowers abound throughout the sanctuary, especially along the cattail marsh and flood plain. In fact, the whole preserve by late spring seems to be a riot of plant life.

A leaflet, available at a mailbox just inside the sanctuary gate, lists plants, birds, mammals and other wildlife to both watch and listen for. Twenty-five identified species of birds, for example, nest within the sanctuary.

Several short trails wind through the preserve. One, which begins at the sanctuary entrance, borders the northern boundary, passes through dense woods, then turns south and intercepts a small creek. A second trail, which also begins at the sanctuary entrance, borders Lake Shannon and the cattail marsh before it, too, reaches the creek. This creek is also a focal point for several other trails. One, along the west side, heads upstream. A second, on the east side, borders the streambed, then heads farther east to an old field and a pine plantation. Bridging the creek near the sanctuary's northern boundary is a fallen tree equipped with handrails and a planked trunk.

COUNTY: Livingston

CITY: Parshallville

FEES: None

SCHEDULE: Open year round.

DIRECTIONS: South of Fenton on US-23, exit onto Center Rd. and go a few hundred feet west to the service road that borders the expressway. Turn left (south) onto this service road and go 2 miles to Faussett Rd. Turn right (west) onto Faussett and drive one mile. The entrance road to the sanctuary is a chain-gated track on the south side of Faussett Rd. just before Faussett crosses the southern end of Lake Shannon. Unhook the chain and drive south ½ mile to the sanctuary parking area.

FURTHER INFORMATION: Michigan Nature Association, P.O. Box 102, Avoca, MI 48006.

Howell Nature Center operates one of the few hospitals where well-wishers can benefit more from visitations than the patients. The center, one of the few Michigan members of the National Wildlife Rehabilitation Association, takes in orphaned, sick, injured and confiscated wildlife with the goal of returning them to the wild. The animals could care less about human visitors, and the hours open to the public are very limited. But it's well worth a trip here to get close-up views of both common and exotic animals and gain a renewed appreciation for the diversity and beauty of the animal kingdom.

Approximately 100 birds and mammals are in treatment at any one time, and the 40-plus pens and cages that hold them line a short trail that circles a pond near the headquarters. A recent patient list included a Turkey Vulture, a coyote, an Arctic fox, raccoons, squirrels, a Bald Eagle, a Golden Eagle, six kinds of owls, four kinds of hawks, a wild turkey, deer, a Great Blue Heron, doves, songbirds, a Kestrel, rabbits, a ferret and a family of ducks. You can never be sure what you might see, because each year the center receives over 500 birds and animals representing approximately 50 different species. Labels at most cages identify each animal and sometimes describe its natural habitat and range.

There's more on Howell Nature Center's 260 gently rolling acres than just an animal hospital. Five miles of hiking and cross country ski trails, which vary from one-half to four miles in length, cut through a mature hardwood forest and cross open fields studded with wildflowers. Cross country ski rentals are available.

In December the center hosts a choose-and-cut Christmas tree sale from their tree nursery.

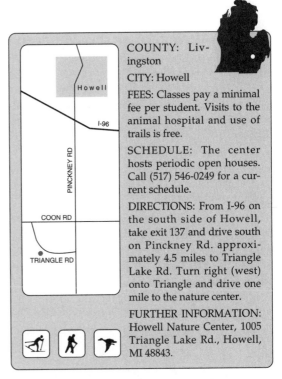

COUNTY: Livingston

CITY: Howell

FEES: Classes pay a minimal fee per student. Visits to the animal hospital and use of trails is free.

SCHEDULE: The center hosts periodic open houses. Call (517) 546-0249 for a current schedule.

DIRECTIONS: From I-96 on the south side of Howell, take exit 137 and drive south on Pinckney Rd. approximately 4.5 miles to Triangle Lake Rd. Turn right (west) onto Triangle and drive one mile to the nature center.

FURTHER INFORMATION: Howell Nature Center, 1005 Triangle Lake Rd., Howell, MI 48843.

The main emphasis at Howell Nature Center, which is owned by the Presbytery of Detroit, is outdoor and environmental education. The center's year-round staff conducts over 75 different programs for student groups who visit the outdoor classroom. The programs can be tailored to students from kindergarten through high school and vary in length from an hour to a several-day stay at the center's lodge.

26 KENSINGTON METROPARK

Mention Kensington Metropark, and most people will probably think of the bustling crowds of swimmers, sunbathers, picnickers, golfers, cross country skiers and sailboaters who flock by the thousands to this popular getaway. Not as well known is a secluded, quiet, much-less-traveled area on the 4,300-acre park's west side where visitors can experience nature and enjoy the out-of-doors on a more intimate basis.

The focal point, there, is a nature center that hugs the shore of Kingfisher Lagoon. Six beautiful hiking and nature trails, four of which are marked with helpful interpretive signs, begin near the Center building. If you're looking for seclusion, take either the Chickadee or Fox Trail, both of which lead to the northern edge of the nature-study area. The best place to enjoy spring wildflowers is on the Deer Run Trail's two loops, and excellent birdwatching possibilities come from the variety of cover and habitat along the 1.25-mile Aspen Trail. Completing the trail system in the nature area are Wildwing Trail, which circles for 2.25 miles around Wildwing Lake, and the half-mile Tamarack Trail, which crosses a tamarack bog.

The Center building houses nature exhibits, including a working beehive, and the center's staff conducts guided hikes, nature workshops and special programs throughout the year.

At Kent Lake, the focal point of most of the park's activities, a paved hiking/bike/jogging trail passes two swimming beaches and 12 scattered picnic areas on its several-mile circuit around the lake. For a different view of the park or to explore Kent Lake's many islands (including Labadie Island and its semiprivate picnic area), use one of the park's rental rowboats or sailboats.

Miles of cross country ski trails, ice fishing, an ice rink and toboggan runs are winter attractions.

COUNTY: Oakland

CITY: Milford

FEES: $2 daily on weekdays, $3 per day on weekends and holidays, or $15 for an annual vehicle permit good at all metroparks. Free admittance on Tuesdays,

SCHEDULE: Open year round except Christmas and Thanksgiving. Trail hours are 6 a.m. - dusk, and park hours are 6 a.m. - 10 p.m.

DIRECTIONS: From I-96 4 miles east of US-23, exit onto either Kensington Rd. or Kent Lake Rd. and go north a few hundred feet to the entrances and the numerous parking lots that ring Kent Lake.

FURTHER INFORMATION: Kensington Metropark, 2240 W. Buno Rd., Milford, MI 48380.

NANKIN MILLS NATURE CENTER 27
& WILLIAM P. HOLLIDAY FOREST

"If only the walls could talk," as the saying goes, the knotted planks of the Nankin Mills Nature Center would whisper several chapters of Michigan history to its 20th-century visitors. Constructed before the Civil War as a gristmill, the building first absorbed the concerns, politics and gossip of farmers who brought in their wheat to be ground. Later within the same walls, escaping slaves huddled as they made their way to Canada via this and other depots along the Underground Railroad. Even Henry Ford — who sometimes seems to have touched everything in Michigan during his lifetime — did in fact remodel this mill in the 1920s to produce electricity.

Today the walls and hand-hewn beams of the restored mill reflect natural history, and visitors now pass by the placid millrace pond to learn from natural displays — including live animal exhibits — and an interpretive program.

The picturesque nature center is also an excellent starting point for a short walk or extensive hike into the adjacent William P. Holliday Forest and Wildlife Preserve. This 540-acre uniquely shaped sanctuary (several miles long and only several hundred yards wide at its broadest point) serpentines its way along Tonquish Creek.

Six nature trails — varying in length from half-mile loops to the 12-mile round-trip Tonquish Trail — follow the stream's course while also making short exploratory circuits away from it. The tree-canopied paths continually cross and recross the creek as they enter then leave a variety of other habitats, including a five-acre marsh, 15 acres of open meadows, the mill pond and several smaller creeks. Comfort stations and shelters are spaced at

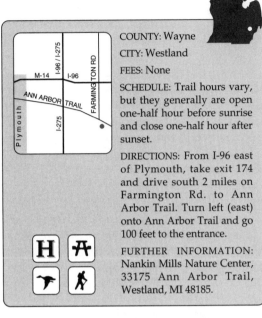

COUNTY: Wayne

CITY: Westland

FEES: None

SCHEDULE: Trail hours vary, but they generally are open one-half hour before sunrise and close one-half hour after sunset.

DIRECTIONS: From I-96 east of Plymouth, take exit 174 and drive south 2 miles on Farmington Rd. to Ann Arbor Trail. Turn left (east) onto Ann Arbor Trail and go 100 feet to the entrance.

FURTHER INFORMATION: Nankin Mills Nature Center, 33175 Ann Arbor Trail, Westland, MI 48185.

regular intervals along the trails, which are also accessible from Cowan Road.

The nature center and wildlife preserve also abut the Middle Rouge Parkway, a 2,250-acre park stretched along the Middle Rouge River from Northville to Dearborn. Facilities there — most scattered along Hines Drive, which runs the length of the park — include ball fields, play areas, picnic areas and several lakes.

28 DEARBORN ENVIRONMENTAL STUDY AREA

Just about anyone who has visited Greenfield Village (along with many who haven't) recognizes that Henry Ford expended a great deal of time, money and energy to preserve the past. What many people don't know, however, is that the great industrialist was almost equally devoted to the conservation and the enjoyment of nature.

When Ford built his Fair Lane Estate along the Rouge River, he set out to create a place where he could retreat from the world in a setting of natural beauty. To do so, he hired then-world-famous landscape architect, Jens Jensen. Ford chose the right person. Jensen's work at Fair Lane — including a lake and a meadow (later renamed in the great architect's honor) linking the lake to Ford's mansion — has been recognized as one of the finest examples of American landscape architecture.

Much of Jensen's work and the Ford estate remains today as a large portion of the University of Michigan-Dearborn Environmental Study Area. Located on campus, this 72-acre sanctuary serves as an outdoor classroom for university students, school children and family groups and as a site for several study projects, including the Rouge River Bird Observatory. It is also a place where the general public can go to enjoy nature as Henry and Clara Ford did more than 60 years ago.

Trails totaling five miles pass by a incredibly diverse array of sights including an abandoned orchard (there long before Ford bought the property), Fair Lane Lake, the Rouge River, a sycamore/willow flood-plain forest, a stand of virgin timber featuring some of the largest beech, maple and burr oak trees in the state. These and other special points of interest, plus a map, are included in a helpful and educational brochure available at the entrance.

The diverse habitat here attracts a wide variety of birds: 240 according to a checklist available at the sanctuary entrance. Local birders know the area as an excellent one for spotting migrating wood warblers in May, and more than 30 species of these brightly colored, energetic little birds have been sighted at the property.

Picnicking is not allowed in the Environmental Study Area, but picnic tables are available in the campus courtyard across the road.

For up-to-date information about all seasonal programs open to the general public, call (313) 593-5338 or write to the address in *Further Information*.

COUNTY: Wayne

CITY: Dearborn

FEES: None

SCHEDULE: Open year round, dawn - dusk.

DIRECTIONS: From M-39 (Southfield Freeway) in Dearborn, exit onto M-153 (Ford Rd.) and go west approximately one mile to Evergreen Rd. Turn left (south) onto Evergreen and go approximately ¾ mile to the University of Michigan-Dearborn campus. The sanctuary is located on the west side of the campus on Fair Lane Rd. Park across from the Henry Ford Estate or farther east on Fair Lane Rd.

FURTHER INFORMATION: University of Michigan-Dearborn, Dept. of Natural Areas, Dearborn, MI 48128.

Belle Isle — at 985 acres, America's largest island urban park — had rather humble origins. Purchased from the Indians for three rolls of tobacco, eight barrels of rum, six pounds of red paint and one belt of wampum, the island was used by early Detroit settlers as a giant pigpen, where porkers could roam free yet remain relatively safe from wolves. It was still known as Hog Island when families first began sailing to it in the mid-1800s for picnics.

Today the only pigs on the island are those being barbecued. Around the turn of the century, well-known landscape architect Frederick Law Omstead, who also created New York's Central Park, fashioned Belle Isle into an urban playground that is so big, with so much to see and do, that you have to come several times to take it all in.

What's immediately evident on your first visit is the unique and unavoidable scenery. Belle Isle is shaped like a giant ore carrier, and it sits in the middle of the Detroit River with its "prow" pointed downstream and tethered to the mainland by the MacArthur Bridge. A multilane one-way road circles the "deck" of this grounded ship, and from the 10-mile route, you're treated to some of the most striking scenery in southeast Michigan. Motorists, as well as joggers and bicyclists, move past quiet lagoons, deep woods, sprawling picnic areas, and Scott Fountain, which stands 38 feet tall and has 109 water outlets. The skylines of Windsor and Detroit make great backgrounds for watching pleasure craft and ore carriers that ply the river. The park also seems to extend an open invitation to walk along the edge of the river or slip down the quiet byways that cut through the heart of the island.

Thousands of visitors come daily to enjoy a meal in the park's almost unlimited picnic areas. The huge grounds can accommodate the largest 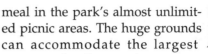 party or family reunion, yet couples and small families can find a spot that offers scenery, seclusion or shade, and sometimes all three. Tables edge the deep woods on the island's east end, they line the riverbank and frame the half-mile-long swimming beach on the north side, and they are scattered over picturesque meadows throughout the rest of the park.

The island is also one of the best birdwatching areas in the state. The park's lagoons and lakes attract numerous ducks in the fall. Many waterfowl winter-over on the Detroit River, and spring brings loons, grebes, warblers, woodpeckers, countless sparrows, and renewed flights of ducks.

Ball diamonds, basketball courts, tennis courts, a 20-station physical fitness trail, a golf

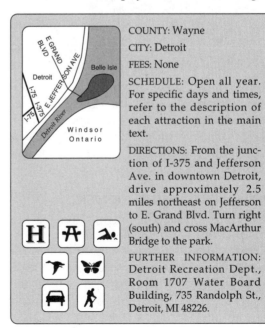

COUNTY: Wayne

CITY: Detroit

FEES: None

SCHEDULE: Open all year. For specific days and times, refer to the description of each attraction in the main text.

DIRECTIONS: From the junction of I-375 and Jefferson Ave. in downtown Detroit, drive approximately 2.5 miles northeast on Jefferson to E. Grand Blvd. Turn right (south) and cross MacArthur Bridge to the park.

FURTHER INFORMATION: Detroit Recreation Dept., Room 1707 Water Board Building, 735 Randolph St., Detroit, MI 48226.

course, and a huge play area with a giant amusement-park slide are among facilities that elevate the park well above the normal.

And there's more. An array of special attractions makes Belle Isle unique in the Midwest, if not the country.

NATURE CENTER

The entire park will delight nature lovers, but they will be especially drawn to the Nature Center, on the northeast end of the island. There, two narrow self-guided footpaths lead away from the island's hustle and bustle into nearly 200 acres of virgin timber and around wetlands filled with wildlife.

Visually handicapped visitors can also experience nature on a sensory trail near the center. Inside the modern building, exhibits and displays showcase Michigan plants and animals, and park naturalists conduct weekend programs. You can walk the trails any time, but the building is only open noon to 4 p.m. on Tuesdays and 10 a.m. to 4 p.m. Wednesday through Sunday.

BELLE ISLE ZOO

East Indian apes, South American bears, kangaroos, sea lions, wolves, big cats and exotic birds are just a few of the fascinating animals you can see wandering their large, barless, natural confines at this 13-acre zoo, located near the center of the island. You get unobstructed, close-up views from an elevated boardwalk that winds through the enclosures, and a trip to the zoo can be the high point of a child's visit to Belle Isle. The zoo is open daily 10 a.m. to 5 p.m. from May through October. Admission is free for children under five and $2 for adults, with discounts for senior citizens and children between the ages of five and 12.

WHITCOMB CONSERVATORY

A quarter of a million plants inside, plus countless others in formal gardens surrounding Whitcomb Conservatory attract a million visitors a year. Inside the towering glass structure, six display rooms showcase tropical plants, ferns, cactus, palms, and special displays that erupt in wild splashes of color. The Tropical Room alone is worth a visit to examine breadfruit, pomegranate, papaya and coffee trees and take in the exquisite beauty of orchids, hibiscus and a variety of exotic plants. Outside, a lily pond, an outstanding display of perennials, and the formal gardens that surround the conservatory are also lovely. And in the spring, 40,000 tulips and 1,250 narcissi paint the landscape with a variety of vibrant colors. The conservatory hosts six major flower shows throughout the year. The building is open daily from 9 a.m. to dusk, and admission is free.

AQUARIUM

Unless you scuba dive, there's no better or easier way to see live fish in their natural element than beneath the sea-green tile of Belle Isle Aquarium's arched ceiling. More than 40 large tanks line the walls of this, the nation's oldest freshwater aquarium. Fish native to the Great Lakes region dominate the collection of 5,000 live specimens representing 118 species. But stingrays, Australian lungfish, and the gourami — a species that has been around for 26 million years and looks it — are just a few of the weird, colorful and remarkably ugly fish from around the world that draw more than their fair share of stares. The aquarium is open daily from 10 a.m. to 5 p.m., and admission is free.

DOSSIN GREAT LAKES MUSEUM

The romance and history of the Great Lakes lives on at the Dossin Great Lakes Museum. The lounge of a Great Lakes passenger ship, an authentic pilot house, artifacts from shipwrecks, a large collection of model ships, and a variety of other special exhibits trace the history of seafaring on the lakes. The museum is open 10 a.m. to 5:30 p.m. Wednesday through Saturday. Admission is free.

30 LOWER HURON METROPARK

This long, relatively narrow, 1,239-acre Huron-Clinton Metropark borders both banks of the Huron River for more than five miles. The river is the thread that binds this beautiful park together, because whether you are picnicking, hiking, birdwatching, biking, or just enjoying a scenic drive, the wide, lazy stream is rarely out of view.

An access road runs through the park, and wide loops of the river continuously curve away from, then back to the edge of the pavement. At about the halfway point, the road crosses over the wide ribbon of water, then the river plays the same game on the opposite side. Strung along the road, nestled in the river's broad loops are picnic areas and playgrounds, a par-3 golf course, hiking trails, nature areas, ball fields, and a large swimming pool.

Bicyclists, joggers and walkers can take in five-plus miles of the beautiful scenery along a wide bike path that parallels the park road.

Hikers and nature lovers can choose from two trails through contrasting environments, and both offer good birding. The Bob White Nature Trail's woodchip-covered path winds for almost a mile through an upland hardwood forest on the side of the road opposite the river. The pleasant walk is especially rewarding in spring when wildflowers blanket the forest floor.

The Paw Paw Nature Trail drops to the flood plain of the Huron River, where the path then weaves through a lowland swamp marked by huge trees — many labeled — and a wild profusion of native Michigan flowers.

The park's picnic areas are the equal of any in southeastern Michigan for beauty and spaciousness. The tables, grills and shelters dot nearly endless expanses of lush grass, and most spots have the river as a backdrop and are shaded by stately trees.

During the winter you can skate on three lighted ponds or cross country ski anywhere other than the golf course.

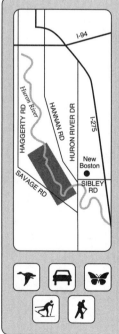

COUNTY: Wayne

CITY: New Boston

FEES: Daily vehicle permit, $2 on weekdays and $3 on weekends and holidays; annual vehicle permit, $15; senior citizen annual permit, $8. Admittance on Tuesdays is free.

SCHEDULE: Open year round, 6 a.m. - 10 p.m.

DIRECTIONS: From the junction of I-94 and I-275, drive south on I-275 4 miles to the Sibley Rd. exit. Go west ½ mile on Sibley to Huron River Dr. Turn left (south) onto Huron River and drive ½ mile to the park entrance.

FURTHER INFORMATION: Lower Huron Metropark, 17845 Savage Rd., Belleville MI 48111.

OAKWOODS NATURE STUDY AREA 31

Oakwoods is a 400-acre nature-study area nestled along the southern shore of the Huron River about 10 miles upstream from its mouth on Lake Erie. More than 3.75 miles of trails explore its variety of scenery and habitats.

The Big Tree Trail, for example, circles for 0.75 miles through a hardwood forest. The one-mile Sky-Come-Down Trail skirts a large pond, but the main attraction along it is a classic display of "edge effect," that is, the meeting, overlapping and blending of two different plant communities — meadows and woods in this case. Formally called *ecotones*, these edge areas support a variety of plant species from both habitats and, as a result, are usually excellent places to observe wildlife, especially birds.

Other trails include the park's longest, the Long Bark Trail, which follows the edge of the Huron River for nearly a mile before winding its way back through deep woods for another mile to the Nature Center.

Numbered posts, which correspond to numbered paragraphs in a pamphlet available at the Nature Center Building, identify and interpret flowers, trees and other natural points of special interest along all trails. A variety of exhibits inside the Nature Center includes a live animal display, and the park's staff conducts nature walks and classes throughout the year. Picnicking is available at a separate nearby area.

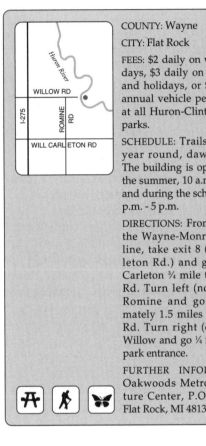

COUNTY: Wayne

CITY: Flat Rock

FEES: $2 daily on weekdays, $3 daily on weekends and holidays, or $15 for an annual vehicle permit valid at all Huron-Clinton metroparks.

SCHEDULE: Trails are open year round, dawn - dusk. The building is open during the summer, 10 a.m. - 5 p.m., and during the school year, 1 p.m. - 5 p.m.

DIRECTIONS: From I-275 on the Wayne-Monroe county line, take exit 8 (Will Carleton Rd.) and go east on Carleton ¾ mile to Romine Rd. Turn left (north) onto Romine and go approximately 1.5 miles to Willow Rd. Turn right (east) onto Willow and go ¼ mile to the park entrance.

FURTHER INFORMATION: Oakwoods Metropark Nature Center, P.O. Box 332, Flat Rock, MI 48134.

32 LAKE ERIE METROPARK

Lake Erie Metropark completes a string of nine Huron-Clinton metroparks that follow the course of the Huron River from its source in northern Oakland County to Lake Erie, 100 miles later. Unlike the other metroparks on the route, Lake Erie Metropark is not on the Huron River, but is located north of the river-mouth along the shore of Lake Erie at the mouth of the Detroit River. This unique location offers a rich mosaic of lakeshore, marsh-land, open water and islands attractive to a wide variety of plant and animal life.

For a glimpse into the natural and cultural history of the region, with a particular emphasis on marsh ecology and the duck hunting tradition, stop at the Marshlands Museum and Nature Center, between two scenic lagoons at the north end of the park.

Also you can explore the varied habitats — such as an oak wood, open field, coastal marsh and lake shoreline — along a system of walking trails.

A natural spectacle of international reputation is the annual fall migration of waterfowl and "hawks" (eagles, falcons, vultures, and true hawks). From late summer through November 16, different species of hawks funnel over Lake Erie Metropark by the tens of thousands. Bald Eagles are a regular sight at all seasons, and you can see thousands of Tundra Swans offshore during the winter months.

Other facilities here include lakeside picnic areas, a wave pool, an 18-hole golf course, a boat launch and a marina.

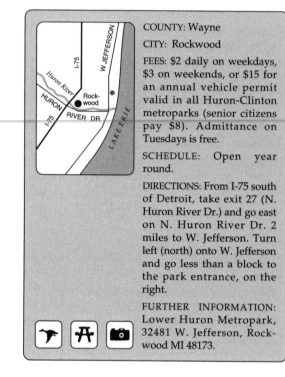

COUNTY: Wayne

CITY: Rockwood

FEES: $2 daily on weekdays, $3 on weekends, or $15 for an annual vehicle permit valid in all Huron-Clinton metroparks (senior citizens pay $8). Admittance on Tuesdays is free.

SCHEDULE: Open year round.

DIRECTIONS: From I-75 south of Detroit, take exit 27 (N. Huron River Dr.) and go east on N. Huron River Dr. 2 miles to W. Jefferson. Turn left (north) onto W. Jefferson and go less than a block to the park entrance, on the right.

FURTHER INFORMATION: Lower Huron Metropark, 32481 W. Jefferson, Rockwood MI 48173.

POINTE MOUILEE STATE GAME AREA 33

Excellent birding plus good hiking are the draws to the Pointe Mouilee State Game Area, which stretches from the Huron River mouth south along nearly four miles of western Lake Erie shoreline.

The vast marsh, open waters, diked ponds and inlets of the game area and its adjoining wildlife refuge attract large numbers of birds year round, but early spring and before the opening of waterfowl hunting season in the fall are the best times to see large concentrations. Ducks, geese, shorebirds, gulls and terns plus many rare and unusual species make stopovers here during spring and fall migrations. The area, which encompasses a significant portion of the Lake Erie marsh system, also provides nesting habitat for many waterfowl and shorebirds during the summer breeding season.

A good place to spot shorebirds, songbirds and waterfowl is in a small section of the game area that lies along Pointe Mouilee Road north of the Huron River in Wayne County. Located on a point within this area, the park headquarters marks the mouth of the Huron River.

Hikers and birders take trails from several parking areas along Dixie Highway and Roberts Road, both of which border the western edge of the area. These trails lead into the woods and marshes and alongside both Mouillee Creek and the Lautenschlager Drain. Trails from a parking area at the end of Sigler Road (which crosses Dixie Highway just south of the Huron River) lead to an extensive dike system, which in turn leads to the wildlife refuges within the game area. There, you can walk for several miles next to marshes, diked pools and open water. A map that marks the parking areas, trails and the dike system is available at the headquarters.

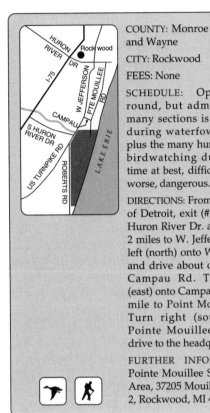

COUNTY: Monroe and Wayne

CITY: Rockwood

FEES: None

SCHEDULE: Open year round, but admittance to many sections is restricted during waterfowl season, plus the many hunters make birdwatching during this time at best, difficult, and at worse, dangerous.

DIRECTIONS: From I-75 south of Detroit, exit (#27) onto S. Huron River Dr. and go east 2 miles to W. Jefferson. Turn left (north) onto W. Jefferson and drive about one mile to Campau Rd. Turn right (east) onto Campau and go ½ mile to Point Mouillee Rd. Turn right (south) onto Pointe Mouillee Rd. and drive to the headquarters.

FURTHER INFORMATION: Pointe Mouillee State Game Area, 37205 Mouillee Rd., Rt. 2, Rockwood, MI 48173.

34 ERIE MARSH PRESERVE

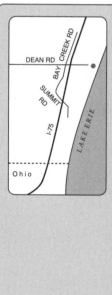

The 2,618-acre Erie Marsh Preserve and the shoreline of Lake Erie from the Ohio border north to Point Mouillee is one of the finest birdwatching regions in the state. The area — one of the last large remnants of a great prehistoric marsh and wetlands that once stretched along the south and west shores of Lake Erie — attracts impressive numbers of waterfowl, shorebirds and other species. Most birds — including hawks and rare terns and gulls, such as Forester's Tern, Great Black-backed Gull and Icelandic Gull — pass through the wet meadows, marshes, diked pools and open waters of North Maumee Bay during spring and fall migration. But a signif-icant number — including Great Blue Herons, Coots, Gallinules, terns, several species of ducks, gulls (including some species rare in the state) and egrets — also nest here in the summer.

The preserve — 11 percent of state wetlands found between Port Huron and the Ohio line — is also home to many rare and interesting plants. The rare swamp rose mallow and the American lotus, for example, grow in the wetlands and bloom in profusion during late summer.

A system of dikes circles the preserve, and miles of trails atop them give access to the area. The Nature Conservancy, owner of the preserve, requests, however, that all visitors use only the inner dikes. Birdwatchers are very visible when walking on the raised dikes and, as a result, should carry binoculars and spotter scopes because waterfowl are difficult to approach. In some areas, the dikes are tree-lined or bordered by brush and shrubs, and birders there have a better chance for close observation.

The entire area surrounding the Erie Marsh Preserve also affords great birdwatching. Mud flats, lagoons, drains and floodings border many local secondary roads such as Dean, Summit and Bay Creek, and you can spot numerous waterfowl, shorebirds, gulls and terns without leaving your car.

COUNTY: Monroe

CITY: Monroe

FEES: None

SCHEDULE: Open year round except for the months of October and December.

DIRECTIONS: From I-75 2 miles north of the Ohio-Michigan state line, exit (#2) onto Summit Rd., which passes over the expressway. Make a U-turn at the bait shop just south of the overpass and head back northeast on Summit Rd. ½ mile to Bay Creek Rd. Turn right (north) onto Bay Creek and drive ½ mile to Dean Rd. Turn right (east) onto Dean and go ½ mile to the parking area at the Erie Shooting Club.

FURTHER INFORMATION: The Nature Conservancy Michigan Chapter, 2840 E. Grand River Ave., Suite 5, East Lansing MI 48823.

What might a daydreaming nature lover in a crowded urban area wish for as a quick and nearby escape from the roads, cars and people? He or she might imagine a small haven where, except for the chatter of birds, quiet would reign in a woods lush with plant life. Trees would shade and cool the forest floor, even on the hottest of days. And a trail, though well-worn, would be crowded with shrubs and trees as it wound through an oak/hickory hardwood forest and along a gently flowing creek.

Such a place exists, and it's called the Searles Natural Area. Only a few miles from downtown Ann Arbor and barely a mile from the busy US-23 expressway, the 50-acre haven, owned by the Washtenaw Audubon Society, offers peace, seclusion, and the opportunity to get away from the urban sprawl. It's the answer to an urban nature lover's wish.

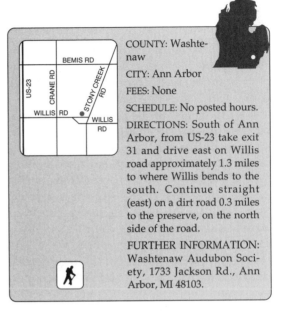

COUNTY: Washtenaw

CITY: Ann Arbor

FEES: None

SCHEDULE: No posted hours.

DIRECTIONS: South of Ann Arbor, from US-23 take exit 31 and drive east on Willis road approximately 1.3 miles to where Willis bends to the south. Continue straight (east) on a dirt road 0.3 miles to the preserve, on the north side of the road.

FURTHER INFORMATION: Washtenaw Audubon Society, 1733 Jackson Rd., Ann Arbor, MI 48103.

36 ROLLING HILLS COUNTY PARK

Carved out of the rolling farmland of southeastern Washtenaw County, this new park has enough facilities and attractions to keep outdoor enthusiasts busy year round

Near the center of the park, a pleasant picnic area snuggles in among a grove of young hardwoods that line one side of an oblong pond. Tables and grills are scattered among the thick-set trees, and from almost every picnic site you get good views of the pond and the rolling land across the narrow body of water. A small concession complex is only a short walk from the picnic grounds.

An approximately half-mile-long nature trail, which circles around and over a wooded hill behind the picnic area, connects to a hiking/cross country ski trail. That three-mile-plus route crosses old farm fields, skirts large meadows, circles the pond, and ducks in and out of small woodlots as it traces the park's periphery.

The area is worth exploring by birders. Ducks visit the pond in spring, and the brushy fringe bordering the open fields, plus the small wooded groves should attract a fair share of songbirds.

Two water slides and a wave pool will have kids clamoring to visit, and the outdoor fun doesn't stop when the snow flies. Three miles of cross country ski trails lace the park, and one loop is lighted for night skiing. A skating rink and two toboggan runs are added attractions. Rental skis are available, and rental toboggans are mandatory.

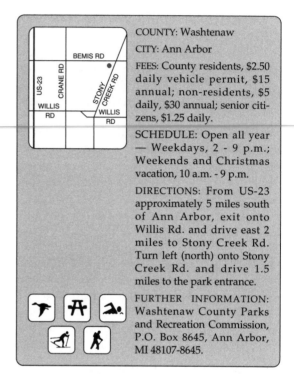

COUNTY: Washtenaw

CITY: Ann Arbor

FEES: County residents, $2.50 daily vehicle permit, $15 annual; non-residents, $5 daily, $30 annual; senior citizens, $1.25 daily.

SCHEDULE: Open all year — Weekdays, 2 - 9 p.m.; Weekends and Christmas vacation, 10 a.m. - 9 p.m.

DIRECTIONS: From US-23 approximately 5 miles south of Ann Arbor, exit onto Willis Rd. and drive east 2 miles to Stony Creek Rd. Turn left (north) onto Stony Creek Rd. and drive 1.5 miles to the park entrance.

FURTHER INFORMATION: Washtenaw County Parks and Recreation Commission, P.O. Box 8645, Ann Arbor, MI 48107-8645.

This small city park on the extreme west side of Ann Arbor packs a lot of habitat diversity into 44 acres. Two lakes, a pond, upland forest, dead forested wetlands, an oak-hickory forest, old fields and areas of dense shrubs and young trees grace the property. This rich diversity makes Dolph Park an urban Noah's Ark that shelters a wide range of wild plants and animals. The City of Ann Arbor has recognized the park's importance as a wildlife preservation site and, except for foot trails and a foot bridge, the city has purposely left the area undeveloped. This is a place for enjoying and studying nature and not for ball games, picnics or exercising your dog.

From the small parking lot on Wagner Road, a well-marked trail leads a short distance to the high ground lying between the park's two most prominent features — First Sister Lake and Second Sister Lake — the only naturally formed lakes in Ann Arbor. The pathway borders Second Sister Lake —

the bigger of the siblings — before crossing a small footbridge and climbing to the highlands and where two overlooks present nice views of a pond, First Sister Lake and a variety of natural habitats. The entire trail system totals only a half mile.

The park is a wonderful location for a pleasant walk amidst a natural setting, but it would almost be a shame not to bring along a bird book and plant identification guide. A walk of only a few steps will take you from one ecosystem and its community of plants to a strikingly different system. An amazing variety of wildflowers, grasses, trees and shrubs constantly demand your attention, and the combination of shelter and food attracts numerous birds.

A park brochure and interpretive panels at the trailhead further help you appreciate the park's natural splendor.

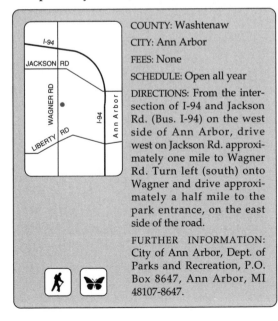

COUNTY: Washtenaw

CITY: Ann Arbor

FEES: None

SCHEDULE: Open all year

DIRECTIONS: From the intersection of I-94 and Jackson Rd. (Bus. I-94) on the west side of Ann Arbor, drive west on Jackson Rd. approximately one mile to Wagner Rd. Turn left (south) onto Wagner and drive approximately a half mile to the park entrance, on the east side of the road.

FURTHER INFORMATION: City of Ann Arbor, Dept. of Parks and Recreation, P.O. Box 8647, Ann Arbor, MI 48107-8647.

38 COUNTY FARM PARK

If you're tired of exercising in the artificial environment of a gym or health club, County Farm Park's outdoor fitness trails, which combine cardiovascular exercise stops with the enjoyment of nature, may be just what the waistline ordered. Or, the gravel paths through the varied and pretty scenery are enjoyable places to simply take a walk.

Three level, wide trails — which loop 0.6, 1.1 and 1.4 miles through the park — skirt deep woods, pass by a perennial demonstration garden and native shrub plantings, and cross meadows where shrubs and brush are filling the open spaces. At numerous stops along the routes, you can perform a variety of exercises on specially constructed equipment. Also, a 0-.4-mile nature trail, with no fitness stops, weaves through a dense hardwood forest with a tangled understory of brush, saplings and wildflowers.

The shrub-filled meadows and wild, overgrown forest, all located within a densely populated urban area, make County Farm a small oasis for wildlife and also a prime birding spot.

A picnic area — tables, grills, and a small pavilion — at the Manchester Street entrance is too small to accommodate large groups, but for a family picnic, it's a nice alternative to busy parks or long drives.

In the winter a 1.5-mile cross country ski trail here is another option for exercising in the out-of-doors.

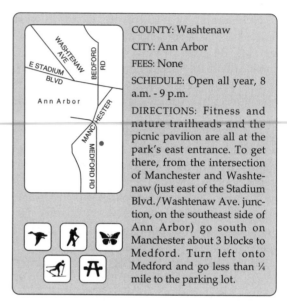

COUNTY: Washtenaw

CITY: Ann Arbor

FEES: None

SCHEDULE: Open all year, 8 a.m. - 9 p.m.

DIRECTIONS: Fitness and nature trailheads and the picnic pavilion are all at the park's east entrance. To get there, from the intersection of Manchester and Washtenaw (just east of the Stadium Blvd./Washtenaw Ave. junction, on the southeast side of Ann Arbor) go south on Manchester about 3 blocks to Medford. Turn left onto Medford and go less than ¼ mile to the parking lot.

Even though the University of Michigan's Nichols Arboretum is hard to get to, it consistently draws 100,000 visitors annually. If you pay even a brief visit, you'll see why. This is one of the premier arboretums in the Midwest, and it's not hard to imagine that Nichols Arboretum spawned the phrase "communing with nature."

Begun in 1907 on 27 acres, Nichols has grown to 123 acres. Its formal and natural settings of mature specimen plants plus large areas of totally untamed vegetation sprawl across a diverse landscape of steep ravines, open prairie and rolling hills, all fronted by a half-mile run of the Huron River.

Among the multitude of fascinating and impressive trees within the arboretum are 64 species labeled with small numbered tags that match a list in a brochure available by writing the university's School of Natural Resources and Environment (see *Further Information*). With the help of that booklet, you can seek out Amur corktrees, cedar of Lebanon, lacebark pine, Japanese umbrella pine, baldcypress, and castor aralia, plus 30 species native to Michigan. Most of the trees are fully mature, and many are flowering varieties that put on a stunning spring show.

In early summer another attraction is worth a special visit. A peony garden contains more than 262 varieties in 27 beds, and in June the 700 plants burst into a spectacular array of color. Another brochure, also available from the School of Natural Resources and Environment, identifies all the plants, some of which date back to 1927.

Several trails not only wind through lush vegetation past the outstanding examples of flora collected from all over the world, but also cross a 10-acre restored prairie, border the Huron River, cut through remnant oak-hickory forests, and skirt small, marshy wetlands.

The arboretum is well-known among local birdwatchers as an excellent area to spot a surprisingly wide assortment of species. Spring migration begins an exceptional number of warblers to the wooded landscape, and Red-tailed Hawks and Cooper's Hawks have been known to nest in the area. Although spring and fall offer the best birding, a trip to the sanctuary any time of the year can be rewarding.

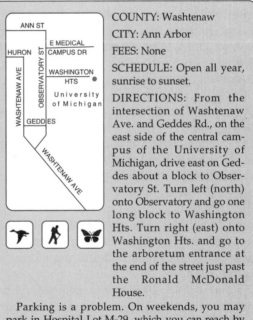

COUNTY: Washtenaw

CITY: Ann Arbor

FEES: None

SCHEDULE: Open all year, sunrise to sunset.

DIRECTIONS: From the intersection of Washtenaw Ave. and Geddes Rd., on the east side of the central campus of the University of Michigan, drive east on Geddes about a block to Observatory St. Turn left (north) onto Observatory and go one long block to Washington Hts. Turn right (east) onto Washington Hts. and go to the arboretum entrance at the end of the street just past the Ronald McDonald House.

Parking is a problem. On weekends, you may park in Hospital Lot M-29, which you can reach by driving on Observatory north a block past Washington Hts. to East Medical Campus Dr. and turning right. During the week, parking may or may not be available in U-M lots on Washington Hts.

FURTHER INFORMATION: Friends of Nichols Arboretum, University of Michigan, School of Natural Resources and Environment, Dana Bldg., 430 E. University, Ann Arbor, MI 48109.

40 PARKER MILL

A fully restored, operating grist mill, which ground the area farmers' feed from 1873 until 1968, is the focal point for most visitors at this Wash-tenaw County park. But nature lovers, birdwatchers, and anyone else who takes pleasure in a stroll through a quiet, pastoral landscape will find much more.

Fleming Creek, which powered the mill, is itself worth a visit. Almost small enough to jump, the exuberant little creek rushes over midstream boulders and recklessly weaves through curves. Mature, staid hardwoods that hover overhead seem to gaze disapprovingly at the stream's constant youthful frivolity. A short trail drops under a bridge that spans Geddes Road, then edges the stream as it tumbles over a short rapids. But if you want to follow the brook through most of the rest of the park, you have to carefully pick your way around and over streamside trees, roots and brush.

Developed trails do step into other areas of the 27-acre park, including a large meadow slowly being reclaimed by shrubs and young trees. The wide, easily walked trails pass through some excellent bird habitat — from dense thickets and open fields to the tree-lined creek — and birders should have good luck filling their binoculars from a variety of choice spots.

Scheduled for a fall 1995 completion is the mile-long Hoyt G. Post Nature Study Pathway, a barrier-free, boardwalked path through the Fleming Creek Southern alluvium forest, composed primarily of black maple, hackberry, burr oak, with southern species like sycamore, bladdernut, wafer ash, and wahoo. Six intrepretive stations on decks will focus on the area's flora and fauna, plus a wildlife observation blind will over-

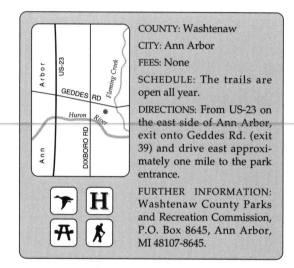

COUNTY: Washtenaw

CITY: Ann Arbor

FEES: None

SCHEDULE: The trails are open all year.

DIRECTIONS: From US-23 on the east side of Ann Arbor, exit onto Geddes Rd. (exit 39) and drive east approximately one mile to the park entrance.

FURTHER INFORMATION: Washtenaw County Parks and Recreation Commission, P.O. Box 8645, Ann Arbor, MI 48107-8645.

look the confluence of Fleming Creek and the Huron River, a favorite winter waterfowl spot.

Adjacent to the parking lot, a small picnic area, consisting of a few tables and no other facilities, overlooks both the mill and Geddes Road.

MATTHAEI BOTANICAL GARDENS
(continued from p. 45)

profusion of plants, is just about a sure antidote to February's gloom. Spring brings abundant wildflowers, flowering shrubs and migrating songbirds, followed by blooming prairie plants in summer. Beautiful fall-color walks are best September through October.

The University of Michigan's Matthaei Botanical Gardens offers one of the most unusual classes conducted at any nature center — or educational facility of any type, for that matter — in the world. Students enrolled in the class Aerial Ecology study botany and wildlife habitats from the basket of a hot-air balloon as it drifts over the countryside. This center for research, education, and the study of nature hosts a wide range of "normal" programming as well. Birdwatching, Edible Wild Plants, Herb Garden Design, Japanese Flower Arranging, and Mushrooms of Michigan are among the many classes available to both the educational community and the public.

But you don't have to ride in a hot-air balloon or sit in a classroom to learn from or simply enjoy this magnificant 250-acre natural area and indoor/outdoor botanical laboratory. Any visit should begin with a stop at the Conservatory building. There, three large rooms — the Warm House, Warm Temperate House and Arid House — hold more than 2,000 different plants. A brochure available at the building entrance briefly describes the rooms and explains and identifies the plants and the ecosystems in which they flourish.

The newest outdoor attraction is the Gateway Garden, where long- and short-term displays interpret plants native to the Americas before 1492. In this one-of-a-kind area, you'll find both ornamental plants and species such as maise that were of econonomic importance to Native Americans.

Matthaei's four nature trails, however, are the reason many nature lovers pay repeat visits. The routes vary in length, terrain and habitat. The 0.6-mile Musclewood Trail, for example, follows Fleming Creek through its flood plain, past thick shrubs, a small stand of tamaracks and a grove of very old burr oaks,

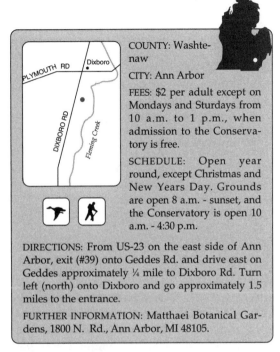

COUNTY: Washtenaw

CITY: Ann Arbor

FEES: $2 per adult except on Mondays and Sturdays from 10 a.m. to 1 p.m., when admission to the Conservatory is free.

SCHEDULE: Open year round, except Christmas and New Years Day. Grounds are open 8 a.m. - sunset, and the Conservatory is open 10 a.m. - 4:30 p.m.

DIRECTIONS: From US-23 on the east side of Ann Arbor, exit (#39) onto Geddes Rd. and drive east on Geddes approximately ¼ mile to Dixboro Rd. Turn left (north) onto Dixboro and go approximately 1.5 miles to the entrance.

FURTHER INFORMATION: Matthaei Botanical Gardens, 1800 N. Rd., Ann Arbor, MI 48105.

then circles through a beautiful wildflower garden. The Fleming Creek Trail winds for 1.2 miles through a prairie area, then follows the east side of the creek past a large, marshy pond. The garden's longest path, 1.8-mile Dix Pond Trail, meanders through a pine plantation and an upland forest, then passes two small ponds. The 0.6-mile Parker Brook Trail circles Willow Pond, crosses its namesake and borders a marsh. Perennial, herb, rose, rhododendron, and other special gardens color the grounds along all trails.

To fully appreciate the dimensions of the Matthaei Botanical Gardens, visit at various times of the year. In the dead of winter, for example, the trails are so quiet, white and peaceful that owls and hawks often perch unconcerned in trees, especially along the Dix Pond Trail. And the Conservatory, with its

(Continued on p. 44)

42 ANNE and LEONARD WING NATURE PRESERVE

A wide variety and large number of plants; the almost constant calls of Red-winged Blackbirds, warblers and herons; the rare opportunity to experience and study a wetlands habitat at very close range; and great natural beauty are reasons why, per square foot, this very small (2.5 acres) area is as much, if not more, of a treat for the senses than some larger, better-known preserves.

Framed on three sides by gently rolling, wooded hills, the entire preserve is set in a small wetlands consisting of a marsh, a pond and a tamarack bog. The marsh supports a profusion of water-loving plants and wild-flowers, and food and shelter at both the marsh and the pond draw a great number of birds. The only trail, an 80-yard-long board-walk, cuts through the heart of the marsh past a small stand of tamarack to the edge of the pond.

The Washtenaw Audubon Society owns the preserve, which is named after a husband and wife who were known respectively as a nationally prominent ornithologist and a nature writer.

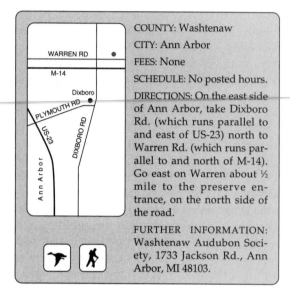

COUNTY: Washtenaw

CITY: Ann Arbor

FEES: None

SCHEDULE: No posted hours.

DIRECTIONS: On the east side of Ann Arbor, take Dixboro Rd. (which runs parallel to and east of US-23) north to Warren Rd. (which runs parallel to and north of M-14). Go east on Warren about ½ mile to the preserve entrance, on the north side of the road.

FURTHER INFORMATION: Washtenaw Audubon Society, 1733 Jackson Rd., Ann Arbor, MI 48103.

Independence Lake Park has all the makings for a good-old-fashioned, something-for-everyone, day-long family picnic. A sprawling picnic grounds, large pavilions, sandy beach, several playground areas, fishing, boating, hiking, volleyball courts, and horseshoe pits — they're all there, spread over 312 beautiful acres.

The park's huge picnic area lines Independence Lake for several hundred yards and reaches back an almost equal distance from the shoreline. You can choose a relatively secluded table, either nestled at the edge of the woods well back from the lake or next to the water. Or you can set up right in the middle of all the action, near the busy swimming beach. (Four large pavilions, which seat from 90 to 480 people, are available on a rental basis and must be reserved in advance.)

The sandy beach indents the meadow in a long, sweeping arc, and if you like to spread a blanket and be slow-roasted by the sun, there's plenty of room to baste yourself on an adjacent, treeless football-field-size grassy lawn.

The park property takes in more than half the shoreline of Independence Lake, and you don't have to get wet to enjoy the emerald-green water. You can launch your boat at a ramp south of the beach, or you can rent a boat or canoe by the hour at the swimming beach. If you like to fish but prefer doing it from a rock-solid base rather than a rocking boat, you can wet your line from a handicapper-accessible fishing pier.

Away from the lake, a mile-plus nature trail probes the park's undeveloped land., including one of the state's finest tall grass prairies, which is burn-managed to protect six species on the threatened or endangered list. The trail ambles from the parking lot down a

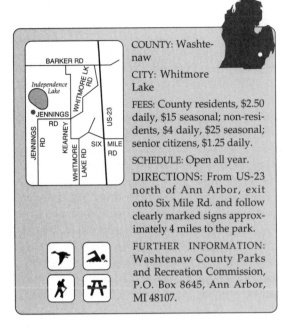

COUNTY: Washtenaw

CITY: Whitmore Lake

FEES: County residents, $2.50 daily, $15 seasonal; non-residents, $4 daily, $25 seasonal; senior citizens, $1.25 daily.

SCHEDULE: Open all year.

DIRECTIONS: From US-23 north of Ann Arbor, exit onto Six Mile Rd. and follow clearly marked signs approximately 4 miles to the park.

FURTHER INFORMATION: Washtenaw County Parks and Recreation Commission, P.O. Box 8645, Ann Arbor, MI 48107.

wide two-track; passes over a marshy pond on a long, elevated boardwalk; then crosses the park road and loops through a succession of old meadows, where shrubs and small trees are slowly filling in the open spaces. Also along that loop, the path edges a lily-pad-choked pond and leads to a tall observation platform that overlooks the surrounding marsh and broken meadows. Except for a few stands of mature hardwoods, most of what passes for woods here is young trees with a dense understory of shrubs and saplings.

Bird life is abundant along the route. Bluebird boxes line parts of the trail, and it's possible to see Woodcock, pheasants, Catbirds, Cardinals, swallows, geese and ducks, all in one 10-minute span.

44 HUDSON MILLS METROPARK

Some of the most picturesque picnic areas in southeast Michigan, scenic trails, and the beauty of the Huron River are good reasons to visit Hudson Mills Metropark.

Two trails, one barrier-free, wind through the former site of a sawmill, a gristmill, a cidermill and a plastermill, the earliest dating back to 1827. Helpful interpretive signs mark the 0.75-mile Acorn Nature Trail, which begins near the Oak Meadows Picnic Area, borders the river, then loops past areas of swamp, marsh and woods. A paved hiking/jogging/bike path, which circles the perimeter of the park, passes through woods, crosses open meadows, traverses a small island via two foot bridges, and for over a third of its approximately two-mile length, borders the river. This trail is easily accessible by wheelchair.

Four of southeast Michigan's most beautiful picnic areas — three near the banks of the river — are spread throughout the 1,545-acre park. The northernmost overlooks one of the few rapids of the Huron River. Another connects, via a small foot bridge, to a small island in the middle of the river. Groves of stately trees and open meadows are the settings for the remaining two.

Several access sites and two overnight campgrounds cater to canoeists, who consider this one of the finest sections of the Huron River to paddle.

Other facilities include several ball diamonds, disc golf, and children's playgrounds (usually near the picnic areas), plus bike and ski rentals and a food concession at an Activity Center on the east side of the park.

The park maintains groomed cross country ski trails in the winter.

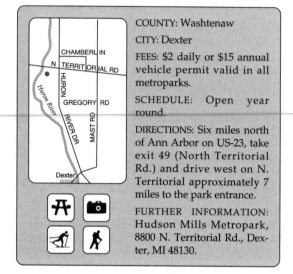

COUNTY: Washtenaw

CITY: Dexter

FEES: $2 daily or $15 annual vehicle permit valid in all metroparks.

SCHEDULE: Open year round.

DIRECTIONS: Six miles north of Ann Arbor on US-23, take exit 49 (North Territorial Rd.) and drive west on N. Territorial approximately 7 miles to the park entrance.

FURTHER INFORMATION: Hudson Mills Metropark, 8800 N. Territorial Rd., Dexter, MI 48130.

Unlike most county parks, Park Lyndon does not cater to hordes of summer picnickers, partiers and water enthusiasts. Its 205 beautiful acres of gently rolling, often steep, hilly terrain contain nearly every type of habitat known to southern Michigan, plus more than 500 species of plants — all nearly undisturbed by man since the passing of the glaciers.

When the glaciers let go of Michigan some 10,000 years ago, they left a rich and varied landscape that Europeans, almost from their first settling, did everything to change. They mined, lumbered, plowed, drained and leveled the land. But Park Lyndon was spared, and today you can witness the work of the glaciers at nearly every turn. Glacial lakes, swamps, bogs, and long, narrow ribbons of gravel called eskers, which were once streams within the mile-thick slabs of ice create an ever-changing landscape.

The park is a naturalist's playground, and with binoculars, bird books, and tree and wildflower identification guides, you can spend a day lost in reverie. You can even sample the edible nuts and berries that grow along the trails, but you can't collect them in bulk or remove them from the park.

North Territorial Road divides Park Lyndon into two distinct north/south sections. Much of the south parcel was used for grazing until the 1940s, but today you'll find little, if any, evidence of its pasture days. A thick, vine-draped oak-hickory forest covers the steep hillsides, and pine plantations, aging meadows and wetlands blanket other parts of the acreage.

Several trails, none longer than a mile and a half, wander through the varying landscape of the park's south section. A few cut through woods so peaceful and quiet that the rustle of

squirrels and chipmunks scurrying across the leaf-covered forest floor may startle you. The shortest trail falls sharply down to lily-pad-covered Lake Genevieve. The lake's shoreline is an indistinct marshy transition between water and terra firma, but two observation decks reach out from the shore to provide excellent views of the glassy-smooth water, which is populated by countless turtles, frogs, dragonflies and an occasional snake.

The main trail into the park's northern acreage, which has barely felt a touch from the hand of man, begins near the parking area on a high, open ridge but quickly plunges into a cool, shaded forest on a long descent that ends at a large expanse of marsh, swamp and wetlands named the Embury Swamp Natural Area. You can get glimpses of tuliptrees, tamaracks, and some of Michigan's rarest flora, including 23 species of ferns and 10 types of orchids, from the combination of corduroy paths, boardwalks and trails that traverse that natural area.

Two small picnic areas — each with tables, grills and a small pavilion — are located at the trailheads, one on each side of North Territorial Road.

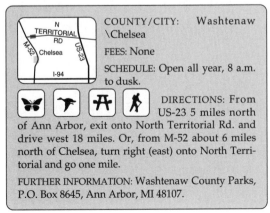

COUNTY/CITY: Washtenaw \Chelsea

FEES: None

SCHEDULE: Open all year, 8 a.m. to dusk.

DIRECTIONS: From US-23 5 miles north of Ann Arbor, exit onto North Territorial Rd. and drive west 18 miles. Or, from M-52 about 6 miles north of Chelsea, turn right (east) onto North Territorial and go one mile.

FURTHER INFORMATION: Washtenaw County Parks, P.O. Box 8645, Ann Arbor, MI 48107.

46 LEFGLEN NATURE SANCTUARY

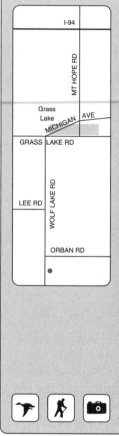

Nearly 700 native Michigan plant species, more than a third found in the state, have been identified in this unique Michigan Nature Association area, where northern and southern fauna coexist. Bring plant and wildflower field guides to fully enjoy and identify the rare wildflowers, including nine species of native orchids.

Birds as well as plants are abundant at Lefglen. More than 50 species, including a pair of Sandhill Cranes at Lake Nirvana, nest in the wide variety of habitats such as swamp, marsh, bogs, true prairie and woods.

Two unconnected mile-long trails, separated by extensive wetlands, provide access to the 210-acre sanctuary. The south trail —

COUNTY: Jackson

CITY: Grass Lake

FEES: None

SCHEDULE: No posted hours.

DIRECTIONS: From I-94 east of Jackson, take the Grass Lake exit (150) and go south to the town of Grass Lake. Turn right (west) onto Michigan Ave., go through town approximately one mile, then turn left (south) onto Wolf Lake Rd. and go 4.5 miles to a small parking area opposite 5344 Wolf Lake Rd. The south trail begins at the back of the parking area.

To reach the northern trail, park at County Park, directly opposite Little Wolf Lake about ½ mile north of the south trail parking lot, and walk north to a Michigan Nature Association cottage at 4583 Wolf Lake Rd. The trail begins there.

FURTHER INFORMATION: Michigan Nature Association, P.O. Box 102, Avoca, MI 48006.

which follows the property's boundary, generally on high ground — skirts marshland, passes through woods, then ends at one of the few areas of native prairie left in the state. The north trail briefly follows the northern boundary, then turns south and follows an esker (a serpentine ridge of gravel and sand left by a glacier) into a large swamp.

HAEHNLE MEMORIAL SANCTUARY 47

The main calling card to the Phyllis Haehnle Memorial Sanctuary is the large number of Sandhill Cranes — some standing four feet tall with wing spans of over six feet — that crowd into the marsh every spring and fall. It is not unusual to see 200 to 400 of these magnificent birds during peak migration periods in the fall, and on one November 1980 day, a record 1,325 were counted. Though some cranes nest here annually, most use the sanctuary as a stopover during their long fall migration flights.

The last two weeks in October and the first two weeks in November, between midafternoon and sunset, have proven to be the best viewing periods. The best observation spot, a high crest overlooking the marsh in the southwest corner of the sanctuary (the only area open to the public) is just a short walk northwest from the parking area. Be sure to bring binoculars, or you may have difficulty spotting the birds in the nearly mile-wide expanse of open water and thick stands of cattails.

Cranes are not the only attraction here. The sanctuary has long been recognized as a spectacular birding site, and its varied habitats — marsh, river, floodplain, climax forest and old farmland — attract a great many other birds. One avid birdwatcher, over a 20-year span from 1935 to 1955, sighted 135 different species, including Yellow Rails, Prairie Chickens and Great Blue Herons. The sanctuary also has a thriving colony of Black Terns.

Casper Haehnle donated the area to the Michigan Audubon Society in 1955 as a memorial to his daughter.

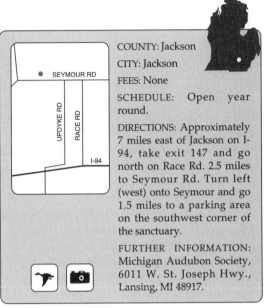

COUNTY: Jackson

CITY: Jackson

FEES: None

SCHEDULE: Open year round.

DIRECTIONS: Approximately 7 miles east of Jackson on I-94, take exit 147 and go north on Race Rd. 2.5 miles to Seymour Rd. Turn left (west) onto Seymour and go 1.5 miles to a parking area on the southwest corner of the sanctuary.

FURTHER INFORMATION: Michigan Audubon Society, 6011 W. St. Joseph Hwy., Lansing, MI 48917.

48 DAHLEM ENVIRONMENTAL EDUCATION CENTER

The Dahlem Environmental Education Center — established in 1973 by Jackson Community College for the improvement, understanding and appreciation of our natural environment — has received national recognition for excellence in science education and for good reason. A wide variety of public programs, workshops, guided hikes, summer camps, classroom visits (elementary through college), and special projects such as the annual Bluebird Festival make this 300-acre preserve an outstanding outdoor classroom for teachers, students, naturalists and the general public.

Five miles of trails and boardwalks wind through gently rolling terrain that features a varied habitat of marshes, wetlands, spring ponds, open fields, evergreen plantings, hardwood forest and a creek. The trails are open in the winter for cross country skiing. Also located on the grounds is the 16-acre Fannie Beach Arboretum.

The center is supported by fund raising, local grants, donations and memberships.

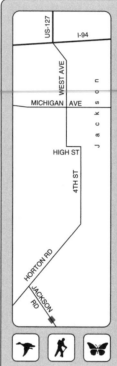

COUNTY: Jackson

CITY: Jackson

FEES: $2 per student for class visits.

SCHEDULE: Nature trail hours are 8 a.m. - 8 p.m. during Eastern Standard Time and 8 a.m. - 8 p.m. during Eastern Daylight Time.

DIRECTIONS: From I-94 in Jackson, exit (#138) onto West Ave. and go south to High St. Turn left (east) onto High and go to 4th St. Turn right (south) onto 4th and go to Horton Ave., which branches off to the west. From Horton Rd. turn left (south) onto Jackson Rd. and proceed to 7117 S. Jackson and the entrance to the center.

FURTHER INFORMATION: Dahlem Environmental Education Center, 7117 S. Jackson Rd., Jackson, MI 49201.

Goose Creek Grasslands is a 69-acre echo of the vast, open prairie that once covered large areas of lower Michigan and extended from the Midwest to the state of New York. This original, untouched Michigan tract, located on the western edge of the Irish Hills, encompasses prairie meadows, marshes and the "largest untouched calcareous fen (low land partially covered by water) known in Michigan."

Amateur and professional naturalists alike will want to pay return visits to Goose Creek. More than 220 plant species — including sedges, rushes, bog plants, native orchids, and several rare and endangered species — have been identified in the preserve. Aquatic plants thrive here, as do 20 different types of grasses, including some spectacular varieties that grow to over five feet tall. Wildflowers cover the area, especially in the spring, and prairie plants reach maturity and flower in mid to late summer. But whether in April, July or August, Goose Creek always has something different and beautiful to show off.

Birds peculiar to open meadows and marshes — such as Bobolinks, wrens, swallows and meadowlarks — inhabit the preserve. Records show that 38 species of birds, including waterfowl and gamebirds, have nested at Goose Creek.

The best way to see and appreciate the area is by boat or canoe, but you can also walk the shoulder of the road and wander through the area north of the bridge on the east side of Cement City Highway. The Michigan Nature Association conducts guided tours of the preserve on several dates throughout the year. Contact them at the address below for a schedule.

Goose Creek recently joined the 18 other original prairie remnants included in the

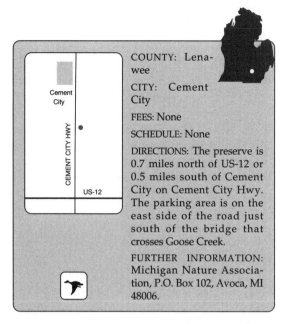

COUNTY: Lenawee

CITY: Cement City

FEES: None

SCHEDULE: None

DIRECTIONS: The preserve is 0.7 miles north of US-12 or 0.5 miles south of Cement City on Cement City Hwy. The parking area is on the east side of the road just south of the bridge that crosses Goose Creek.

FURTHER INFORMATION: Michigan Nature Association, P.O. Box 102, Avoca, MI 48006.

more than 200 nature preserves owned by the Michigan Nature Association. As part of its ongoing efforts to acquire and preserve important natural areas in the state, the 32-year-old non-profit organization is currently attempting to raise funds to purchase land in a 700-acre tract adjacent to Goose Creek that private companies are offering for development.

50 HIDDEN LAKE GARDENS

With the retreat of glaciers from northwest Lenawee County, nature slowly unveiled the rounded hills, steep valleys, conical depressions and sweeping vistas it had painstakingly created over millenniums. Centuries later, man applied strokes of his own: thousands of trees, shrubs and other plantings. Together they created a living work of art framed by the untouched woodlands and open meadows of the Irish Hills and titled, "Hidden Lake Gardens."

Harry A. Fee, a prominent Adrian businessman who was interested in scenic beauty and landscaping, began man's involvement in 1926 when he personally planned and implemented plantings on 226 acres of land he had purchased. Nineteen years later, he donated his gardens to Michigan State University and also established a trust to ensure their further development. Since then, the gardens have tripled in size, plantings have multiplied

(more than 2,500 species planted since 1960), and Mr. Fee's desire "to create landscape pictures ... (and) attract anyone interested in the out-of-doors" has been carried out brilliantly by Michigan State University.

You don't even have to leave your car to appreciate the beauty of the 760-acre area. Six miles of one-way drives wind through the gardens past thousands of labeled plants and trees — massed plantings of azaleas, crab apples, cherries, lilacs, magnolias, rhododendrons, roses, spruces, a wide variety of hardwoods, and the outstanding Harper Collection of dwarf and rare conifers, to name just a few. If you would like to temporarily lose sight of the asphalt, park in any of 10 different areas spaced along the drives and wander among a variety of collections — spruces, willows, a demonstration perennial garden and All American Trials of bedding annuals, again to name just a few.

Those who would like to explore the farther reaches of Hidden Lake Gardens can do so on any of four nature trails. The trails, totaling five miles in length, pass through oak upland forests, border old fence rows and cross rolling countryside. An extensive, in-depth 28-page trail guide points out plants and natural features along the routes and makes the walks and nature study, including some excellent birdwatching and wildflower identification, even more enjoyable.

Three separate rooms in the conservatory, located near the center of the gardens, feature a fascinating array of plants — bamboo, cactus, banana, cocoa, coffee, fig, palm tapioca and others — in their respective tropical, desert or temperate environments. A short walk from the conservatory, more indoor plant displays plus gardening and landscaping information — including programs on gardening and nature study — is available at the Gardens Center Building. A small but beautiful picnic area is located just west of the Conservatory.

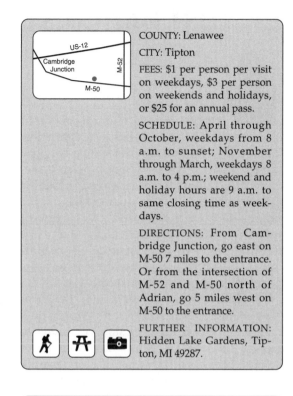

COUNTY: Lenawee

CITY: Tipton

FEES: $1 per person per visit on weekdays, $3 per person on weekends and holidays, or $25 for an annual pass.

SCHEDULE: April through October, weekdays from 8 a.m. to sunset; November through March, weekdays 8 a.m. to 4 p.m.; weekend and holiday hours are 9 a.m. to same closing time as weekdays.

DIRECTIONS: From Cambridge Junction, go east on M-50 7 miles to the entrance. Or from the intersection of M-52 and M-50 north of Adrian, go 5 miles west on M-50 to the entrance.

FURTHER INFORMATION: Hidden Lake Gardens, Tipton, MI 49287.

HIDDEN LAKES GARDENS COLOR SCHEDULE

April - Autumn: Ornamental shrubs and wildflowers.

Mid-April - Early May: Narcissus, Forsythias, Primroses

Early May - Mid-June: Tulips, cherries, redbuds, crab apples, dogwoods, azaleas, rhododendrons, lilacs

Mid-September - Early November: Autumn colors

51 LOST NATION STATE GAME AREA

Even the area's oldest residents argue over the origin of the mysterious, rather romantic name of this wild and rugged section of Hillsdale County. Speculation has swung between the practical — it was "a good place to get lost in" — to wild fantasies, perhaps kindled by the prehistoric Indian mounds that dot the area, that it once harbored a lost tribe of mankind. Another theory has it that "lost nation" refers to the last remnant of Pottawatomi Indians that lived here before the government removed them to the west.

No matter how it got its name, the 2,374-acre checkerboard tract of land, which on a map looks like a flight of stairs climbing to the city of Hillsdale, is a wild and beautiful natural retreat in the heart of rich farming country. The heavily wooded terrain is criss-crossed by glacial ridges and pierced by the swift-flowing St. Joseph of the Maume River. The landscape constantly changes as you travel even short distances on the narrow dirt roads that subdivide the area. Occasional stretches of very rugged terrain alternate with low hills covered with mature stands of hardwoods, small lakes, swamps, and bright, little streams. In the 1850s Silas Doty, a notorious outlaw and self-proclaimed Robin Hood, used the area as a hideout, and it's easy to see why. On either foot or by car, you can become momentarily disoriented by the dense thickets and small pockets of wilderness that seem more appropriate to northern Michigan.

Raccoon, fox, pheasant and opossum roam the area, and birdwatching is good throughout. Wild Turkeys have recently been released here, and you could have your day made by catching a glimpse of one. Two endangered species — a small, white lady's slipper and Kirtland's water snake — have been recorded in the area.

You can easily enjoy the scenery from a slow-moving car on the narrow dirt roads that grid the state game area. The lush vegetation, moving water, and occasional decaying structures that date back to the earliest settlers are among the ever-changing sights.

But the best way to appreciate and enjoy Lost Nation is on foot. There are no officially marked trails, but the combination of old roads now closed to motor traffic and many well-worn footpaths provide plenty of hiking opportunities. The state game area lies within a V formed by highways M-99 and M-34, and nearly all roads within the V that cross state land are dotted by parking areas from which you can head into the woods.

Jeff Greene from District 13 of the DNR, which administers Lost Nation, recommends several good areas for hikers. The nicest and easiest walking is on Way Road. To reach it drive about 3.5 miles east of the intersection of M-99 and M-34 on M-34 to Rumsey Road. Turn south onto Rumsey and go one mile to

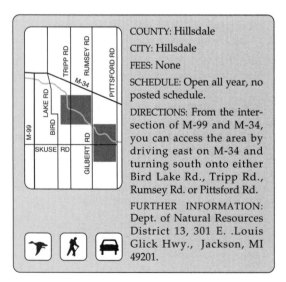

COUNTY: Hillsdale

CITY: Hillsdale

FEES: None

SCHEDULE: Open all year, no posted schedule.

DIRECTIONS: From the intersection of M-99 and M-34, you can access the area by driving east on M-34 and turning south onto either Bird Lake Rd., Tripp Rd., Rumsey Rd. or Pittsford Rd.

FURTHER INFORMATION: Dept. of Natural Resources District 13, 301 E. .Louis Glick Hwy., Jackson, MI 49201.

Way Road. Turn west onto Way and drive 0.4 mile to a small pulloff on the north side of the road where a barricaded gully and two-track come in from the north. Greene says the trail from there "follows a high ridge with mature oaks and hickories and ends when following the lefthand fork in the trail at the St. Joe of the Maume River."

You can reach another especially pretty site by driving farther west on Way Road until it ends at Tripp Road. Turn north onto Tripp and drive almost a mile to where a narrow dirt road intersects from the west. Within a few hundred yards of that intersection are four parking areas from which several unmarked trails lead into the forested hills.

Just east of Tripp Road, almost opposite the intersection, are the ruins of what looks like an old mill. You can see the stonework of the millrace, and the foundation of the mill itself rises a few feet above the ground. It is a delightful spot to pull off the road, enjoy the view of the river, eat a picnic lunch, and wonder about who, why and how someone long ago started a business in this remote place.

Other suggested hikes by Greene begin at a parking area on Gilbert Road just south of Skuse Road and on an old two-track on Bowditch Trail a half mile east of Bird Lake Road.

Hikers may have even more choices in the near future, because the state game area is on the proposed route of the North Country Trail, which when completed will completely traverse both of Michigan's peninsulas.

52 SLAYTON ARBORETUM

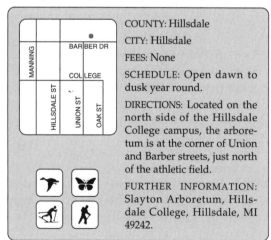

Slayton Arboretum, on the campus of Hillsdale College, proves that an arboretum can have value far in excess of its scientific and educational purposes. The 72 acres of natural plantings, naturalistic landscaping and outstanding examples of fieldstone masonry is an aesthetic delight.

From a narrow, grass-covered plain enclosed by a fieldstone wall and marked by groupings of ornamental shrubs, mature trees and several ponds, the preserve climbs a hill blanketed by low-growing evergreens and tall pines, all accented by wildflowers. Most shrubs and trees bear identifying labels. A steep trail with large stone steps winds up the hill, which is also cut by a small manmade stream that ripples down the slope, tumbles over a waterfall, and comes to rest in a small, hidden pool. At the crest of the hill, a well-worn path follows the boundaries of the arboretum and offers good views of the grounds and plantings below.

Two fieldstone gazebos are the arboretum's two most distinctive manmade features. One overlooks the preserve from the top of the hill

and, except for the profusion of trees and shrubs, may remind you of a German castle perched above the Rhine. The second gazebo is set beside a rock garden at the base of the hill within sight of a picturesque goldfish pond. A footbridge, amphitheater, fieldstone retaining walls, and two small fieldstone buildings add their charm to the surroundings.

You're welcome to wander anywhere along the grassy plain, and in addition to the main stone walkway, a series of other short trails wander up the hill and border its crest. The east edge of the arboretum ends at a wild, overgrown swamp pierced by a trail that can be wet and muddy in the spring.

The wide diversity of plant life, the good cover interspersed with open areas, and the marsh on the east attract a relatively large number of birds for such a small area, and the arboretum has long been a favored bird-watching site for area residents.

In addition to birds, the arboretum also draws brides and is a popular location for outdoor weddings. And when the snow flies, cross country skiers make tracks through the striking scenery.

COUNTY: Hillsdale

CITY: Hillsdale

FEES: None

SCHEDULE: Open dawn to dusk year round.

DIRECTIONS: Located on the north side of the Hillsdale College campus, the arboretum is at the corner of Union and Barber streets, just north of the athletic field.

FURTHER INFORMATION: Slayton Arboretum, Hillsdale College, Hillsdale, MI 49242.

KOPE KON NATURE SANCTUARY 53 and ADALINE KERSHAW WOODS

The last untouched shoreline on a lake shared with Ohio plus an adjacent parcel representing one of Michigan's last virgin wilderness areas combine for a total of 56 acres of unique natural beauty. Second-growth forest and open fields add to the variety of habitat, and more than 50 birds, including five species of woodpeckers, nest within the area.

Named after a Potawatomi Indian chief whose people lived in this Michigan/Ohio border area, Kope Kon Nature Sanctuary hugs a small inlet on Lake George's northern shore. There, cattail marshes, water lilies and shallow coves attract many shorebirds and waterfowl, including Green Herons, Great Blue Herons and Canadian Geese. Wood Ducks nest in hollow trees in a red-maple swamp back from the shoreline.

The unusual Kentucky coffee tree — with its double compound leaves and seeds that early pioneers used to make a substitute coffee — grows in Kope Kon as does the rare king-nut (a member of the hickory family). More common of the 30 different species found here are pawpaw, red maple, tulip, sassafras, beech, basswood, and three species of elm.

Just back from Lake George and adjoining Kope Kon Nature Sanctuary is Kershaw Woods, named after the woman who deeded this land to the Michigan Nature Association in 1979. In sharp contrast to the modern homes built just across the road, much of Kershaw Woods — with its towering oaks, flowering dogwood, rare plants, wildflowers and ferns — remains as it was before settlers came to the state.

From the end of Kope Kon Road, two trails circle into Kope Kon Sanctuary and two others lead several hundred feet into Kershaw Woods.

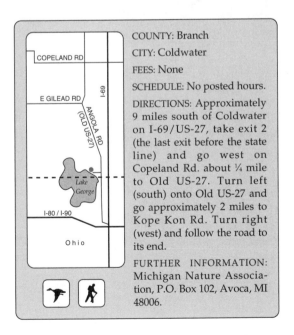

COUNTY: Branch

CITY: Coldwater

FEES: None

SCHEDULE: No posted hours.

DIRECTIONS: Approximately 9 miles south of Coldwater on I-69/US-27, take exit 2 (the last exit before the state line) and go west on Copeland Rd. about ¼ mile to Old US-27. Turn left (south) onto Old US-27 and go approximately 2 miles to Kope Kon Rd. Turn right (west) and follow the road to its end.

FURTHER INFORMATION: Michigan Nature Association, P.O. Box 102, Avoca, MI 48006.

54 PAHL POINT PARK

On the face of it, this small St. Joseph County park hardly seems worth going out of your way to visit. At three acres in size and with only three picnic tables, it doesn't appear to have much to offer. But if you want to experience small slices of diverse habitat without large expenditures of energy, if you like to picnic in private, or if you're after maximum bird sightings with minimum effort, this vest-pocket park will suit you just fine. And there's an added bonus: You get a striking view of one of only two historic covered bridges in the state, only a short walk away.

The park's lone nature trail can hardly be more than 100 yards long, but within that distance it cuts through a small stand of mature hardwoods, bisects a reedy wetlands and tiny marsh, and takes you out onto a dock that extends into a backwater of the St. Joseph River formed by the Sturgis Dam. On the brief walk, you'll pass a fine sampling of wildflowers and native Michigan plants and move through an area with good birding possibilities. The extensive open water attracts waterfowl, the dense marsh and brush edging the backwater draws other species, and the woods and open fields surrounding the park shelter even more varieties.

The picnic grounds, with its three tables and grills, flanks the nature area, and you can almost always be assured of having the place to yourself.

Visible from the dock at the end of the nature trail and only a couple of hundred yards walk from the park entrance on Silver St. is the Langley Covered Bridge. Built in 1887, the old, red structure with white trim is the longest covered bridge in the state.

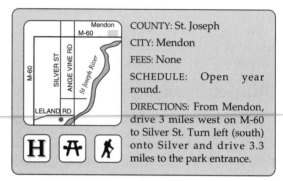

COUNTY: St. Joseph

CITY: Mendon

FEES: None

SCHEDULE: Open year round.

DIRECTIONS: From Mendon, drive 3 miles west on M-60 to Silver St. Turn left (south) onto Silver and drive 3.3 miles to the park entrance.

WHITE PIGEON RIVER 55
NATURE SANCTUARY

Fifty-eight acres of steep hillsides, old river channels, flooded bottomlands, lagoons and riverbanks, plus a riot of plant and animal life are good reasons to visit and explore this premier example of the work of the Michigan Nature Association.

The sanctuary is quickly and justifiably earning a reputation as a great birding spot, especially at the height of activity in May and June. According to a 24-hour bird count by the M.N.A. in 1975, 55 species — including warblers, vireos, kingfishers and two species of flycatchers — nest in the sanctuary's varied habitats. Prothonotary Warblers, which winter in South America, also make their summer home in wooded swamps at White Pigeon River. A glimpse of this rare Michigan nester, whose deep, brilliant yellow head and breast are set off by contrasting blue-gray wings, would, alone, make a visit here worthwhile. Great Blue Herons from a rookery just to the north of the sanctuary, plus gloriously colored Cerulian Warblers, Scarlet Tanagers, Indigo Buntings, Rose-breasted Grosbeaks and Wood Ducks are prominent spring and summer visitors to the sanctuary.

A tremendous diversity of plant life also covers the sanctuary. Shrubs, vines, trees, aquatic plants and wildflowers compete for space along the riverbanks. Back from the river, wild roses, violets, May-apple, Solomon's seal, Jack-in-the-pulpit, and other wildflowers blanket the hillsides in spring and are scattered throughout the property spring through fall. Six species of oak, four of ash, three kinds of maple, plus honey locust, hackberry, basswood, black willow, sycamore, redbud and mulberry are among the many trees that thrive here.

White-tail deer, rabbits, fox, squirrels, woodchucks, raccoons, numerous toads and frogs, Massasauga rattlesnakes and prodigious snapping turtles are among the wildlife that call the White Pigeon River area home. Twenty-seven species — including giant swallowtail, tiger swallowtail, viceroy, bronze-copper and hackberry — make up a partial list of butterflies found at the sanctuary.

The easiest way to negotiate the area's extremes in terrain and habitat is on a nature trail that begins at the intersection of Burke and Silver Creek roads, follows closed-and-gated Burke Road south then turns east into the sanctuary. This easy-to-walk trail generally travels through high, dry hillsides except near the river, where the sanctuary is overgrown and somewhat difficult to get through.

This sanctuary is just one of many examples of the outstanding work done by the non-profit Michigan Nature Association in preserving our state's natural heritage.

COUNTY: St. Joseph

CITY: White Pigeon

FEES: None

SCHEDULE: No posted hours.

DIRECTIONS: From the junction of US-12 and US-131 just west of White Pigeon, drive 2 miles west on US-12 to Burke Rd. Turn left (south) onto Burke and drive one mile to the intersection with Silver Creek Rd. Burke Rd., which marks the sanctuary's western boundary, is closed south of this intersection. Park off the road at the intersection but do not block the gate because, local farm tractors occasionally use the road.

FURTHER INFORMATION: Michigan Nature Association, P.O. Box 102, Avoca, MI 48006.

56 DR. T.K. LAWLESS COUNTY PARK

If you think that our state's southern tier of counties are rather flat and featureless, this Cass County park will pleasantly surprise you. A covey of knobby hills and deep hollows ripple the park's landscape. Open fields dot the grounds, but a dense hardwood forest covers most of the park. Two small lakes, a pond and a stream that hide amid the folds and depressions add their charm to the landscape.

The park's seven trails all begin and end in the central parking area, and their long, leisurely loops trace across the property. The nearly five miles of wide, well-marked paths involve plenty of up and down walking as they cut through the heart of the wooded hills, cross the stream, and lead to both Hogback and Doane lakes. A paved handicap-access nature trail was completed in 1994.

Trail maps are available at the park entrance and the County Road Commission office, 340 North O'Keefe Street, Cassopolis.

The combination of deep cover, open fields and sheltered lakes holds out the promise of good birdwatching. Deer are plentiful, and if you walk quietly and keep a sharp lookout, you're likely to spot more than one whitetail moving through the woods.

A picnic area and two pavilions border the parking lot, and other facilities include ball diamonds and a soccer field.

In winter, beginner through advanced cross country skiers set tracks on the wide paths. Kids especially love the manmade tubing hill, and the park even supplies the tubes.

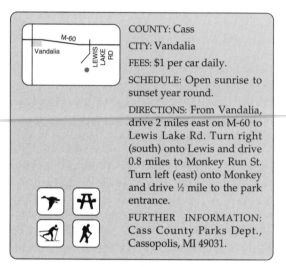

COUNTY: Cass

CITY: Vandalia

FEES: $1 per car daily.

SCHEDULE: Open sunrise to sunset year round.

DIRECTIONS: From Vandalia, drive 2 miles east on M-60 to Lewis Lake Rd. Turn right (south) onto Lewis and drive 0.8 miles to Monkey Run St. Turn left (east) onto Monkey and drive ½ mile to the park entrance.

FURTHER INFORMATION: Cass County Parks Dept., Cassopolis, MI 49031.

At this Cass County park, you have the rare opportunity to picnic, hike and study nature in a national Natural Landmark that also serves as a living research laboratory. The 10-acre park occupies a small corner of Newton Woods, one of the few stands of original Eastern hardwood forest left in Michigan. Dominated by sugar maple, beech and a few monstrous tuliptrees, Newton Woods' 580 acres contains a significant portion of all that remains of the rich broad-leaf forests that covered much of southern Michigan before the coming of European settlers. The woods are owned by the Forestry Department of Michigan State University, and scattered through the ancient woods are demonstration plantings, tree plantations, and research areas where scientists are studying the natural process of the forest and developing methods for improving forest management.

But you don't have to be a scientist to appreciate or enjoy the area. You can hike three trails, ranging from one to slightly more than a mile and a half in length, that pass underneath towering stands of old-growth hardwoods, cross a picturesque trout stream, and take in a variety of interesting tree plantations. Within a short walk of the east entrance, for instance, a white-pine stand planted in 1945 and a grove of black walnut, white ash, red oak and black cherry planted in 1946 edge the trail. Other specimen trees are labeled along the routes.

The biggest tuliptree east of the Mississippi grew here until blown down in 1984 by a great storm. A 16-foot section of that 400-year-old monster is one display near the park's east entrance, and you can see its stump at the end of an 0.8-mile trail. Close to it is a living relative that some day may inherit the downed giant's title.

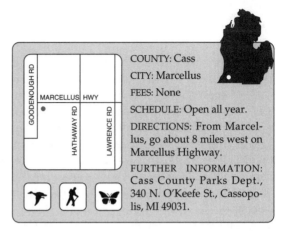

COUNTY: Cass

CITY: Marcellus

FEES: None

SCHEDULE: Open all year.

DIRECTIONS: From Marcellus, go about 8 miles west on Marcellus Highway.

FURTHER INFORMATION: Cass County Parks Dept., 340 N. O'Keefe St., Cassopolis, MI 49031.

At the park's east entrance, a small picnic grounds and pavilion nestles beside a sparkling, little creek. A much bigger picnic area, with a large playground and pavilion, hides beneath the forest canopy of a dense grove of hardwoods on the other side of the creek. A road from the west entrance circles through those deeply shaded grounds, and you'll find individual parking spots next to most tables and grills. A short path and wood bridge that crosses the stream join the two picnic areas.

58 DOWAGIAC WOODS

Barely touched by man, this 220-acre tract is so fertile you can often find more than a dozen plants growing in a single square foot. The land here has never been farmed, grazed or, except for sporadic lumbering operations, otherwise disturbed. Its owner, the Michigan Nature Association, in fact, believes that Dowagiac Woods may be the largest moist virgin-soil woodland left in Michigan.

You might expect such an area to support a profusion of plants and animals, and it does. Four hundred identified plants — hepatica, bloodroot, anemones, trilliums, five species of orchids, and more than 20 kinds of ferns, to name just a few — thrive in Dowagiac Woods. The area also shelters nine plants and animals — including swallowtail butterflies, spotted turtles and marsh blue grass — that are endangered in Michigan. The sanctuary is, in fact, a giant living outdoor natural history museum.

Spring is without a doubt the best time to visit. Fifty different blooming species of wildflowers literally carpet the forest floor then in a spectacular display. The star of the show? — the blue-eyed Mary, a delicate blue-and-white flower that blooms from April to June in the damp, open woods of only four southern Michigan counties.

Although Dowagiac Woods puts on its greatest show in spring, visits in summer and fall pay dividends, too. Prairie grasses and wildflowers, for example, bloom in July and August. And 45 different kinds of trees — including blue beech, chinkapin oak, cork elm, hackberry, and Ohio buckeye, which is endangered in Michigan — just about guarantee beautiful autumn color.

Birdwatchers, too, will not be disappointed. Forty-nine species nest in the sanctuary, and many more pass through, especially during spring migration. Northern Yellowthroats, Acadian Flycatchers, woodpeckers, Wood Ducks, Scarlet Tanagers, grosbeaks, and Indigo Buntings are just a few of the many species birders might spot here.

Hikers can use three trails to explore the sanctuary. The main trail begins at the north edge of the parking lot, then circles for 1.5 miles through the sanctuary. An extension of this loop reaches to the northern limits of the sanctuary. Both trails occasionally cross wet ground, especially in the spring. A short, easy trail — especially beautiful in the spring when the woods are blanketed with wildflowers — begins on Frost Road west of the parking area in the extreme southwest corner of the sanctuary.

The Michigan Nature Association purchased this area in 1983 with funds from 550 individual contributors plus a grant from the Kresge Foundation.

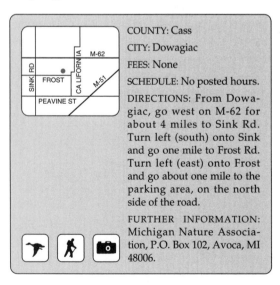

COUNTY: Cass

CITY: Dowagiac

FEES: None

SCHEDULE: No posted hours.

DIRECTIONS: From Dowagiac, go west on M-62 for about 4 miles to Sink Rd. Turn left (south) onto Sink and go one mile to Frost Rd. Turn left (east) onto Frost and go about one mile to the parking area, on the north side of the road.

FURTHER INFORMATION: Michigan Nature Association, P.O. Box 102, Avoca, MI 48006.

FERNWOOD, INC. 59

Nature provided the raw materials: ravine-cut hills that sharply rise 125 feet from the St. Joseph River to a gently rolling terrain of woodland, open fields and a tall-grass prairie. Later, man added some finishing touches of his own: numerous gardens, plantings and an arboretum. Together, they created Fernwood, a 105-acre privately owned preserve and botanical garden on the east bank of the St. Joseph River where you can enjoy the peace and beauty of nature from a garden gazebo, a riverbank, the midst of a garden, or a hillside full of azaleas.

Twelve nature trails, though totaling only three miles, pass by a startling array of mini-ecosystems that results from the great difference in elevation and soil types here. The River Trail, for example, switchbacks down the steep fern-covered banks of the St. Joseph River. The Wilderness Trail, on the other hand, wanders through 18 acres of untouched forest. Other trails — including one guided by a helpful brochure, available at the entrance — probe a cattail marsh, a trout pond, a creek, a lily pond and steep ravines.

Trails also lead to a 45-acre arboretum and a five-acre tall-grass prairie. The Arboretum Trail (the longest in the park) wanders through carefully arranged plantings of ornamental and native shrubs and trees. To reach the tall-grass prairie, north of the arboretum in the extreme northeast corner of the preserve, take a cutoff from either the Arboretum or Wilderness trails. The best views of this small sample of the great prairie system that once spanned large areas of the Midwest come from an observation platform located at the midpoint of a trail that skirts the prairie's southern edge.

Flower trees, shrubs, annuals and perennials fill a large main garden, located near the

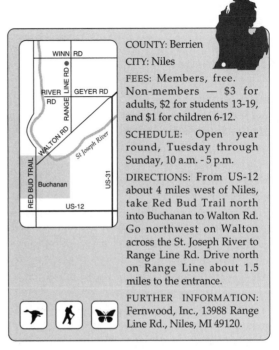

COUNTY: Berrien

CITY: Niles

FEES: Members, free. Non-members — $3 for adults, $2 for students 13-19, and $1 for children 6-12.

SCHEDULE: Open year round, Tuesday through Sunday, 10 a.m. - 5 p.m.

DIRECTIONS: From US-12 about 4 miles west of Niles, take Red Bud Trail north into Buchanan to Walton Rd. Go northwest on Walton across the St. Joseph River to Range Line Rd. Drive north on Range Line about 1.5 miles to the entrance.

FURTHER INFORMATION: Fernwood, Inc., 13988 Range Line Rd., Niles, MI 49120.

entrance. Throughout the preserve, smaller specialized gardens include a children's Discovery Garden and the Rock and Bog gardens, which display unusual and rare ferns, dwarf conifers, and plants from around the world. Hanging and potted tropical plants fill a greenhouse, and wildflowers, herbs, perennials, lilac, boxwood, iris and daylily cover other special planting areas scattered throughout the grounds.

60 TRILLIUM RAVINE PLANT PRESERVE

It's just a short, pleasant stroll through a small stand of mature hardwoods to the focal point of this 15-acre Michigan Nature Association parcel. Problem is, by late spring the walk passes through such a profusion of delicate beauty, you may have trouble reaching the most memorable spot in the preserve.

So on your way to the main attraction, try to ignore the imposing, downright huge beech trees and don't get suckered into kneeling among the riot of wildflowers everywhere underfoot. Press on through all this natural beauty until you get to a V-shaped ravine with almost geometrically perfect sides. By late spring its steep slopes are blanketed in a rich, dense green that from a distance looks like the felt covering on a pool table. The panoramic view is captivating, but a closer look is what you're here for.

Covering the ravine's slopes are two flowers seldom found in Michigan — toadshade and prairie trillium. These wildflowers, which bloom as early as April 9th, have dark-red stalkless flowers that rest directly on the deep-green mottled leaves. Their rarity, exquisite beauty, and unusual setting in the ravine combine to make this tiny corner of the state a uniquely beautiful spot.

Once you have soaked in the view and studied the flowers, you can turn to the preserve's other treasures. Basswood, ironwood and red oak share the forest with beech and maple. Closer to the ground, mosses and ferns are scattered among wildflowers. In late spring, May-apples, violets, yellow trout lilies, wood poppies and other wildflowers grow so thick that it's almost impossible to walk the preserve without stepping on them.

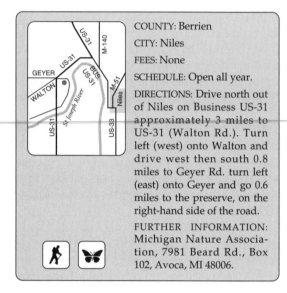

COUNTY: Berrien

CITY: Niles

FEES: None

SCHEDULE: Open all year.

DIRECTIONS: Drive north out of Niles on Business US-31 approximately 3 miles to US-31 (Walton Rd.). Turn left (west) onto Walton and drive west then south 0.8 miles to Geyer Rd. turn left (east) onto Geyer and go 0.6 miles to the preserve, on the right-hand side of the road.

FURTHER INFORMATION: Michigan Nature Association, 7981 Beard Rd., Box 102, Avoca, MI 48006.

This heavily wooded 121-acre Berrien County park is as pleasing to the senses today as it must have been to the Indians who passed through it on the Sauk and Chicago trails and to the French voyageurs who paddled their fur-laden canoes down the historic St. Joseph River, which marks the park's west boundary.

Today, foot travelers in the park can follow the course of the slow-moving river for almost half a mile on a trail atop steep-sided bluffs that line the water. Other of the park's four-plus miles of scenic hiking routes skirt several open meadows and cut narrow corridors through a dense second-growth forest. Birding is excellent along all the paths, and sharp eyes and quiet steps may also reward you with glimpses of the deer that inhabit the park. For even more hiking options, you can take a trail that connects to Indiana's St. Patrick County Park, across Bertrand's south boundary. A detailed brochure, available at Bertrand's visitor center, maps the hiking trails in both parks and also highlights the Hoosier park's other facilities.

Madeline Bertrand Park, is named after a Potawatomi woman, but the French traders called the area Parc aux Vaches ("cow pasture") because they regularly spotted buffalo grazing in a meadow here. Today, the pasture where buffalo roamed is a broad, grassy picnic grounds ringed by trees. Most tables and grills there are within easy walking distance of playgrounds, ball fields, hiking trails and the park's most unusual feature, an 18-hole disc golf course, where players use frisbee-like discs instead of balls and clubs to reach from tees to holes. Scattered throughout the park are several picnic shelters, including one built out over the side of a bluff with a commanding view of the 50-yard-wide St. Joseph

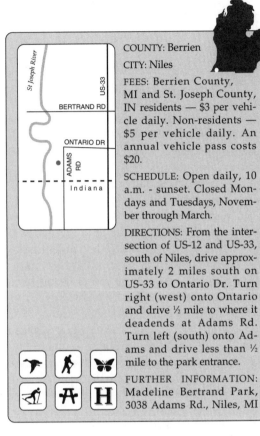

COUNTY: Berrien

CITY: Niles

FEES: Berrien County, MI and St. Joseph County, IN residents — $3 per vehicle daily. Non-residents — $5 per vehicle daily. An annual vehicle pass costs $20.

SCHEDULE: Open daily, 10 a.m. - sunset. Closed Mondays and Tuesdays, November through March.

DIRECTIONS: From the intersection of US-12 and US-33, south of Niles, drive approximately 2 miles south on US-33 to Ontario Dr. Turn right (west) onto Ontario and drive ½ mile to where it deadends at Adams Rd. Turn left (south) onto Adams and drive less than ½ mile to the park entrance.

FURTHER INFORMATION: Madeline Bertrand Park, 3038 Adams Rd., Niles, MI

River.

The visitor center is the staging area for a variety of nature programs, which range from night nature walks to fall color tours. A window wall on one side of the building looks out onto a bird feeding area.

During the winter months, you can cross country ski over 3.5 kilometers of groomed trails. Fires blaze in trailside warming shelters, and a mile of trail is lit at night.

62 DAYTON WET PRAIRIE PRESERVE

This quietly spectacular preserve holds one of the last vestiges of a 15,000-acre prairie that at one time spread over much of the Michigan/Indiana border. The 47-acre parcel survived the plow and passed almost untouched into the hands of the Nature Conservancy because numerous small ponds and countless ground seepages made it unsuitable for farming. A jungle of wildflowers, however, thrives in the moist, rich soil.

No trails have made their way into the sanctuary, since most of the land is a checkerboard of small, relatively dry hummocks; wet, soggy depressions; and waist-high grass. About the only place from which to appreciate the colorful profusion of plant life is from Curran Road, which bisects the preserve from east to west. With a wildflower guide you can identify and photograph plants — including rare and threatened species such as rosin weed, Jacobs ladder, spotted phlox and numerous grasses — within a few feet of the road. The preserve area south of the road is higher and drier than the north, and you can walk several yards into and over the primeval prairie there.

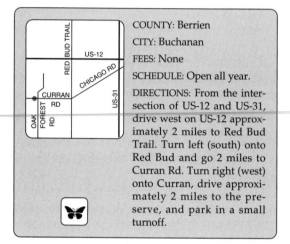

COUNTY: Berrien

CITY: Buchanan

FEES: None

SCHEDULE: Open all year.

DIRECTIONS: From the intersection of US-12 and US-31, drive west on US-12 approximately 2 miles to Red Bud Trail. Turn left (south) onto Red Bud and go 2 miles to Curran Rd. Turn right (west) onto Curran, drive approximately 2 miles to the preserve, and park in a small turnoff.

LOVE CREEK NATURE CENTER 63

Be sure to bring your camera when you visit this plant and wildlife sanctuary. Then step up to a one-way wildlife observation window in the center's interpretive building and photograph a variety of animals and birds from a closeness you may never approach again.

Your camera will also come in handy during walks down any of the 200-acre center's 13 nature trails. In spring and summer, an abundance of wildflowers — from Dutchman's breeches and trillium to marsh marigolds — line nearly six miles of trails interrupted now and then by wooden bridges and trailside benches. At any time of year, the beech/maple climax forest, open fields, pond, small two-acre marsh, Love Creek and observation tower overlooking a marsh provide not only a variety of photo opportunities but also an ideal setting to simply contemplate the quiet beauty of nature.

Love Creek personnel conduct guided field trips, programs for school children, and classes on wildlife and ecology plus year-round nature walks and slide shows. Other natural displays and exhibits complement the interpretive center's main window attraction. Birdwatching here is rated good, especially during the spring migration season.

Hiking and snowshoeing, plus more than five miles of groomed cross country ski trails of varying difficulty are winter attractions.

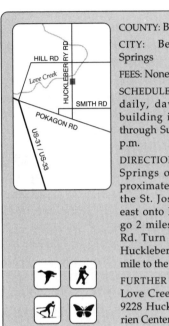

COUNTY: Berrien

CITY: Berrien Springs

FEES: None

SCHEDULE: Trails are open daily, dawn - dusk. The building is open Tuesday through Sunday, 11 a.m. - 5 p.m.

DIRECTIONS: In Berrien Springs on US-31/33 approximately ½ mile east of the St. Joseph River, turn east onto Pokagon Rd. and go 2 miles to Huckleberry Rd. Turn left (north) onto Huckleberry and drive one mile to the entrance.

FURTHER INFORMATION: Love Creek Nature Center, 9228 Huckleberry Rd., Berrien Center, MI 49102.

64 SARETT NATURE CENTER

Those who like to view the natural world from as many angles as possible will enjoy the Sarett Nature Center. There, in a gallery of manmade structures — towers, elevated platforms, benches boardwalks and an extensive system of woodchip-covered paths — you can view 350 acres of swamp and floodplain forest, cattail marshes, tamarack bogs, meadows, streams, manmade ponds and upland forest from a wide range of perspectives. Plus, a beautifully illustrated guide advises what to look for at each stop along five trails totaling more than six miles.

And there is much to see. Located on the banks of the Paw Paw River, this fine sanctuary is composed of many different habitats that support a wide variety of plant and animal life. Tamarack, willow, alder, spice bush, hardwoods, wild swamp rose, multiflora rose, ferns, sedges, and a multitude of wildflowers, for example, are among the flora found here.

Shorebirds and waterfowl are attracted to Sarett's extensive wetlands, and rails, marsh wrens and ducks nest in its cattail marshes. Hawks and owls, too, are common visitors to the sanctuary, owned by the Michigan Audubon Society, and spring migration is an excellent time to spot songbirds here. Sarett Nature Center encourages those visits through an extensive program of wildlife plantings to provide food and shelter for birds and animals.

To attract human visitors and to meet its stated goal to "provide quality environmental education to the community," Sarett offers a wide range of facilities — meeting rooms, exhibits, a book shop, a library and an observation room — plus quality public programs, including natural history classes and guided field trips and expeditions. And attract people it does. In 1985, alone, more than 19,000 school children from southwestern Michigan took part in the center's programs.

Trails are open for cross country skiing in the winter.

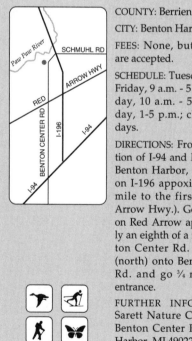

COUNTY: Berrien

CITY: Benton Harbor

FEES: None, but donations are accepted.

SCHEDULE: Tuesday through Friday, 9 a.m. - 5 p.m.; Saturday, 10 a.m. - 5 p.m.; Sunday, 1-5 p.m.; closed Mondays.

DIRECTIONS: From the junction of I-94 and I-196 east of Benton Harbor, drive north on I-196 appoximately one mile to the first exit (Red Arrow Hwy.). Go southwest on Red Arrow approximately an eighth of a mile to Benton Center Rd. Turn right (north) onto Benton Center Rd. and go ¾ mile to the entrance.

FURTHER INFORMATION: Sarett Nature Center, 2300 Benton Center Rd., Benton Harbor, MI 49022.

ALLEGAN STATE GAME AREA 65

Scenic beauty, easy hiking, two campgrounds, and some of the state's best bird-watching are good reasons to pay a visit to the Allegan State Game Area.

In this large area of marshlands, the Kalamazoo River branches into many bayous, and during fall migration, waterfowl by the thousands stop along the river, marshes, streams and ponds. Some — including Canada Geese and even a few Snow, Ross', and White-fronted geese — winter over in the area.

In May during spring migration, large numbers of warblers, including Golden-winged Warblers and Hooded Warblers, move through the area. The Allegan State Game Area also is one of the few places in the state that hosts large numbers of Prothonotary Warblers. Best locations to spot the warblers plus other songbirds are along creeks near the river and at Swan Creek Pond. Among the many other birds to look for here are Pileated Woodpeckers, several different thrushes, Scarlet Tanager and Wild Turkeys.

An 18-mile web of well-marked, level, easily walked hiking trails laces through a beautiful setting of streams, marshes, lakes, forests and open fields. Most of the trails are included in the Swan Creek Foot Trails System. This trail network is composed of several one- to two-mile loops that variously follow the course of Swan Creek, circle Swan Creek Pond, skirt wetlands and thrust into other areas of the game area. Thirty-three sites at Pine Point Campground, located on Swan Creek Pond accommodate campers.

To the west of the Swan Creek System, one 10-mile circuit loops past the park's other campground. Hikers who enter this trail from the north end of Swan Creek Pond will reach the 80-site Ely Lake Campground after a 6.5-mile walk. Another 3.5-mile trail connects

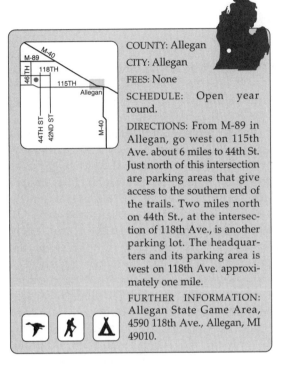

COUNTY: Allegan

CITY: Allegan

FEES: None

SCHEDULE: Open year round.

DIRECTIONS: From M-89 in Allegan, go west on 115th Ave. about 6 miles to 44th St. Just north of this intersection are parking areas that give access to the southern end of the trails. Two miles north on 44th St., at the intersection of 118th Ave., is another parking lot. The headquarters and its parking area is west on 118th Ave. approximately one mile.

FURTHER INFORMATION: Allegan State Game Area, 4590 118th Ave., Allegan, MI 49010.

back from Ely Lake Campground to the south end of the Swan Creek Pond trail network.

All hiking trails and campgrounds are clearly marked on a map available at the park headquarters, on 118th Avenue.

66 KALAMAZOO NATURE CENTER

A wide variety of demonstration projects — from a 128-year-old functioning pioneer farm to a modern Solar Homestead and Solar Garden — are the main attractions to one of Michigan's premier nature centers.

Eleven trails totaling 8 miles lead to a natural spectrum of special projects and demonstrations. Nine hundred native Michigan-area trees and shrubs, for example, fill a 25-acre arboretum. A formal garden and a prairie restoration project have their own reserved sites within the 640-acre center, too. Early American crafts and early rural Michigan life are played out at the DeLano Homestead, a completely restored functioning pioneer farm, originally built in 1858. Modern gardening and farming techniques, on the other hand, are demonstrated at the Youth Solar Garden and the Tillers Small Farm Program. And at yet another demonstration project, easy-to-install, low-cost energy conservation equipment has turned a drafty old house into an energy-efficient Solar Homestead.

A variety of exhibits that interpret Michigan's natural history plus a live-animal display, an extensive nature library and a book shop compete for space inside the busy interpretive center. The building is also the focal point for an ambitious number of programs — ranging from summer camps and family picnics to conservation and natural history workshops — geared to students, educators and the general public.

Not lost among the dazzle of the exhibits and outdoor projects and displays is the quiet beauty of nature. Most of the outstanding natural features — including the Kalamazoo River and more than 200 acres of mature beech/maple forest — that drew James Fenimore Cooper as a regular visitor to the area more than 100 years ago are even more impressive today. Walkers can also stroll along forest paths, explore the banks of a small stream or investigate marshes and ponds. And both birdwatchers and wildflower enthusiasts will pay return visits here.

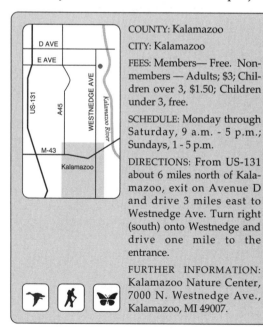

COUNTY: Kalamazoo

CITY: Kalamazoo

FEES: Members— Free. Non-members — Adults; $3; Children over 3, $1.50; Children under 3, free.

SCHEDULE: Monday through Saturday, 9 a.m. - 5 p.m.; Sundays, 1 - 5 p.m.

DIRECTIONS: From US-131 about 6 miles north of Kalamazoo, exit on Avenue D and drive 3 miles east to Westnedge Ave. Turn right (south) onto Westnedge and drive one mile to the entrance.

FURTHER INFORMATION: Kalamazoo Nature Center, 7000 N. Westnedge Ave., Kalamazoo, MI 49007.

For the closest and clearest look you may ever get at a virtual Audubon's Who's Who of birds of prey, visit the Kellogg Bird Sanctuary, northwest of Battle Creek. The sanctuary has become one of the Midwest's largest havens for magnificent avian predators, many of which, because of injury or because they were raised as pets, can no longer survive in the wild. Outdoor flight cages here, for example, house hawks such as Cooper's, Rough-legged, Red-shouldered, Red-tailed, Broad-winged and Goshawk. Representatives from the owl family include Great Gray, Barred, Great Horned and Screech. And a Bald Eagle is on loan from the U.S. Fish and Wildlife Service.

In spite of that awesome display of power and predatory efficiency, the overall atmosphere at Kellogg is one of peace and serenity. Even "hiking" seems to be too strong a term to use here. "Leisurely stroll" seems more appropriate to the beautifully landscaped, paved paths that curve gently through the sanctuary, where Wild Turkeys and peafowl freely roam the grounds along with flocks of geese, ducks, swan, and even white-tail deer. Ducks dabble and dive practically within arm's reach in display ponds around the edge of Wintergreen Lake. In fact, more than 20 species of ducks and geese plus five different species of swan — the North American native Trumpeter, Tundra, Mute, Whooper and Australian Black — are residents.

This large number of different birds, their closeness to the visitor and the hand feeding of the Canadian Geese make the Kellogg Sanctuary an ideal place for a first exposure to nature study and birding, especially for children.

Kellogg Sanctuary, begun by cereal magnate W.K. Kellogg in 1927 as a private refuge,

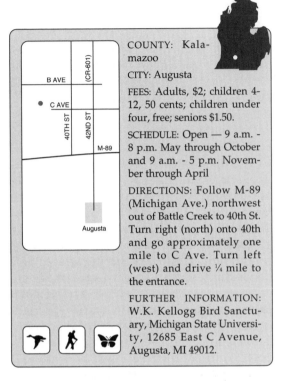

COUNTY: Kalamazoo

CITY: Augusta

FEES: Adults, $2; children 4-12, 50 cents; children under four, free; seniors $1.50.

SCHEDULE: Open — 9 a.m. - 8 p.m. May through October and 9 a.m. - 5 p.m. November through April

DIRECTIONS: Follow M-89 (Michigan Ave.) northwest out of Battle Creek to 40th St. Turn right (north) onto 40th and go approximately one mile to C Ave. Turn left (west) and drive ¼ mile to the entrance.

FURTHER INFORMATION: W.K. Kellogg Bird Sanctuary, Michigan State University, 12685 East C Avenue, Augusta, MI 49012.

is also an excellent place for a continuing education in nature study. For casual learners, the Overlook Museum at Wintergreen Lake features self-guiding displays and exhibits. For more serious students, Michigan State University — which received the sanctuary from Kellogg in 1928 and has maintained and operated it since — offers college classes, adult education programs and summer day camps, all available to the general public. The sanctuary also serves as a wildlife-management research center and field laboratory for MSU.

68 BERNARD W. BAKER SANCTUARY

This 871 acres of swamp and wetlands near Battle Creek probably is the nation's first Sandhill Crane sanctuary and definitely is the first and largest of the Michigan Audubon Society's 10 sanctuaries.

During the first three decades of this century in Michigan, the number of Sandhill Cranes diminished at an alarming rate, mainly due to the draining of marshland throughout the state. Many voiced concern; Bernard W. Baker, a Muskegon businessman, artist and conservationist, took action. In 1941 he purchased 491 acres that made up part of the swampland known as the Big Marsh and donated it to the Michigan Audubon Society as a refuge for the cranes. The establishment of this and subsequent sanctuaries throughout the state helped the Sandhill Crane population to slowly recover to normal levels.

Today, though virtually within sight and sound of I-69, the sanctuary is quiet, beautiful and little-used by the general public. For panoramic views of the lowlands, close-up looks at native Michigan wildflowers, and good birding for a variety of species in addition to cranes, walk along the Iva E. Doty Native Flower Trail. This nature path begins to the left of a small interpretive building near the entrance, then cuts through open fields, crosses a marsh boardwalk, and enters deep woods along 1.5 miles of the sanctuary's eastern edge.

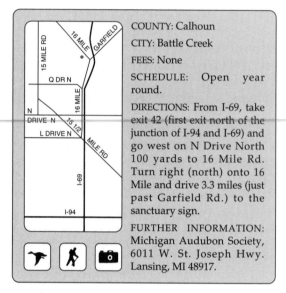

COUNTY: Calhoun

CITY: Battle Creek

FEES: None

SCHEDULE: Open year round.

DIRECTIONS: From I-69, take exit 42 (first exit north of the junction of I-94 and I-69) and go west on N Drive North 100 yards to 16 Mile Rd. Turn right (north) onto 16 Mile and drive 3.3 miles (just past Garfield Rd.) to the sanctuary sign.

FURTHER INFORMATION: Michigan Audubon Society, 6011 W. St. Joseph Hwy. Lansing, MI 48917.

JENNEY WOODS PRESERVE 69

If you don't like to be restricted to well-worn paths or be guided through natural areas by signs and guideposts, this Nature Conservancy preserve will suit you to a tee. The wild, untamed 142-acre tract of swamp, old-growth hardwoods and swamp forest has no trails, no interpretive signs, no restrooms and no parking lot. In fact the only concession to visitors is a sign that lets you know you've found the preserve.

To get into the sanctuary, you have to shoulder your way through a dense understory of young trees, tall grass and shrubs. Once in the preserve, which fronts C Road for several hundred yards and fans out to the south, you are free to wander to your heart's content or until your stamina gives out. Be sure to take a compass, however, because it's easy to become disoriented, especially deep into the area.

A stand of mature silver maple and oaks somehow escaped the axe and have grown to truly impressive dimensions on 20 acres of Jenney Woods. The preserve is also home to a variety of animals and birds, including Acadian Flycatchers and Cerulean Warblers, which are at the extreme northern limits of their range in Calhoun County.

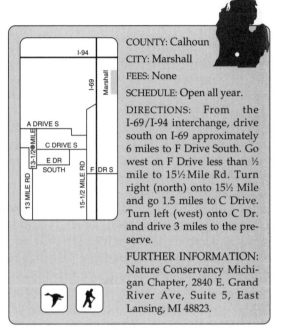

COUNTY: Calhoun

CITY: Marshall

FEES: None

SCHEDULE: Open all year.

DIRECTIONS: From the I-69/I-94 interchange, drive south on I-69 approximately 6 miles to F Drive South. Go west on F Drive less than ½ mile to 15½ Mile Rd. Turn right (north) onto 15½ Mile and go 1.5 miles to C Drive. Turn left (west) onto C Dr. and drive 3 miles to the preserve.

FURTHER INFORMATION: Nature Conservancy Michigan Chapter, 2840 E. Grand River Ave, Suite 5, East Lansing, MI 48823.

70 WHITEHOUSE NATURE CENTER

Though relatively young, this nature center has, especially through its energetic and growing reclamation and restoration projects, earned a respected position on the roster of outstanding Michigan nature areas.

The center's transformation of an unsightly garbage dump and gravel pit, for example, into an 8-acre wildlife habitat is an excellent example of performing reconstructive surgery on land scarred by man, then returning it to nature. Food, shelter and water — the three essential ingredients for wildlife maintenance and sustenance — were provided by the creation of shallow ponds and the planting of selected grasses, legumes, shrubs and trees.

Also typical of the center's ongoing work is the restoration of a tall-grass prairie area and the creation of a native wildflower garden. Tall-grass prairie once covered extensive portions of Michigan and the Midwest until farmers plowed it under to the point of near extinction. Whitehouse has re-established this threatened ecosystem by taking seeds from native plants along railroad tracks in Michigan and from areas in Indiana and Illinois, then planting them in a special 3-acre site. Adjacent to the prairie are wildflower specimens that have been transplanted from natural habitats that are being destroyed. Both projects are tucked between a marsh at the edge of the Kalamazoo River and another of the center's developments, an arboretum that will eventually include nearly 100 different native Michigan trees and shrubs.

Located on the campus of Albion College, the 125-acre center's other varied habitats — including open fields, farmland, marshy areas along the edges of the east branch of the Kalamazoo River, and 25 acres of woodland — support nearly 400 kinds of plants and more than 175 species of birds.

Printed guides (available at the interpretive building) to the center's five trails, do an excellent job of explaining the various ecological communities and special features found along each trail. Hiking opportunities here total more than six miles and vary in length from the half-mile Marsh Trail, a boardwalk path along the Kalamazoo River, to the 2.4-mile Ecology Trail, which follows the center's boundaries.

The center also serves as an outdoor classroom for college biology courses, individual field studies and public school visitors.

COUNTY: Calhoun

CITY: Albion

FEES: None

SCHEDULE: Open year round, dawn - dusk. The Interpretive Building is open Monday through Friday, 9:30 a.m. - 4:30 p.m., and on Saturday and Sunday, 10:30 a.m. - 4:30 p.m.

DIRECTIONS: From I-94, exit (#121) onto Business Rte. I-94 and follow the route (which becomes Michigan Ave.) into Albion to Albion College. At the college campus, turn south onto Hannah, then turn left immediately after crossing the railroad tracks and follow the road and signs to the nature center parking lot.

FURTHER INFORMATION: Whitehouse Nature Center, Albion College, Albion, MI 49224.

FOX PARK 71

Activity at this 35-acre Eaton County park centers around a long, narrow manmade lake. A beach — which edges the west side of the small, oblong body of water — is backed by a gently rising grassy area where swimmers and sunbathers can spread their blankets and parents can keep a sharp eye on their children. At the top of the hill, a large playground overlooks the grassy slope and water. On the opposite shore, a picnic grounds reaches down to the lake, and shore fishermen can try their luck at several spots around the water's edge.

Two miles of hiking trails all begin near the picnic area. One that makes the less than one mile trip around the lake is good for little more than exercise. The paths that slip into the woods guarding the back of the picnic area, however, reveal an interesting mix of wildflowers, flowering shrubs, some impressively large hardwoods, and a diverse forest landscape. One trail, just east of the picnic area, crosses a low, wet forested area on an elevated boardwalk with close-up views of swamps typical of those that covered much of Michigan before settlers cleared the timber and drained the land. North of the lake, another trail borders a quiet tree-lined pond that is home to turtles, frogs, and occasional ducks and herons. On all trails, walking is easy over gently rolling terrain, and the woods are lovely in spring, summer and fall.

In the winter, cross country skiers can explore the same landscape on two miles of soft, groomed trails.

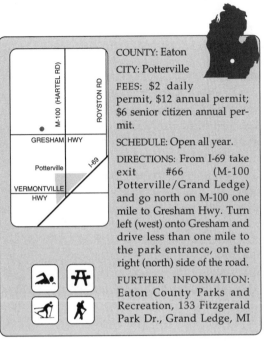

COUNTY: Eaton

CITY: Potterville

FEES: $2 daily permit, $12 annual permit; $6 senior citizen annual permit.

SCHEDULE: Open all year.

DIRECTIONS: From I-69 take exit #66 (M-100 Potterville/Grand Ledge) and go north on M-100 one mile to Gresham Hwy. Turn left (west) onto Gresham and drive less than one mile to the park entrance, on the right (north) side of the road.

FURTHER INFORMATION: Eaton County Parks and Recreation, 133 Fitzgerald Park Dr., Grand Ledge, MI

72 FITZGERALD COUNTY PARK

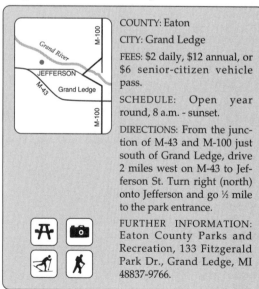

Erosion doesn't have to be ugly, as evidenced by the quiet, patient work of the Grand River, which over the past several thousand years, has slowly carved one of the most unique spots in southern Michigan. A place so compelling that Indians and early settlers went miles out of their way to view nature's handiwork; a place so mystic that an 18th-century religious group constructed a building there to conduct seances; and a place so beautiful that turn-of-the-20th-century tourists flocked to resorts here by the thousands.

What is the magnet that has attracted such a diverse group of visitors? The answer can be summed up by the name of the nearby city: Grand Ledge. Eons ago, what is now Michigan was covered by a great sea. Time and pressure slowly changed its beaches and bottom to sedimentary bedrock. Then recently, geologically speaking, the Grand River cut through the rock and left a mile-long series of magnificent 270-million-year-old sandstone outcroppings.

In addition to the sheer beauty and distinctive geological character of these ledges, another attraction to nature lovers is an ecosystem that is unique to Lower Michigan. Eastern hemlocks and other evergreens seem to grow right out of the rock. And mosses, lichens and liverworts — some of which are found nowhere else in the Lower Peninsula — cover the edges.

The best views of the Fitzgerald County Park's 80 acres come from the half-mile self-guiding Ledges Trail. A large red barn — built and used in the late 1800s by the Grand Ledge Spiritualists Association for meetings and seances — marks the trail's beginning. The trail then follows the 270-million-year-old sandstone ledges that border the river before ending at the park's boundary, marked by a railroad trestle. The trail continues across private property for another 0.6 miles to Island Park in downtown Grand Ledge. Three other nature trails, totaling about two miles, wind through steep ravines, into woods, around ponds and past a dam.

Other facilities here include a nature center, athletic fields, picnic areas, a winter sledding hill and cross country ski trails. Canoe and cross country ski rentals are all available at the park.

COUNTY: Eaton

CITY: Grand Ledge

FEES: $2 daily, $12 annual, or $6 senior-citizen vehicle pass.

SCHEDULE: Open year round, 8 a.m. - sunset.

DIRECTIONS: From the junction of M-43 and M-100 just south of Grand Ledge, drive 2 miles west on M-43 to Jefferson St. Turn right (north) onto Jefferson and go ½ mile to the park entrance.

FURTHER INFORMATION: Eaton County Parks and Recreation, 133 Fitzgerald Park Dr., Grand Ledge, MI 48837-9766.

Located on an old farm amid expressways, residential areas and urban sprawl, the 188-acre Woldumar Nature Center is an oasis to both wildlife and people. Open fields, 100 acres of woodland, marshes, ponds, two streams and the Grand River attract a wide variety of animal life including 125 species of birds. Deer, for example, feed in an old apple orchard; raccoons and opossum, on the other hand, find food an shelter in the woods. And migrating waterfowl make regular spring and fall stopovers at the ponds and lagoon.

A mature oak/beech climax forest is an excellent example of the Eastern woodland forest that covered great portions of the eastern United States before the arrival of European settlers. This hardwood stands in sharp contrast to the white pine and spruce also planted at the center.

Five nature trails totaling five miles make full exploration of the Center's different environments a pleasure.

The farm's barn now houses the Center's administrative offices, meeting room, library, nature exhibits and gift shop. A wide variety of programs, including guided field trips and day camps, for preschoolers through adults are available.

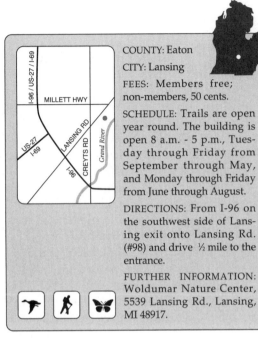

COUNTY: Eaton

CITY: Lansing

FEES: Members free; non-members, 50 cents.

SCHEDULE: Trails are open year round. The building is open 8 a.m. - 5 p.m., Tuesday through Friday from September through May, and Monday through Friday from June through August.

DIRECTIONS: From I-96 on the southwest side of Lansing exit onto Lansing Rd. (#98) and drive ½ mile to the entrance.

FURTHER INFORMATION: Woldumar Nature Center, 5539 Lansing Rd., Lansing, MI 48917.

74 RIVERBEND NATURAL AREA

If you could create a natural area, you would probably first find an out-of-the-way area. Then you might take a flood plain, a creek and a pond and place them among 285 acres of mature forests and open fields. To complete your creation, you could nestle it all in a sweeping bend of a large river, then lace the parcel with five miles of nature trails.

You could, but you don't have to. It's already there, on the east bank of the Grand River on the western edge of Ingham County, and it's called Riverbend Natural Area.

At Riverbend, there are plenty of opportunities for solitary walks, nature study, photography or the search for wildflowers and birds along seven trails, which vary in length from the quarter-mile Timber Doodle Trail to the 1.3-mile Deer Run Trail. The trails are open to mountain bikers in the summer and cross country skiers in the winter.

There are no picnic facilities in this quiet, picturesque area, but a drive a quarter mile east on Nichols Road, then a mile north on Grovenburg Road leads to a large picnic area at Grand River Park.

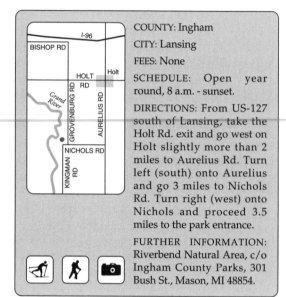

COUNTY: Ingham

CITY: Lansing

FEES: None

SCHEDULE: Open year round, 8 a.m. - sunset.

DIRECTIONS: From US-127 south of Lansing, take the Holt Rd. exit and go west on Holt slightly more than 2 miles to Aurelius Rd. Turn left (south) onto Aurelius and go 3 miles to Nichols Rd. Turn right (west) onto Nichols and proceed 3.5 miles to the park entrance.

FURTHER INFORMATION: Riverbend Natural Area, c/o Ingham County Parks, 301 Bush St., Mason, MI 48854.

Meridian Township's Legg Park preserves the natural splendor of one of southern Michigan's most picturesque rivers. The Red Cedar River is a relatively small — a good high school broad jumper could clear it in most places — swift-moving stream that almost twists itself in knots as it passes through deep woods southeast of Okemos. The river flows westerly toward Lansing, but anyone looking at a map can see the river had a tough time making up its mind. Tight, tortuous loops cut through the thick-forested flood plain, and within a half mile the river flows toward every point on the compass. The primeval woods form a dense canopy of green and almost lead you to imagine the river has lost its way in the forest.

From the Sloan Creek Trailhead, you step into a cool, shaded world, and everything else but the river and the woods is lost to view. The almost three miles of trails closely border the twisting river and present explorers with one memorable scene after another. By early summer, shoulder-high ferns crowd the trail, creating a lush understory from which enormous trunks of old-growth hardwoods rise to support the leafy roof. It's a quiet world of green, with only the moving water breaking the silence.

The trails are level and well-marked and invite you to quietly and slowly stroll the woods rather than work up a sweat with vigorous walking. Even the most dedicated and devoted aerobic walker will find it all but impossible to ignore the views when the trail crosses the stream. The trail is divided into three loops with the shortest being slightly longer than half a mile.

A small picnic area rests in an open field near the parking lot, and Bluebird boxes dot nearby open spaces. In the winter the trails are open and groomed for cross country skiers.

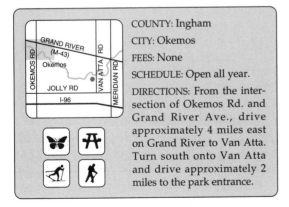

COUNTY: Ingham

CITY: Okemos

FEES: None

SCHEDULE: Open all year.

DIRECTIONS: From the intersection of Okemos Rd. and Grand River Ave., drive approximately 4 miles east on Grand River to Van Atta. Turn south onto Van Atta and drive approximately 2 miles to the park entrance.

76 BAKER WOODLOT

Michigan State University's 173-acre Baker Woodlot holds a soul-stirring fragment of the great beech/maple climax forest that once blanketed much of southern Michigan. Imposing specimens of oak, basswood, ash, cherry, maple, beech, tuliptree and elm compete for space and a piece of the sky everywhere you look. Many of the largest trees are between 100 and 150 years old, and a few grand, old elms have been around for 300 years. Some visitors say they feel almost reverent when they walk beneath the trees, which have stood in silent witness to the passing of so much human and natural history.

You can easily experience the sanctuary by hiking any of several wide, level paths that circle its perimeter and cut through the heart of the forest. Five major ponds and several seasonal swamps add variety to the landscape, and be sure to bring tree and plant guides to help identify the 357 species of vascular plants that grow here.

Baker Woodlot, the largest natural area on the MSU campus, has not escaped unscathed over the years from the intrusion of man. Selective timber cutting has occurred, some species foreign to the area have been introduced, and the construction of a drainage ditch across a corner of the natural area has altered, to some degree, the natural evolution of the forest. Although that may detract somewhat from the scientific value of the area, it's all but undetectable to most of us, who simply wish to savor the magnificence of a mature woods. And Baker Woodlot is protected from further intentional alteration by man.

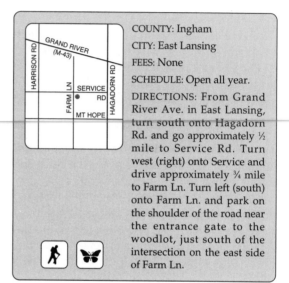

COUNTY: Ingham

CITY: East Lansing

FEES: None

SCHEDULE: Open all year.

DIRECTIONS: From Grand River Ave. in East Lansing, turn south onto Hagadorn Rd. and go approximately ½ mile to Service Rd. Turn west (right) onto Service and drive approximately ¾ mile to Farm Ln. Turn left (south) onto Farm Ln. and park on the shoulder of the road near the entrance gate to the woodlot, just south of the intersection on the east side of Farm Ln.

You would expect one of the nation's premier agricultural colleges to have an impressive botanical garden. But 5,000 different kinds of plants artfully arranged in hundreds of carefully tended beds in just five acres?! W.J. Beal Garden, located in the heart of the Michigan State University campus, is a living tribute to a long line of talented gardeners and botanists. It is beautiful, peaceful, fascinating and, no matter how hard you try, impossible to take in or fully appreciate in just one visit. If you looked at each type of plant for just one minute, it would take more than 83 hours to see them all. But even a brief visit will bring you into contact with a surprising number and variety of growing things from all over the world.

The plant collections are organized into four broad categories. In one, families of plants are systematically arranged according to botanical relationships. Don't understand this category? Don't worry, the other three groupings make more sense. The economic group features plants of direct use to humans, such as for food, fiber, perfume and medicine. That grouping also includes plants that are dangerous to people. Native Michigan plants make up another collection, and the last broad grouping showcases ornamental and landscape plants. Most specimens are accompanied by small signs that give the plant name and its history and habitat.

There are no formal paths through the garden, but you are free to stroll across the lush lawn from one rank of beds to another. One of the joys of Beal is the tight-packed variety. You can move only a few steps from a zucchini to a coffee plant, black gum tree or Rose of Sharon, then turn again and come face to face with a weeping maidenhair tree, at 150 million years old, one of the two most ancient

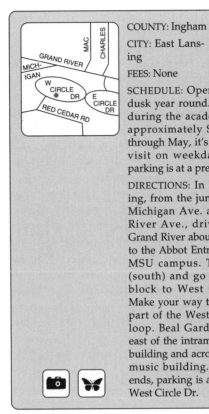

COUNTY: Ingham

CITY: East Lansing

FEES: None

SCHEDULE: Open dawn to dusk year round. However, during the academic year, approximately September through May, it's best not to visit on weekdays, when parking is at a premium.

DIRECTIONS: In East Lansing, from the junction of E. Michigan Ave. and Grand River Ave., drive east on Grand River about one block to the Abbot Entrance to the MSU campus. Turn right (south) and go about one block to West Circle Dr. Make your way to the south part of the West Circle Dr. loop. Beal Gardens is just east of the intramural sports building and across from the music building. On weekends, parking is available on West Circle Dr.

tree species still in existence. And from the exotic to the practical, the many shrubs, perennials and annuals will trigger gardening and landscaping ideas for your own yard.

If you need a break from bending over to find out the name of yet another strange plant, an ideal place to sit and enjoy this enclave of pastoral beauty, which has enchanted visitors since its founding in 1873, is at a goldfish pond near the center of the garden.

78 SANFORD NATURAL AREA

Squeezed between the bustling Michigan State University campus on the south and a commercial strip bordering Grand River Avenue on the north is an exceptional wilderness area. Take one step off the sidewalk on Hagadorn Road, which marks the Sanford Natural Area's east side, and you enter a hardwood forest of towering trees the likes of which covered much of lower Michigan before the coming of Europeans.

And this remnant of native Michigan forest will remain untouched. Sanford is one of a few spots on the MSU campus that are managed at "the highest level of protection and the lowest level of use." A Campus Natural Areas Committee must approve any collecting or other scientific study by professors, and class projects are limited to observations only. In addition, all downed trees are left where they fall, and there is no control of insects or poisonous plants within the natural area's boundaries.

As a result, at Sanford Natural Area and a

few other locations on Campus (see Baker Woodlot and Red Cedar Natural Area), you can come closer to experiencing the untouched splendor of a natural forest stuck smack dab in a major urban setting than in any other large city in the state.

Broad, easily walked paths circle the area and penetrate to the heart of the dark, quiet woods. The Red Cedar River forms Sanford's 3,000-foot north boundary, and the abrupt border between the trees and moving water creates the most-memorable scenery in the preserve. Old cedars and gnarled, aging hardwoods lean out over the water. In many instances the current has undercut the trees to expose crazy latticeworks of huge roots over the water. Numerous exceptionally picturesque views come from a well-worn path that edges the river.

Sanford Natural Area holds the promise of good birdwatching, especially on the edges of the preserve and the area bordering the river. Belted Kingfishers are common along the river, warblers stop in the woods during spring migration, and you can observe thrushes busily investigating the leaf-strewn forest floor.

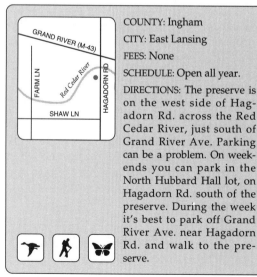

COUNTY: Ingham

CITY: East Lansing

FEES: None

SCHEDULE: Open all year.

DIRECTIONS: The preserve is on the west side of Hagadorn Rd. across the Red Cedar River, just south of Grand River Ave. Parking can be a problem. On weekends you can park in the North Hubbard Hall lot, on Hagadorn Rd. south of the preserve. During the week it's best to park off Grand River Ave. near Hagadorn Rd. and walk to the preserve.

RED CEDAR NATURAL AREA 79

The Red Cedar and Sanford natural areas are wilderness outposts that guard the west and east flanks of beautiful Michigan State University. They are nearly twins. Both are covered by towering hardwoods, and the Red Cedar River defines their north boundaries. Both are managed at a high level of protection and low level of use. That is, visitors are allowed to wander the preserves, but all other activities, including scientific research, must be approved by a Campus Natural Areas Committee. Both are primal sanctuaries that stand in silent tribute to the great forests that covered southern Michigan before they were cleared by farmers and lumbermen.

But the Red Cedar Natural Area — because it's much less accessible and, thus, less frequently used — seems much more remote and wild. There are no marked entrances to the natural area, not even a sign identifying its existence. To explore the preserve, park alongside Kalamazoo Street near the bridge that crosses the Red Cedar River and enter the forest on either side of the road. The paths are not well-defined, but that adds to the feeling of the area's untouched uniqueness.

Birdwatching possibilities along the edges of the forest and near the river are excellent.

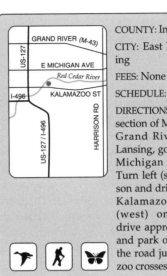

COUNTY: Ingham

CITY: East Lansing

FEES: None

SCHEDULE: Open all year.

DIRECTIONS: From the intersection of Michigan Ave. and Grand River Ave. in East Lansing, go 2 blocks west on Michigan to Harrison Rd. Turn left (south) onto Harrison and drive three blocks to Kalamazoo St. Turn right (west) onto Kalamazoo, drive approximately ½ mile, and park on the shoulder of the road just before Kalamazoo crosses the river.

80 FENNER NATURE CENTER

The opportunity for solitude along an extensive system of nature trails within a city limits, plus a wide variety of fascinating exhibits and programs are reasons to visit Fenner Nature Center, a 120-acre city park located on the eastern edge of Lansing.

Five miles of trails — lined with many species of trees, lush plant life and wildflowers — wind through diverse habitat to a variety of attractions. The Pioneer Trail, for example, skirts the northwestern edge of the park and passes through meadows as it leads to a centennial cabin and pioneer garden. Con-structed in 1959, the cabin is a replica of homes found in the area 100 years earlier. The garden, too, is typical of one planted in the pioneering days. The Prairie Trail crosses grassland to a pond with a photoblind, then meanders through a field that home to tree swallows and blue birds. The mile-long Tamarack Trail passes through a swamp and borders a secluded pond. The Sugar Bush Trail, as the name implies, passes a maple grove in its 0.75-mile paved circuit from the Visitor Center, where all trails originate. And another paved trail circles a pond just outside the Center.

Exhibits and facilities inside the interpretive center, located up a long driveway from the park entrance, include small-animal displays, a wildlife feeding station, a touch table for hands-on experience with nature, trail maps, a gift shop and a nature library. Bird talks and nature walks are among the regular programs conducted at Fenner throughout the year. Special programs include the Apple Butter Festival, held in October, and the Sugar Bush Festival, held in March.

A pleasant grass-covered picnic area shaded by large, stately trees is located next to the parking lot.

COUNTY: Ingham

CITY: Lansing

FEES: None

SCHEDULE: The park is open year round, 8 a.m. - dark. The Visitor Center is open Tuesday through Friday, 9 a.m. - 4 p.m. Weekend schedule for the building is December through March, 11 a.m. - 4 p.m.; other months Saturday, 10 a.m. - 5 p.m., and Sunday, 11 a.m. - 5 p.m.

DIRECTIONS: From US-127 / I-496 in Lansing, take the Trowbridge Rd. exit and go east on Trowbridge to Harrison Rd. Turn right (south) onto Harrison and drive ½ mile to Mt. Hope Rd. Turn right (west) onto Mt. Hope and drive 1.5 miles to the entrance (just before Aurelius Rd.)

FURTHER INFORMATION: Fenner Nature Center, 2020 E. Mt. Hope, Lansing, MI 48910.

ROSE LAKE WILDLIFE 81 RESEARCH CENTER

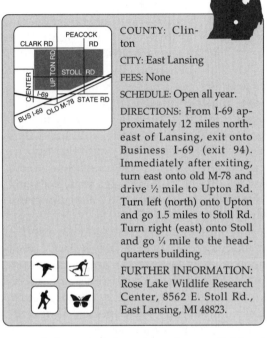

The Rose Lake Wildlife Research Center is one of the most underrated and overlooked great birdwatching areas in the state. The Department of Natural Resources purchased the 3,646-acre tract in the 1930s for use as a research station and management area to study farm-habitat wildlife.

The Center's rolling farmland, old fields, upland and lowland woods, brushy areas, wetlands and five lakes offer plenty of food and shelter to a wide variety of birds. And man has improved upon nature's work by creating ponds, flood areas, brush piles, and tree and shrub plantings to make the area even more attractive to wildlife. The work has obviously paid off, because the Center's checklist numbers 231 bird species observed here since 1960. The impressive list includes more than 30 kinds of warblers, six species of woodpeckers, 23 varieties of ducks and geese, and nesting Sandhill Cranes. The handy checklist, available at the headquarters building, also notes each species' abundance and rates the likelihood of spotting them during each season.

You'll also want to pick up the brochure, "Mammals of Rose Lake Wildlife Research Area," and then keep your eyes peeled for the 41 mammals — from masked shrews and silver-haired bats to red fox and long-tailed weasels — found in the area. The annotated list tells where you're most likely to spot each animal, how abundant or rare it is in the area, and a bit of its natural history.

Rose Lake has no dedicated hiking trails, but you can choose from plenty of short or long walks along several narrow work roads that wind through the landscape. Also, public roads that crisscross the area provide good vantage points for birding. A free, detailed map of the research center, also available at the headquarters building, clearly marks all work roads and points out parking lots where you can leave your car and explore the area on foot.

The Center is also open to hunters, fishermen and cross country skiers and contains both a rifle and skeet range.

COUNTY: Clinton

CITY: East Lansing

FEES: None

SCHEDULE: Open all year.

DIRECTIONS: From I-69 approximately 12 miles northeast of Lansing, exit onto Business I-69 (exit 94). Immediately after exiting, turn east onto old M-78 and drive ½ mile to Upton Rd. Turn left (north) onto Upton and go 1.5 miles to Stoll Rd. Turn right (east) onto Stoll and go ¼ mile to the headquarters building.

FURTHER INFORMATION: Rose Lake Wildlife Research Center, 8562 E. Stoll Rd., East Lansing, MI 48823.

82 MAPLE RIVER STATE GAME AREA

The 1,200 acres of the Wetland Wildlife Management Units of the Maple River State Game Area make up the largest wetland complex in central Michigan. That alone just about guarantees good birdwatching, and there's even an added plus: This parcel isn't hidden away in some hard-to-find geographic nook or cranny. The major north-south highway in central Michigan, US-27, cuts through the game area, so during peak migration periods, even speeding motorists get some outstanding views of hundreds of waterfowl and shorebirds.

The wetlands habitat — composed of meadows, forest, river, marshes, pools, canals and adjoining farmland — attract huge numbers of birds throughout the year. Egrets, Great Blue Herons, Whistling Swans, Canada Geese, numerous duck species, songbirds, and shorebirds also nest here or stop briefly on their migrations. Best birding is from March to May and September to November, when thousands of migrating birds pass through the area. But because of the many nesting birds, even midsummer holds good possibilities.

The Maple River State Game Area is an excellent example of what can be accomplished when groups and agencies combine forces toward a common goal. In this case, the groups and agencies included the Michigan Duck Hunters Association, the Audubon Society, the Michigan Wildlife Habitat Foundation, and the Department of Natural Resources, to name just a few. Their goal: to help restore an area of Michigan's original, vitally important wetlands habitat. Some donated money; most donated time and sweat to improve this ecosystem. Many, for example, built or improved dikes, channels and spillways; erected Osprey nesting platforms; or placed numerous Wood Duck nesting boxes throughout the area.

Wildlife photographers, birdwatchers, nature lovers or hikers can enjoy the groups' and individuals' extraordinary efforts from the tops of several miles of dikes. The level, easy-to-walk dikes penetrate the heart of the area and offer spectacular close-up views of the countless birds that pervade the flooded pools, marshes, meadows and woods.

To reach the dikes, park at any of three different areas, all reached via US-27 north of the Maple River. The easiest to get to is a half mile north of the river on the east side of US-27. The dikes from this lot lead to a panoramic view of the area from atop a 15-foot observation tower. To reach the other two parking areas, drive about a mile north of the river on US-27 to Ranger Road. Turn either east or west onto Ranger Road, drive to the first crossroad in either direction, then turn south and go approximately one-half mile to the parking area.

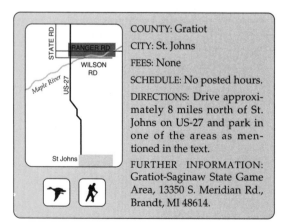

COUNTY: Gratiot

CITY: St. Johns

FEES: None

SCHEDULE: No posted hours.

DIRECTIONS: Drive approximately 8 miles north of St. Johns on US-27 and park in one of the areas as mentioned in the text.

FURTHER INFORMATION: Gratiot-Saginaw State Game Area, 13350 S. Meridian Rd., Brandt, MI 48614.

BROCK PARK 83

This forest-shrouded Ionia County park hugs busy highway M-21, but most motorists zip by, only aware of its presence if they spot the entrance sign. Those in the know turn off M-21 and slip under the canopy of thick, towering hardwoods and evergreens that shelter a sprawling, secluded campground and a beautiful picnic area bisected by a bright, swift-moving stream.

The park road snakes through the deep forest and skirts openings in the woods that are sprinkled with picnic tables and grills. Nearly all picnic spots are private and shady, and many are within sight and sound of the stream. Two picturesque fieldstone footbridges that arch over the stream lead to exceptionally private picnic areas, tennis courts, and the start of the park's nature trail.

The trail begins at a staircase that climbs a steep hill trapped within a narrow loop of the creek, and from the top of the stairs, you can work your way along the ridge of the high, thin finger of land. The valley falls steeply away from both sides of the trail, and sharp-edged gullies score the sides of the hill. Near the "finger's" tip, the trail forces you to turn around and retrace your steps to the trailhead.

Other faint, unmarked trails head every

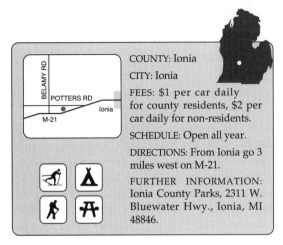

COUNTY: Ionia

CITY: Ionia

FEES: $1 per car daily for county residents, $2 per car daily for non-residents.

SCHEDULE: Open all year.

DIRECTIONS: From Ionia go 3 miles west on M-21.

FURTHER INFORMATION: Ionia County Parks, 2311 W. Bluewater Hwy., Ionia, MI 48846.

which-way through the park and include several that edge the stream.

In the winter, nine miles of track-set cross country ski trails lace the hilly terrain.

At the park's primitive camping area, you can choose from plenty of scenic and secluded spots to set up. The campground road is, itself, quite scenic as it winds up and down hills and around hairpin curves in a dense old-growth forest dotted with small openings that can hold a single tent or trailer. Dozens of yards of deep woods often separate the sites, which means you'll have both privacy and shade.

84 BLANDFORD NATURE CENTER

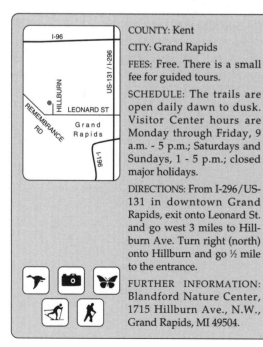

When you enter the interpretive building at the Blandford Nature Center, don't be shocked if you come almost eyeball to eyeball with a live owl, hawk, crow or other form of wildlife that may be perched on bookshelves, desks, pieces of driftwood or light fixtures. One of the Center's rooms, you see, serves as a wild-animal hospital and the patients are sometimes given the run of the building. On a recent visit they included more than half a dozen Screech, Barred, Great Horned and long-eared owls, which were loose and within hand-shaking distance. Also recuperating out of their cages that day were a Red-tailed Hawk and a crow. Several songbirds completed the patient list.

A visit with sick animals probably isn't why most people come to Blandford, however. Most visitors would rather spend an after-noon or a day exploring the Center's variety of natural attractions and displays. And the best way to do that is on seven trails totaling 4.5 miles that wind through the Center's 143 acres of woodland, open fields, marsh and farmland plus by several ponds and Brandy-wine Creek. The trails include two short self-guided paths that circle a heavily wooded ravine.

Still other trails lead to a variety of outdoor exhibits such as the Pioneer Heritage Complex. Fully restored and furnished buildings there include a homesteader's log cabin built in 1866, a school house and various outbuildings. Planted around the structures are an herb garden, a dye-plant garden and a family garden typical of the era. Or along another path, sample rural life at a small family farm, complete with barn, farm animals and gardens.

Facilities at the interpretive building include a meeting room, a book shop and large viewing windows that overlook a wildlife feeding station and wooded ravine. A 1.5-mile cross country ski trail is open in

COUNTY: Kent

CITY: Grand Rapids

FEES: Free. There is a small fee for guided tours.

SCHEDULE: The trails are open daily dawn to dusk. Visitor Center hours are Monday through Friday, 9 a.m. - 5 p.m.; Saturdays and Sundays, 1 - 5 p.m.; closed major holidays.

DIRECTIONS: From I-296/US-131 in downtown Grand Rapids, exit onto Leonard St. and go west 3 miles to Hillburn Ave. Turn right (north) onto Hillburn and go ½ mile to the entrance.

FURTHER INFORMATION: Blandford Nature Center, 1715 Hillburn Ave., N.W., Grand Rapids, MI 49504.

This Grand Rapids city park's' quiet beauty, pleasant trails, and colorful array of plant life is the perfect antidote for a hectic lifestyle.

Beautiful Sand Creek winds through the heart of the park and dominates its landscape. The tiny creek almost ties itself in knots on its passage through Aman, and over the eons has carved a narrow, little valley that overlays the property with a large S.

You can get some impressive overlooks of the area from the park's three trails, which total nearly five miles. The paths dip in and out of the valley, cross the creek on two footbridges, skirt a tamarack bog and a small lake, and cut through a mature beech/maple forest and stands of aspen and hemlock.

No matter what the terrain — woods, fields or wetlands — the one constant at Aman is the brilliant and continual show of wildflowers from early spring through fall. Skunk cabbage and pussy willow herald spring in late March. Trout lily, marsh marigolds and Dutchman's breeches add their color to the surroundings in late April. And in May, violets, false Solomon's seal and many others burst into bloom. More flowers and brilliant berries continue the display through late summer and fall.

The wide diversity of food and shelter attract a fair number of birds throughout the year, with the peak of birding occurring during spring migration.

And in the winter — when most birds have headed south and the dry wildflowers are buried beneath a soft blanket of snow — cross country skiers take over the occasionally groomed trails.

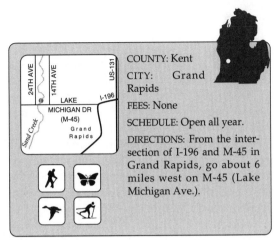

COUNTY: Kent

CITY: Grand Rapids

FEES: None

SCHEDULE: Open all year.

DIRECTIONS: From the intersection of I-196 and M-45 in Grand Rapids, go about 6 miles west on M-45 (Lake Michigan Ave.).

86 DEGRAAF NATURE CENTER

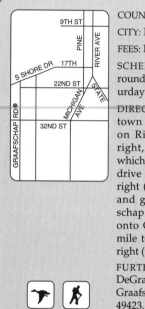

The DeGraaf Nature Center is a perfect example of the old adage, "good things come in small packages." Though only 15.5 acres big, the area is packed with a wide variety of habitats and plant and animal life.

As a result, visitors receive great rewards for little effort. Trillium, lady's-slippers, wild roses and other wildflowers, plus a variety of shrubs and trees line the six short trails that lead variously to a stream, a pond, woodland, a meadow and a marsh. A wide range of animals and birds — including Great Blue Herons, Green Herons and Belted Kingfishers — find food and shelter in these diverse habitats.

Self-guiding brochures for all trails are available at the trailhead, and groups can arrange for guided tours of the center, which is operated by the city of Holland.

COUNTY: Ottawa

CITY: Holland

FEES: None

SCHEDULE: Open year round, Tuesday through Saturday.

DIRECTIONS: From downtown Holland, drive south on River Ave., then bear right, onto Michigan Ave., which angles southwest, and drive to West 22nd St. Turn right (west) onto West 22nd and go 1¼ miles to Graafschap Rd. Turn left (south) onto Graafschap and go ½ mile to the entrance, on the right (west) side of the road.

FURTHER INFORMATION: DeGraaf Nature Center, 600 Graafschap Rd., Holland, MI 49423.

KITCHELL DUNE PRESERVE 87

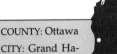

Tucked away on the north shore of the Grand River a few hundred yards from where it empties into Lake Michigan at Grand Haven, the Kitchell Dune Preserve is a living showcase for a typical Michigan dunal ecosystem, where nature patiently and efficiently changes a sandy, barren dune into a hardwood forest.

For a walking textbook tour of the progressive stages of this dunal plant succession, take the 0.75-mile Connie Lindquist Trail through the 52-acre sanctuary. Dune grass, which stops erosion and stabilizes the sand, dominates at the trails beginning. Farther inland along the trail, cottonwoods and shrubs have displaced the dune grass, and near the end of the hike, oak and maple mark the climax of the natural succession process. This easy-to-walk trail also skirts several interdunal ponds, briefly cuts through an area of pine plantings and passes many plants typical of this ecosystem, including sassafras, bearberry, horsetails, sand cherries and the rare pitchers thistle, found only along Great Lakes shores.

A self-guiding brochure, an excellent aid to the enjoyment and understanding of the fragile and fascinating environment, is available by mail from the Nature Conservancy, which owns and maintains this preserve.

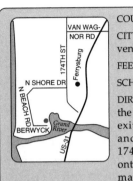

COUNTY: Ottawa

CITY: Grand Haven

FEES: None

SCHEDULE: No posted hours.

DIRECTIONS: From US-31 on the north side of Ferrysburg, exit onto Van Wagnor Rd. and drive west ½ mile to 174th St. turn left (south) onto 174th and go approximately one mile to North Shore Dr. Turn right (west) onto North Shore and go 1½ miles to North Beach Rd. Turn left (south) onto North Beach and drive approximately 1½ miles to Berwyck St., just before the Grand River. Turn left (east) onto Berwyck and park at the marina just a few hundred yards east. The trail begins on the north side of Berwyck where it curves sharply in front of a "Captain Cove" sign.

FURTHER INFORMATION: Nature Conservancy Michigan Chapter, 2840 E. Grand River Ave., Suite 5, East Lansing, MI 48823.

88 FIVE LAKES MUSKEGON NATURE SANCTUARY

To the untrained eye, the Five Lakes Muskegon Nature Sanctuary appears to be not much more than a pleasant, attractive and peaceful place to walk. Naturalists and conservationists, on the other hand, shake their heads in wonder and amazement at the tremendous number of unusual and rare grasses, sedges and rushes that thrive here. Outside of this area, many of the species grow only along the Atlantic Coast.

Why here? The gradual drying of large lake that once covered the entire area in the early 1800s created near-perfect growing conditions — an open sunny area of wetlands ringed by trees — for an incredible variety of grasses, sedges, rushes and prairie plants.

So be sure to bring plant and wildflower identification guides to fully enjoy your visit. And though you can spend as little as an hour on an enjoyable walk, you may end up taking an entire day — spring, summer or fall — identifying and marveling at the rich diversity of plant life virtually always underfoot. Birders will find hawks as well as a wide variety of waterfowl and songbirds, including herons and bluebirds, that visit or nest in the sanctuary.

Access into the sanctuary is through a 200-yard long panhandle-shaped easement from Evanston Road. At the end of the easement, two mile-long trails — one leading east, the other heading northeast — branch into the 53-acre sanctuary.

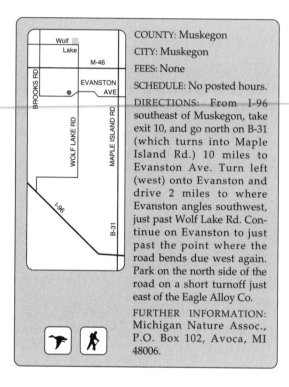

COUNTY: Muskegon

CITY: Muskegon

FEES: None

SCHEDULE: No posted hours.

DIRECTIONS: From I-96 southeast of Muskegon, take exit 10, and go north on B-31 (which turns into Maple Island Rd.) 10 miles to Evanston Ave. Turn left (west) onto Evanston and drive 2 miles to where Evanston angles southwest, just past Wolf Lake Rd. Continue on Evanston to just past the point where the road bends due west again. Park on the north side of the road on a short turnoff just east of the Eagle Alloy Co.

FURTHER INFORMATION: Michigan Nature Assoc., P.O. Box 102, Avoca, MI 48006.

MUSKEGON WASTEWATER 89
TREATMENT AREA

"Hold it right there!" you're probably thinking. "What in the name of all that's holy to nature lovers is a sewage treatment plant doing in a book on natural attractions?" Well, the fact is, this is one of the state's great bird-watching areas, a place where year after year you can, with little effort, observe a staggering number of birds rare to Michigan.

Each spring the broad, flat, sandy plains that surround the treatment facility are planted with cash crops. The recycled wastewater from the plant, which is collected in two 800-acre diked lagoons, is used to irrigate the farmland. The extensive fields, shallow lagoons, dikes and small woodlots at the fields' edges draw an enormous number and variety of birds, especially shorebirds and waterfowl. And, almost as though they were made for birders, one-lane roads follow the top of the dikes to make spotting easy.

Baird's Sandpiper, Buff-breasted Sandpiper, Stilt Sandpiper, Willet, American Avocet and Red Phalaropes are just some of the unusual and rare shorebirds you might spot along the edges of the lagoons. In late September through October, thousands of ducks and geese congregate on the holding ponds. Western Grebes and Eared Grebes call each spring and fall, as do such rare-to-Michigan gulls as the Glaucous, Iceland, Thayer's and Little.

Vultures and birds of prey, including Gyrfalcons and Peregrine Falcons, have been spotted in the area, and in spring the small woodlots attract good numbers of songbirds.

Yellow-headed Blackbirds, Wilson's Phalaropes, Upland Sandpipers, Bobolinks, Grasshopper Sparrows and Eastern Bluebirds are just a partial list of other interesting birds you will most likely see while slowly driving

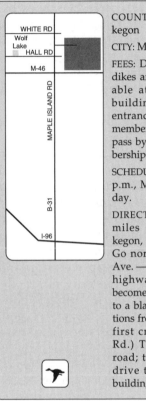

COUNTY: Muskegon

CITY: Muskegon

FEES: Daily passes onto the dikes are free and are available at the headquarters building, near the plant's entrance. Audubon Society members can obtain a yearly pass by showing their membership cards.

SCHEDULE: Open 8 a.m. to 5 p.m., Monday through Friday.

DIRECTIONS: From I-96 9 miles southeast of Muskegon, take exit 10 (Nunica). Go north 9 miles on 112th Ave. — marked B-31 on state highway maps and which becomes Maple Island Rd. — to a blacktop road that junctions from the east. (You will first cross M-46 and Hall Rd.) This is the entrance road; turn right (east) and drive to the headquarters building.

atop the narrow dikes. This is not only a great area for avid birdwatchers, but also an ideal location for novice birders to get hooked on America's fastest-growing sport. Needless to say, it would be a crime to arrive here without binoculars and bird identification books. Peak season for birding runs from mid-July until the ponds freeze over.

90 CHRISTENSEN NATURE CENTER

Though relatively small, this 128-acre nature preserve takes in a remarkable range of scenery and habitat — upland forests, open fields, a swamp, a marsh, a bog, a creek, a pond, a lake, a pine plantation, a wildflower garden and an arboretum — and they're all easily accessible.

Eight well-marked trails, totaling six miles and ranging in length from a quarter mile to a mile and a half, lace the property and probe its every corner. Also, the nature preserve is surrounded by the Rogue River State Game Area, and trails extend into that 5,000 acre parcel. Where the land gets soft, soggy or downright wet, you can — from elevated boardwalks, a floating bridge, and observation towers — get close-up views of landscape and habitats not usually observable without hard walking and waterlogged boots. The variety and lushness of habitat, good cover, and abundant food sources all make for good birdwatching.

The Kent Intermediate School District, which owns the Howard Christensen Nature Center, focuses its services and facilities on educating school children about nature and the environment. This is especially evident in the Center's interpretive building, where several exhibits and learning stations help nurture an appreciation of nature's fascinating diversity and interdependence. Mammal and bird specimens are also set up for detailed study and examination. The interpretive center, which is open to the public, also houses a nature library.

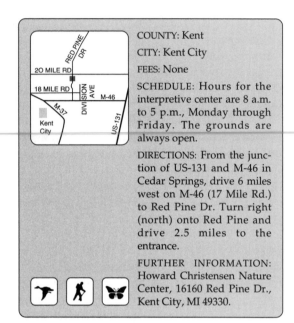

COUNTY: Kent

CITY: Kent City

FEES: None

SCHEDULE: Hours for the interpretive center are 8 a.m. to 5 p.m., Monday through Friday. The grounds are always open.

DIRECTIONS: From the junction of US-131 and M-46 in Cedar Springs, drive 6 miles west on M-46 (17 Mile Rd.) to Red Pine Dr. Turn right (north) onto Red Pine and drive 2.5 miles to the entrance.

FURTHER INFORMATION: Howard Christensen Nature Center, 16160 Red Pine Dr., Kent City, MI 49330.

NEWAYGO PRAIRIE PLANT PRESERVE 91

Prairies are one of the rarest ecosystems in Michigan. Only an estimated 0.3% of the state's total land mass, or about 100,000 acres, was originally prairie. And with the coming of European settlers, it quickly disappeared under the plow because farmers didn't have to clear trees to start planting crops. But in many cases, the prairie soil was sandy, dry and ill-suited for cash crops, and farmers abandoned it.

Such was the case at the Newaygo Prairie Plant Preserve, now owned by the Michigan Nature Association. The land was last worked in the late 1800s, and since then prairie plants have slowly reclaimed the area. Today this 110-acre preserve reveals one of the few remaining large expanses of dry prairie in the state, and it's a strange sight for those of us used to seeing a landscape filled with trees, vast lakes or wetlands.

The main portion of the sanctuary fills a shallow tree-fringed bowl with a wide assortment of grasses and sun-loving wildflowers. The more than 100 plant species that populate the preserve put on a colorful show from early spring through late fall. In spring the prairie is covered with delicate wildflowers that hug the earth. As summer arrives, taller plants and grasses reach maturity. By late summer and early fall, the heavyweights put on a spectacular display, with eight-foot-tall big bluestem, Indian grass, goldenrod and sunflowers dominating the plain.

Poplar Avenue borders the west side of the preserve, so even from your car you can appreciate the prairies unique features. But take at least a few steps into the entirely different environment of strange grasses, plants and flowers. You don't have to bring a plant identification guide to enjoy the area, but it will certainly make for a richer experience.

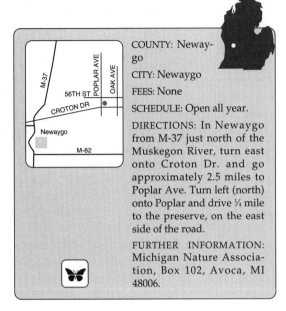

COUNTY: Newaygo

CITY: Newaygo

FEES: None

SCHEDULE: Open all year.

DIRECTIONS: In Newaygo from M-37 just north of the Muskegon River, turn east onto Croton Dr. and go approximately 2.5 miles to Poplar Ave. Turn left (north) onto Poplar and drive ¼ mile to the preserve, on the east side of the road.

FURTHER INFORMATION: Michigan Nature Association, Box 102, Avoca, MI 48006.

92 YWCA'S CAMP NEWAYGO WETLAND TRAIL

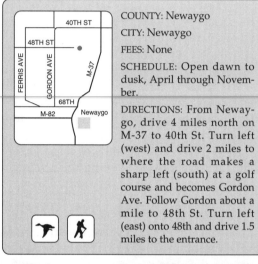

For nature lovers the YWCA's Camp Newaygo boardwalk beats Atlantic City's hands down. The one-mile wood trail treats you to some truly unusual scenery while taking you across a huge marsh and bog and into the heart of a fascinating environment. The dead-level, easily walked boardwalk, which is wide enough for wheelchairs, is elevated just inches above a riot of vegetation sprouting from "land" that perpetually has the consistency of a water-laden sponge,.

Delicate, vibrant and colorful wildflowers grow within inches of the boardwalk, and the lacy leaves of giant ferns crowd its edges. Unusual and fascinating plants seem to be everywhere, and when you lift your eyes from the wonders at your feet, you are assailed by the striking beauty of the cumulative effect of the low-growing jungle of plant life.

From several places where the trail widens, you get views usually only available from a boat or after a long, wet wade through dense vegetation. One of the observation platforms overlooks a bog that has reduced a lake to a small, dark pond ringed by sphagnum moss. The still, reflective waters ringed by green looks like a setting out of a fantasy where someone comes to cast a spell.   From benches at another platform, you can relax and enjoy a panoramic view of the marsh and a grove of dead trees drowned by the wetlands.

The area is as rich in wildlife as it is in plant life. Woodpeckers hammer at dead trees; Great Blue Herons, Kingfishers and other birds hunt the shallow waters for fish; you can see turtles sunning themselves; and you might even spot a muskrat or raccoon slipping through the water or grass.

COUNTY: Newaygo

CITY: Newaygo

FEES: None

SCHEDULE: Open dawn to dusk, April through November.

DIRECTIONS: From Newaygo, drive 4 miles north on M-37 to 40th St. Turn left (west) and drive 2 miles to where the road makes a sharp left (south) at a golf course and becomes Gordon Ave. Follow Gordon about a mile to 48th St. Turn left (east) onto 48th and drive 1.5 miles to the entrance.

MANISTEE TRAIL 93

The crossing of several roads and one Michigan highway keeps this 30-mile pathway from being a 100 percent wilderness experience. But because of the beautiful scenery along the other 99.99 percent of the route, hikers and backpackers usually voice no complaints, and in one way the trail-road intersections are a plus, because they provide a choice of access and stopping points that allow you to tailor an outing to your liking.

The trail, which runs generally north and south through the Manistee National Forest and the heart of Newaygo County, creases high, rolling country dotted with fields, pine forests, large stands of mixed hardwoods with a sometimes-dense understory of ferns, and large openings in the forest created by clear-cut lumbering. Footbridges and even logs carry hikers over numerous streams that cut across the trail. Deer are plentiful, and it's rare if you don't see or at least hear them moving through the forest.

Three rustic campgrounds are all located along the southern third of the route. You can also backcountry camp anywhere along the pathway as long as you set up at least 200 feet off the trail and 200 feet from lakes or streams.

You don't have to walk the entire trail, which starts at 40th Street about five miles north of Newaygo. You can also step onto it at Pierce Drive, M-20 and other east-west roads. For a complete trail guide and map that marks all access points. write to the address in *Further Information*.

The Manistee Trail has been incorporated into what when completed will be the longest hiking route in the U.S. — the North Country Trail, which will run from Maine to North Dakota.

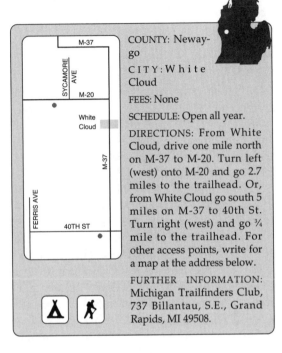

COUNTY: Newaygo

CITY: White Cloud

FEES: None

SCHEDULE: Open all year.

DIRECTIONS: From White Cloud, drive one mile north on M-37 to M-20. Turn left (west) onto M-20 and go 2.7 miles to the trailhead. Or, from White Cloud go south 5 miles on M-37 to 40th St. Turn right (west) and go ¾ mile to the trailhead. For other access points, write for a map at the address below.

FURTHER INFORMATION: Michigan Trailfinders Club, 737 Billantau, S.E., Grand Rapids, MI 49508.

94 LODA LAKE WILDFLOWER SANCTUARY

This 1,000-acre haven for native Michigan plants is both a treat for the senses and highly educational.

A one-mile-long trail, with 39 numbered posts, wanders through a collective microcosm of Michigan habitats — including a small lake, a bog, marshes, meadows and forests — filled with an astounding number of both common and endangered native plants.

The Federated Garden Club of Michigan, in cooperation with the U.S. Forest Service, began development of the sanctuary in 1938. Native Michigan plants were transplanted into the preserve, and those already there were nurtured and identified. But don't come expecting to see an arboretum, flower gardens or even informal plantings. The preserve is wild with flowers, shrubs and trees scattered across the landscape in a completely natural setting. The only concessions to people are a small picnic area at the trailhead, a boardwalk that crosses a wide marsh, the one-mile trail that partly follows an old two-track, and the numbered posts and a few benches along the path.

Be sure to draw your eyes away from the sweep of Loda Lake or the dense forest and take a close look at the delicate beauty underfoot. A brochure, available at the trailhead and the U.S. Forest Ranger Station on M-37 in White Cloud (chances are better for getting it there than at the trailhead), will help you identify ferns, violets, swamp rose, wild orchids, carnivorous plants, trillium, and many other delicate, beautiful species. Numbers in the pamphlet correspond to the numbered posts.

As you would expect in an area of such rich and diverse habitats, birds find the sanctuary to their liking. Waterfowl call at the lake, shorebirds and marsh birds nest and feed in the wetlands, and songbirds flit among the trees. If you pick up the interpretive brochure, you won't need to bring a wildflower guide, but until such time as birds can be induced to sit on numbered posts, be sure to bring binoculars and a bird book.

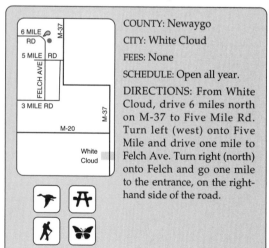

COUNTY: Newaygo

CITY: White Cloud

FEES: None

SCHEDULE: Open all year.

DIRECTIONS: From White Cloud, drive 6 miles north on M-37 to Five Mile Rd. Turn left (west) onto Five Mile and drive one mile to Felch Ave. Turn right (north) onto Felch and go one mile to the entrance, on the right-hand side of the road.

The picturesque White River and the dense lushness of the Manistee National Forest create a quiet, pastoral mood at this little-used national recreation area.

A day-use area lies tight against the north bank of the clear river. The apparently little-used picnic grounds there are wedged into a narrow isthmus that barely keeps a long loop of the river from forming a complete circle. Picnic tables are scattered under a tent of pines and hardwoods on a low bank that overlooks the river. Tubers and canoeists love the spot, because they can launch their craft on the north side of the picnic grounds, drift for half an hour with current, then land on the south end of the picnic area only a few yards on land from where they started.

From the back of the picnic area, the seldom-trod, one-mile-long Pines Point Trail cuts a lazy oval through the forest. Except for areas where the route crosses a mature pine plantation or follows an old two-track, ferns and low-growing plants crowd the path so tightly they will brush your legs. At times, in fact, the trail appears to be only a crease in the green carpet that covers the forest floor, but it is well-marked and easily walked over the rolling terrain.

Not far from the day-use area, 32 widely spaced and well-shaded campsites — many with excellent privacy, with several accessible to the physically challenged — rest on a low bluff that overlooks the White River. Pressurized water and a flush toilet are available.

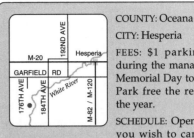

COUNTY: Oceana

CITY: Hesperia

FEES: $1 parking fee during the managed season, Memorial Day to Labor Day. Park free the remainder of the year.

SCHEDULE: Open all year. If you wish to camp outside the managed season, contact the White Cloud Ranger District, address below.

DIRECTIONS: From Hesperia, drive 2 miles west on M-20 to 192nd Ave. Turn left (south) onto 192nd and go one mile to Garfield Rd. Turn right (west) onto Garfield, go 3 miles, then follow the signs to the recreation area.

FURTHER INFORMATION: Manistee National Forest, White Cloud Ranger District, 12 N. Charles, White Cloud, MI 49349.

96 WALKINSHAW WETLANDS

This 1,000-acre expanse of marsh and wet meadow rates as a pretty undistinguished stretch of landscape. But people don't drive out of their way — and the wetlands *are* out of the way from practically any place in the state — for the scenery. They come to see the unusual visitors that return here spring through fall, year after year.

America's third-largest bird, the Sandhill Crane, favors the area as a courting grounds, nesting site, and staging area for fall migrations. Cattle graze part of the refuge, which is part of the old Walkinshaw farm, now run by Merle Lass. Lass also manages the area for the Forest Service to support the cranes, and the birds evidently like the accommodations. Their numbers have steadily grown over the years, and Lass says he has noticed a marked increase in breeding pairs in the many years he's been at the farm.

The cranes arrive in mid-March and stay through mid-October. During nesting season, in early summer, the 40-inch-tall birds with seven-foot wing spans can be rather secretive, but in spring and fall they put on a spectacular show. In the spring, young birds try to attract a mate for life through a dance that involves strutting, bowing, jumping, and even stick tossing, all of which is accompanied by a great deal of cackling. And in the early fall, more than 200 cranes gather here, like a giant tour group preparing to go south for a winter vacation.

You can observe the birds from the road that borders the wetlands, and you're also welcome at the farm. Sightings are never guaranteed, but the best time for ensuring a successful visit falls between late September and early October. And for best results then, as in spring and summer, arrive early in the morning or late afternoon.

You can spot other birds in the wetlands, too, such as Marshhawks, American Bitterns and White Egrets.

COUNTY: Oceana

CITY: Hesperia

FEES: None

SCHEDULE: Mid-March to mid-October.

DIRECTIONS: From Hesperia, drive 2 miles west on M-20 to 192nd Ave. Turn right (north) onto 192nd and drive 6 miles to where the road bends sharply right (east). Follow the bend and drive approximately ½ mile to 198th Ave. Turn left (north) onto 198th and drive 2 miles to the wetlands, which start just north of the intersection of Fox Rd.

It's not often that we're blessed by somebody else's financial ruin, but that's the case for hikers who walk the Sheep Ranch Pathway. As in most of northern Michigan, the area through which this trail passes was heavily lumbered in the late 1800s. But the lumber company that felled the white pine here went bust before they could level all the trees. As a result, you can enjoy a few imposing specimens of Michigan's state tree while walking the trail.

There's plenty of other memorable scenery along the pathway's two loops through this corner of the Pere Marquette State Forest. The trails cross several small streams, edge swamps, climb low hills, and traverse several pine plantations and stands of jack pine and oak.

The one-mile-long Lake Loop connects Big Leverentz and Little Leverentz lakes and the state forest campgrounds nestled next to them. Ten sites make up the campground at the larger lake, and at the south end of the loop, you'll find seven sites at Little Leverentz Lake. Neither lake, with their muddy bottoms, is suitable for swimming, but fishermen will find perch, bluefish, pike and bass awaiting their bait.

The pathway's River Loop swings in a 2.3-mile arc to the north of the smaller Lake Loop. At the farthest point, just before the trail turns back south, you reach an overlook with picturesque views of the Baldwin River, the first river in the state in which German brown trout were released.

In winter the pathway expands to 4.5 miles of ungroomed cross country ski trails.

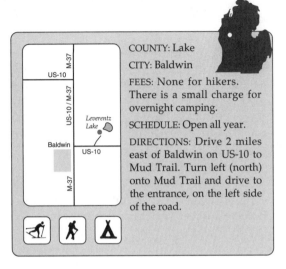

COUNTY: Lake

CITY: Baldwin

FEES: None for hikers. There is a small charge for overnight camping.

SCHEDULE: Open all year.

DIRECTIONS: Drive 2 miles east of Baldwin on US-10 to Mud Trail. Turn left (north) onto Mud Trail and drive to the entrance, on the left side of the road.

98 NORDHOUSE DUNES WILDERNESS AREA

If your main requirement of an outdoor area is the opportunity to get away from the hustle and hassle of modern life, you'll like the Nordhouse Dunes Wilderness Area. The rugged trails, extensive beach and other facilities in this 3,450-acre area of the Manistee National Forest at times appear to be lightly used.

You can backcountry camp at many sites along the more than 10 miles of hiking trails that wind through an area rich in animal and bird life and abundant with wildflowers. Campfires and campsites must be set up more than 400 feet from Lake Michigan and the wilderness boundary and no closer than 200 feet to Nordhouse Lake. No trails in this out-of-the-way area are marked, so carry a compass.

You can reach the south side of the wilderness area from a parking area at the end of Nurnberg Road. Perhaps the best access is from a campground at the Lake Michigan Recreation Area on the north end of Nordhouse Dunes. This campground not only makes a good base camp for hikers, but also is the only spot in the area that has potable water. Adjacent to the campground is a beautiful, secluded picnic area.

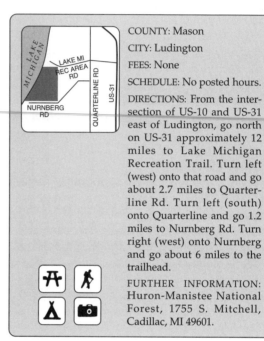

COUNTY: Mason

CITY: Ludington

FEES: None

SCHEDULE: No posted hours.

DIRECTIONS: From the intersection of US-10 and US-31 east of Ludington, go north on US-31 approximately 12 miles to Lake Michigan Recreation Trail. Turn left (west) onto that road and go about 2.7 miles to Quarterline Rd. Turn left (south) onto Quarterline and go 1.2 miles to Nurnberg Rd. Turn right (west) onto Nurnberg and go about 6 miles to the trailhead.

FURTHER INFORMATION: Huron-Manistee National Forest, 1755 S. Mitchell, Cadillac, MI 49601.

Many immigrants have taken root at this "Ellis Island" of Michigan arboretums. In 1940 the United States Forest Service planted this out-of-the-way arboretum in the Manistee National Forest to determine the adaptability and growth potential of trees from Europe, Asia and various non-Michigan climate areas of the United States. After more than 40 years, the impressive survivors of that experiment stand tall here.

A nearly mile-long self-guided trail leads to all the major stands of specimen trees, which include Scotch, pinon, pitch, white, red, table top, jack, Balkan and Austrian pine; white, blue and Norway spruce; and Darvain larch, hemlock, Douglas fir, and black cherry. Interpretive signs identify the trees and explain the natural setting, and several benches scattered throughout the grounds allow for long, relaxed looks.

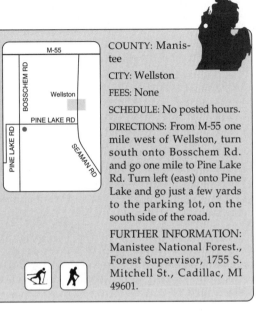

COUNTY: Manistee

CITY: Wellston

FEES: None

SCHEDULE: No posted hours.

DIRECTIONS: From M-55 one mile west of Wellston, turn south onto Bosschem Rd. and go one mile to Pine Lake Rd. Turn left (east) onto Pine Lake and go just a few yards to the parking lot, on the south side of the road.

FURTHER INFORMATION: Manistee National Forest., Forest Supervisor, 1755 S. Mitchell St., Cadillac, MI 49601.

100 BIG MANISTEE RIVER STATE GAME AREA

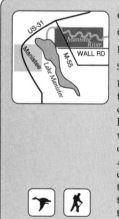

This is one of the hottest birding spots in their county, says the Manistee County Audubon Society. Wood Ducks, warblers, owls, terns, wrens, and a surprising variety of other shorebirds and waterfowl all pay visits to this state game area, through which the last six miles of the Manistee River flows before emptying into Manistee Lake. Highway M-55 cuts through the heart of the area, and you have excellent chances of spotting birds just by pulling off to the side of the pavement and sweeping the wetlands with a pair of binoculars. Spring and fall visits will result in the most sightings, but any time of the year can be rewarding.

The game area is kept flooded to create a wetland habitat, and the dikes that help control water level provide ready-made walkways. From just south of the bridge that carries M-55 over the river, one broad dike forms a large half moon of dry land between grassy wetlands and the swift-moving Manistee River. That easily walked dike makes a fine vantage point for searching the marshy area that, in addition to birds, also shelters numer-ous fur-bearing animals. A canal that hugs the dike for several hundred yards harbors frogs, turtles, and small birds, which hide in the vegetation that crowds the lily-pad-dotted ditch.

A three-quarter-mile walk down the half-moon dike takes you to an observation platform built by the Manistee Audubon Society. The tower rises about 15 feet above the dike and offers a sweeping view of the wetlands to the west and the tree-lined Manistee River to the east.

COUNTY: Manistee

CITY: Manistee

FEES: None

SCHEDULE: Open all year.

DIRECTIONS: From the junction of M-55 and US-31, drive ½ mile south on M-55. Park along the shoulder anywhere south of where M-55 crosses the Manistee River. A one-car parking area at the dike with the observation tower is 200 yards south of the river on the west side of the highway.

MAGOON CREEK NATURAL AREA 101

This 97-acre tract of land overlooking Lake Michigan from atop a wooded bluff has felt the soft tread of moccasin-clad Indians who camped here each summer, the hobnail boots of lumberjacks who felled white pine that once grew here, and the iron-shod hooves of plow horses that worked the land at the turn of the century. But humans haven't touched the area for the past 50 years, and today, people are only occasional visitors to the dense woods and meadows that are slowly being returned to nature.

Magoon Creek offers so many options that it induces "cross training" in outdoor enthusiasts. Picnickers won't be able to resist the nature trail or the beach. Hikers will have trouble maintaining an even pace as they pass interpretive signs, and beachcombers will find the woods and meadows as compelling as the lakeshore.

A one-mile self-guided nature/hiking trail winds throughout the preserve, including the picnic area and beach. Forty-four stops along the route make learning tree and shrub identification easy. At each stop a plaque identifies an important tree, shrub or fern in the immediate area — paper birch, red oak, red maple, juniper, Norway spruce, black willow, white oak, tamarack, poison ivy, white pine, beech, blackberries, horse chestnuts and wild grapes, to name a few — then explains both its natural history and importance to people and wildlife. You can also pick up an interpretive brochure, which has the same information as the plaques, from the Manistee Area Chamber of Commerce, on US-31 just south of the bridge over the Manistee River.

The trail pierces some prime wildlife habitat, where fox and deer are plentiful, and also passes through an area that contains the largest concentration of Bluebirds in Manistee

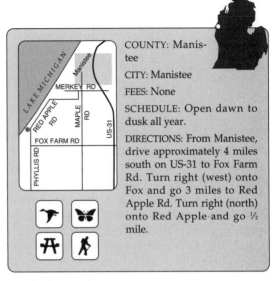

COUNTY: Manistee

CITY: Manistee

FEES: None

SCHEDULE: Open dawn to dusk all year.

DIRECTIONS: From Manistee, drive approximately 4 miles south on US-31 to Fox Farm Rd. Turn right (west) onto Fox and go 3 miles to Red Apple Rd. Turn right (north) onto Red Apple and go ½ mile.

County. The local Audubon chapter also rates Magoon Creek as an excellent birdwatching spot for warblers, upland birds, woodland species and birds of prey.

A small, secluded picnic area, accessible either by the trail or by road, is set in a dense stand of second-growth trees at the very edge of the bluff. The canopy of trees completely shades the area, and with the cooling effect of Lake Michigan at your very feet, you'll rarely feel the full brunt of Michigan's midsummer heat.

From a parking lot a quarter of a mile south of the picnic area, a several-hundred-yard downhill tramp ends at a little-used stretch of sand and surf. If you plan to spend a day on the beach there, pare what you want to take down to the bare essentials, because you'll have to haul it all back uphill to your car.

102 LAKE BLUFF AUDUBON CENTER

One of the most unusual trees in Michigan grows at the Lake Bluff Audubon Center, on Lake Michigan. Relatively speaking it's still a baby, even at more than 100 feet tall and four feet in girth at its base. Its size, however, isn't what makes it particularly unusual, because it's a member of one of the longest-lived and largest species on earth — Sequoia redwoods. A Sequoia redwood? In Michigan!?

Lake Bluff began in 1936 as the private estate of M.E. and Gertrude E. Gray, and they spent years developing their acreage into a beautiful combination of natural landscaping and a carefully planned arboretum. In 1949 they brought several species of redwood seedlings to Lake Bluff in a single one-pound coffee can. Three, including the large Sequoia, survived their cross-country transplanting and continue to grow to maturity in our state.

But these "Baby Hueys" of the plant kingdom aren't the only outstanding natural attraction at the 70-acre estate— including a third of a mile of Lake Michigan shoreline — that was donated to the Michigan Audubon Society in December 1987 upon the death of Mrs. Grey. More than 150 varieties of shrubs and trees surround the estate house and grace the well-kept grounds, which run to the edge of a bluff that rises above Lake Michigan. Telephone-pole-size Douglas firs, white spruce, alder, huge old cottonwoods, black locust, white ash, weeping beech, red maple, Chinese juniper, spindle tree, Norway spruce, gingko, English holly and many others join the redwoods.

All shrubs and trees are labeled, and most are close enough together that you can take in a continent's worth of species in a very short walk. Adding to the enjoyment of a stroll through this unusual and magnificent collection are views of Lake Michigan, which come from almost everywhere within the arboretum.

Open meadows and wood lots make up the acreage away from the estate house. A large, open meadow studded with Bluebird boxes edges the southern boundary of the estate's formal lawn, and across M-110 a 40-acre wood lot holds a dense stand of second-growth maple, beech, hemlock, birch and oak.

Two trails probe the woodlot; a third heads to the beach.

The sanctuary's location on the Lake Michigan Flyway, the wide variety of flora, and the good cover all attract a great many birds. During spring and fall migrations, waterfowl and accipiter movement can be heavy.

Future use at this newest (as of 1995) Audubon nature center is in the planning stages, but most assuredly, opportunities for enjoying Lake Bluff will improve each year.

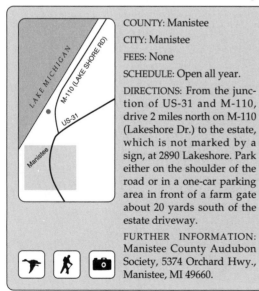

COUNTY: Manistee

CITY: Manistee

FEES: None

SCHEDULE: Open all year.

DIRECTIONS: From the junction of US-31 and M-110, drive 2 miles north on M-110 (Lakeshore Dr.) to the estate, which is not marked by a sign, at 2890 Lakeshore. Park either on the shoulder of the road or in a one-car parking area in front of a farm gate about 20 yards south of the estate driveway.

FURTHER INFORMATION: Manistee County Audubon Society, 5374 Orchard Hwy., Manistee, MI 49660.

TOWER PRESERVE 103

A variety of dunal habitats, the glistening shore of Lake Michigan, and the absence of any concession to human use (except for several small property signs), make the 21-acre Lucia K. Tower Preserve a small gem of untouched beauty.

No trails mar the pristine beauty of this impressive Nature Conservancy preserve. A two-track briefly crosses the southeast corner of the property but quickly wanders off to the south. So if you want to experience the full flavor of the area, you need to take a compass and strike out on your own. Steep hills and the lack of well-trod paths require some strenuous walking, but you will be repaid with peace, solitude, and some unforgettable scenery.

The interior of the preserve holds a stand of large white cedar, several small swamps that darkly reflect the images of nearby trees, and hillsides covered with beech, birch and maple, In many places the overhead canopy so effectively blocks out the sun that you almost have to use a flash on your camera at noon, even in midsummer.

High dunes line the lakeshore, with Mt. Baldy, at 200 feet above Lake Michigan, presenting the most-breathtaking view of the wide explanse of watery blue that extends out to the horizon.

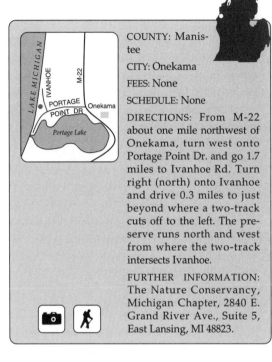

COUNTY: Manistee

CITY: Onekama

FEES: None

SCHEDULE: None

DIRECTIONS: From M-22 about one mile northwest of Onekama, turn west onto Portage Point Dr. and go 1.7 miles to Ivanhoe Rd. Turn right (north) onto Ivanhoe and drive 0.3 miles to just beyond where a two-track cuts off to the left. The preserve runs north and west from where the two-track intersects Ivanhoe.

FURTHER INFORMATION: The Nature Conservancy, Michigan Chapter, 2840 E. Grand River Ave., Suite 5, East Lansing, MI 48823.

104 WOODLAND MANAGEMENT TRAIL

Whether you have a wood lot to manage or not, this easy walk through a beautiful natural setting is a fascinating educational experience. And when you do complete the three-quarter-mile-long trail, with its 22-page interpretive guide, you should merit an honorary diploma in wood lot management. The guide, compared to most interpretive brochures, looks like a textbook (study questions included). But don't be put off by its size; it's easy to use.

The guide's 19 numbered stops correspond to posts along the pathway, and at each you get a detailed but uncomplicated lesson on how forests can be managed for both wildlife and commercial interests. You learn, for instance, why aspen seedlings are important to deer and Ruffed Grouse, why Woodcocks need open fields, how often pine plantations should be harvested, the significance of a wolf tree, the importance of wood lot ponds, and how to select hardwoods for thinning and harvesting.

Using the booklet, you can also determine which trees are healthy and which benefit wildlife the most. You can get the guide in advance by writing the Manistee County Soil Conservation District (see *Further Information*), or you can pick it up there during normal business hours.

Education aside, the trail presents a great opportunity to explore a beautiful and remote corner of the Manistee National Forest. The woodchip-covered path encounters a deep hardwood forest carpeted with ferns, a quiet pond, military-straight rows of red pines, open fields, an eerie swamp, and a slow-moving stream crossed by rough-hewn planks. Deer, raccoon, Wild Turkey, Woodcock, woodpeckers, squirrels and other wildlife inhabit the area.

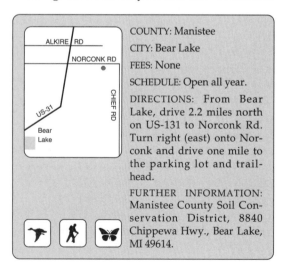

COUNTY: Manistee

CITY: Bear Lake

FEES: None

SCHEDULE: Open all year.

DIRECTIONS: From Bear Lake, drive 2.2 miles north on US-131 to Norconk Rd. Turn right (east) onto Norconk and drive one mile to the parking lot and trailhead.

FURTHER INFORMATION: Manistee County Soil Conservation District, 8840 Chippewa Hwy., Bear Lake, MI 49614.

Most northbound motorists who crest the hill that overlooks Arcadia Lake 16 miles north of Manistee on M-22 will dismiss the view as merely pleasant when compared with the more-stunning scenery just a few miles up the road at Sleeping Bear Dunes. But bird-watchers will instinctively ease off the accelerator as the car comes off the hill and approaches the shallow, marshy lake. They will immediately recognize the lake as a potentially great birdwatching area and one where birding can be productive from the roadside rather than after or during a long walk. If they stop, they will prove their instincts right. The Manistee County Audubon Society rates Arcadia Marsh one of the best birdwatching sites in their county.

M-22 crosses the lake on a long causeway, and only a short bridge near the middle actually spans the water. The wide shoulders on either side of the highway permit easy pulloffs at what is, in fact, the middle of the lake. From the rock-steady roadway, you have a panoramic view of the lake and the marshy fringe that rings most of its shore.

Be sure to bring binoculars and, for best results, also a spotting scope to search the lake for the numerous waterfowl and shore-birds that migrate through the area every spring and those that take up residence here during the summer months. Sandhill Cranes, teal, Buffleheads, swans, Marsh Hawks, Red-tail Hawks and eagles have all been sighted here in addition to a wide variety of song-birds.

Children, however, may find more interest in the turtles that line every log near the road-side or the carp that churn throughout the shallow water.

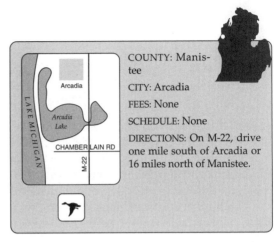

COUNTY: Manistee

CITY: Arcadia

FEES: None

SCHEDULE: None

DIRECTIONS: On M-22, drive one mile south of Arcadia or 16 miles north of Manistee.

106 POINT BETSIE DUNES PRESERVE

After you've walked a quarter mile down the beach from a Nature Conservancy sign at the end of Point Betsie Road, you can almost convince yourself you have discovered a stretch of Lake Michigan shoreline all but untouched by man. True, the stroll does take you past a few homes (set well back from the beach) and the Point Betsie Lighthouse may still be visible over your shoulder. But the 71-acre Point Betsie Dunes Preserve, with its 1,100 feet of prime lake frontage, still appears primeval.

Lake Michigan rolls in on soft, white sand interrupted by bands of stones and pebbles that have been polished by the sand, wind and water. The beach gently rises 25 yards from the water line to low-lying dunes that begin marching inland.

The preserve's exposed position on the tip of Point Betsie makes life hard for the plants that try to colonize the area. Sand cherries and dune grass hug the front of the dunes and are the first to put down roots and stabilize the sand. Farther inland, stunted trees and shrubs claw at the sand. But the precari-

ousness of their situation is evident by the numerous blowouts, areas where strong winds have undermined the plants and then blown bare the face of the dune. These are ideal spots to study plant succession.

Life may be harsh for the plant kingdom, but people and animals find it quite hospitable. Inland, the line of successively higher dunes cup interdunal ponds that shelter frogs, toads, turtles, other amphibians and shorebirds. The lakeshore invites waders and beachcombers to search for unusual stones and driftwood that has been sculpted by the elements then tossed ashore. And the commanding, panoramic view of the great lake can lure you into simply sitting and contemplating the sweeping sea of blue.

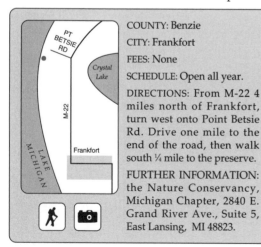

COUNTY: Benzie

CITY: Frankfort

FEES: None

SCHEDULE: Open all year.

DIRECTIONS: From M-22 4 miles north of Frankfort, turn west onto Point Betsie Rd. Drive one mile to the end of the road, then walk south ¼ mile to the preserve.

FURTHER INFORMATION: the Nature Conservancy, Michigan Chapter, 2840 E. Grand River Ave., Suite 5, East Lansing, MI 48823.

PLATTE SPRINGS PATHWAY 107

Hikers will find that the Platte Springs Pathway is a great place to "get their feet wet." No, this is not necessarily the best place in Michigan for someone to take their first hike. Hikers here really do have to get their feet wet, because to both reach and leave the trail they have to take off shoes and socks, roll up pant legs and cross the Platte River. The ford is usually less than a foot and a half deep, but the sandy riverbed and the fairly strong current make it an exhilarating way to begin and end this hike.

Even without its unusual beginning/end, this short but strenuous, rugged and scenic trail would be a magnet to hikers. The 1.25-mile main trail plus several shorter loops border the picturesque Platte River and climb steep ridges — with abrupt elevation gains of up to 150 feet — to the hills overlooking its valley. Free-flowing springs and several small streams occasionally interrupt the trail on their way down the hillside to join the Platte. Hikers must often climb under or over fallen trees that block the way. The trail also crosses old logging roads, follows game trails and passes through small stands of virgin hardwood where the terrain is so rugged, lumbermen couldn't fell and drag the trees out. One grand old sugar maple, which took root when Michigan became a state, measures two and a half feet in diameter.

Blue paint blazes and 26 numbered posts mark the trail. Corresponding numbers in a pamphlet available from any DNR office identify and interpret special points of interest. Many trees and shrubs are also marked and identified.

Attractions to anglers include excellent trout fishing and heavy fall salmon runs. A secluded, quiet state-forest campground completes this near-perfect outdoor spot.

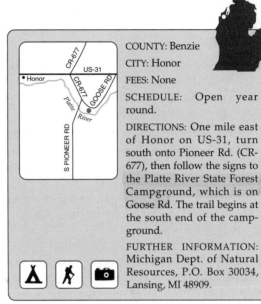

COUNTY: Benzie

CITY: Honor

FEES: None

SCHEDULE: Open year round.

DIRECTIONS: One mile east of Honor on US-31, turn south onto Pioneer Rd. (CR-677), then follow the signs to the Platte River State Forest Campground, which is on Goose Rd. The trail begins at the south end of the campground.

FURTHER INFORMATION: Michigan Dept. of Natural Resources, P.O. Box 30034, Lansing, MI 48909.

108 LAKE ANN PATHWAY

Before hiking here, be sure to stop at the Platte River Hatchery, on US-31 east of Honor, and pick up an excellent printed guide to the area. The pamphlet includes not only a trail map but also 20 numbered descriptions of special points of interest that correspond to numbered posts along the Pathway's two trails. Blue paint spots also mark the routes, and are especially welcome where they pass through sometimes thick undergrowth and clusters of 100-year-old white-pine stumps, reminders of the area's lumbering past.

The Lake Ann (formerly Chain O' Lakes) Pathway's two loops begin and end at the Lake Ann State Forest Campground, on the west shore of Lake Ann. Both the 1.25- and 2-mile loop probe a variety of habitats including the Platte River, bogs, two lakes, and several clearings over rolling terrain. Stands of maple, birch, aspen, blackberry and white pine cover the higher ground, while the vegetation changes to cedar, spruce, tamarack, dogwood, mosses and ferns as the land drops to the bogs and natural springs that flow near the Platte River. Many of the trees and shrubs are labeled for easy identification.

The trails are open in the winter for cross country skiing.

Sites at the Lake Ann State Forest Campground are grass-covered, shady and fairly private.

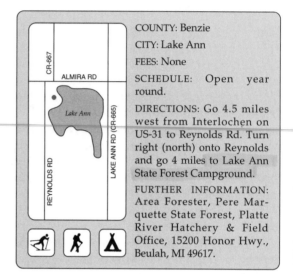

COUNTY: Benzie

CITY: Lake Ann

FEES: None

SCHEDULE: Open year round.

DIRECTIONS: Go 4.5 miles west from Interlochen on US-31 to Reynolds Rd. Turn right (north) onto Reynolds and go 4 miles to Lake Ann State Forest Campground.

FURTHER INFORMATION: Area Forester, Pere Marquette State Forest, Platte River Hatchery & Field Office, 15200 Honor Hwy., Beulah, MI 49617.

LOST LAKE NATURE PATHWAY 109

When you're walking on this trail system past Lake Dubonnet, don't think your eyes are playing tricks on you if you happen to see a chunk of land moving across the water. It probably is.

In 1956 controlled flooding from a dam created Lake Dubonnet from two smaller lakes, and in the process, large areas of lowland along the former shorelines were uprooted. Today, one of those chunks remains as a one-acre floating island, complete with 40-foot trees and brush, that gets blown back and forth across the lake at the wind's whim. Other evidence of the extent of that flooding comes from the dead trees sticking out of the water on the north end of the lake. Waterfowl nest in the habitat, and beaver, too, have built a house there.

The "bottom" (and the shortest, at 1.5 miles) loop of the Pathway's three circular trails, which are "stacked" south to north, begins at the Lake Dubonnet State Forest Campground, in the Fife Lake State Forest, then follows the Lake Dubonnet shoreline for half its length.

The 3.5-mile middle loop passes blueberry bogs, a beaver dam, red-pine plantings and white-pine stumps, evidence of the area's involvement in the lumbering era.

The 5.5-mile "top" loop crosses an abandoned logging railroad grade, then at its northern rim, skirts the lake from which the Pathway gets its name. Lost Lake is an excellent example of the slow process of natural plant succession that eventually fills in all lakes. More than half of its original area has turned into bog, and over the next several hundred years, the bog will replace the entire lake.

Orange paint spots mark the Pathway, and 28 numbered posts along all loops correspond

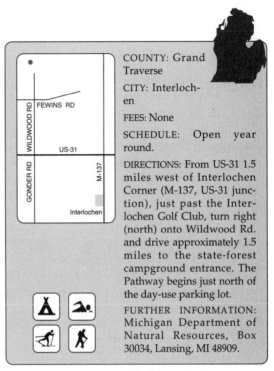

COUNTY: Grand Traverse

CITY: Interlochen

FEES: None

SCHEDULE: Open year round.

DIRECTIONS: From US-31 1.5 miles west of Interlochen Corner (M-137, US-31 junction), just past the Interlochen Golf Club, turn right (north) onto Wildwood Rd. and drive approximately 1.5 miles to the state-forest campground entrance. The Pathway begins just north of the day-use parking lot.

FURTHER INFORMATION: Michigan Department of Natural Resources, Box 30034, Lansing, MI 48909.

to descriptions in a self-guiding brochure available at any DNR office. The brochure, however, is not entirely necessary here because the same information is attached to several of the numbered stops, plus many of the trees and shrubs are also labeled.

The trail system is open for cross country skiing and has a winter extension that adds one mile to the total distance of each loop.

110 MUNCIE LAKES PATHWAY

If there were a printed menu for hikers to select from when they come to Muncie Lakes Pathway, it would probably read something like: "From column A pick a length, from a short 1.5-mile walk to a demanding 9-mile overnighter. Then from column B, choose a destination — secluded lake, beautiful forest, or crystal-clear stream."

Over nine miles of hiking and cross country ski trails divided into a number of loops make up this hiker's smorgasbord in the Pere Marquette State Forest. Maps posted at all trail intersections orient the hiker and note mileage to various points. Blue triangular markers then guide the way over gently rolling wooded terrain.

And there are a variety of distances and destinations to choose from. For example, Muncie Lakes, a cluster of small lakes and marshy area rich in wildlife, is 2.5 miles from the parking lot on Ranch Rudolf Road. Dollar Lake, at the extreme northeastern edge of the trail system, is another two miles farther. The southern loop of the pathway is rarely more than half a mile from the shallow, crystal-clear Boardman River, one of the most scenic streams in the Lower Peninsula. In two places the trail brushes the heavily wooded banks of this twisting, turning excellent trout stream.

Backpackers can camp anywhere off the trails and back from the lakes. Also, Sheck's State Forest Campground connects to Muncie Lakes Pathway's south trail via a hiking/riding path that passes the camping area and joins the Pathway about 0.2 miles north of the campground parking lot.

In winter the trails are marked for cross country skiers by green, blue or black markers, which indicate increasing difficulty.

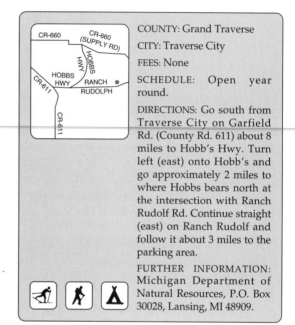

COUNTY: Grand Traverse

CITY: Traverse City

FEES: None

SCHEDULE: Open year round.

DIRECTIONS: Go south from Traverse City on Garfield Rd. (County Rd. 611) about 8 miles to Hobb's Hwy. Turn left (east) onto Hobb's and go approximately 2 miles to where Hobbs bears north at the intersection with Ranch Rudolf Rd. Continue straight (east) on Ranch Rudolf and follow it about 3 miles to the parking area.

FURTHER INFORMATION: Michigan Department of Natural Resources, P.O. Box 30028, Lansing, MI 48909.

GRAND TRAVERSE 111
NATURAL EDUCATION PRESERVE

Strung like a ribbon along the west bank of the Boardman River, the 370-acre Grand Traverse Education Preserve wraps a peaceful, natural package of hiking trails, dams, ponds and scenic picnic areas, all only two miles from the heart of Traverse City.

The preserve hugs the river for over two miles and in many places, especially when squeezed between river and railroad tracks, is only 100 yards wide. Scenic rest areas and picnic grounds are often located in the broader areas. Two dams on the river within the park have created large ponds that attract waterfowl. A pair of Mute Swans, for example, which nest in and around the Grand Traverse region, can usually be spotted along the Boardman here.

Four trails, including one that is self-guided, wind for six miles along the river through marshes, grasslands and forest areas, and across several small streams that empty into the Boardman.

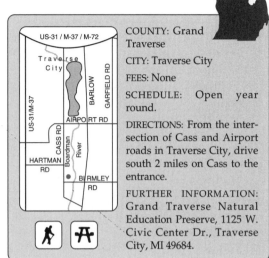

COUNTY: Grand Traverse

CITY: Traverse City

FEES: None

SCHEDULE: Open year round.

DIRECTIONS: From the intersection of Cass and Airport roads in Traverse City, drive south 2 miles on Cass to the entrance.

FURTHER INFORMATION: Grand Traverse Natural Education Preserve, 1125 W. Civic Center Dr., Traverse City, MI 49684.

117

112 LIGHTHOUSE PARK

This memorably beautiful piece of Michigan landscape is also a singular geographic location. When you arrive, not only have you reached the tip of Old Mission Peninsula, but also you are standing exactly halfway between the equator and the North Pole. A big, impossible-to-miss sign notifies you of the fact, and if there's more than four cars in the parking lot, you can lay odds that sometime during your visit somebody will have their picture taken as they "straddle" the 45th Parallel.

The next most-popular attraction here is the picturesque lighthouse that overlooks Grand Traverse Bay. The white clapboard-sided light was constructed in 1870 to mark the end of the long finger of land that divides Grand Traverse Bay into East and West arms.

But the reason nature lovers come here is the sublime beauty of the surroundings. The end of the peninsula is lushly forested. The palisade of trees ends abruptly at a ribbon of soft sand bordering the water, and where the land dips beneath the bay, the sand gives way to cobblestone-size and larger rocks that litter the shallows. The variety of natural colors and textures create an endlessly fascinating scenic panorama.

Several short trails cut through the thick inland vegetation and lead along the shoreline where you can gaze both east and west at the green hills across the waters of the bay. A few picnic tables lay scattered along the beach, attracting both picnickers and those who just want to sit and contemplate the beauty of their surroundings.

An added inducement is that the park is at the end of one of the most beautiful highways in the state. The park marks the end of M-37, which heads north out of Traverse City and for 17 miles treats motorists to one breathtaking view after another. When the road isn't bordering the shoreline or tunneling through huge cherry orchards, it follows the spine of the peninsula and presents spectacular views of both arms of the bay. It is one of the most celebrated drives in Michigan, especially in May when the orchards are in full bloom and the peninsula lies under a soft blanket of blossoms.

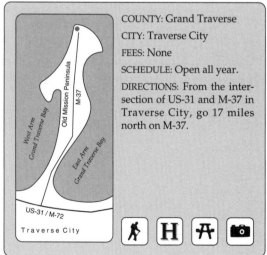

COUNTY: Grand Traverse

CITY: Traverse City

FEES: None

SCHEDULE: Open all year.

DIRECTIONS: From the intersection of US-31 and M-37 in Traverse City, go 17 miles north on M-37.

SAND LAKES QUIET AREA 113

Sand Lakes Quiet Area is rated "G," that is, suitable for even very young children. Easy walking over rolling, sandy hills and through a mixed hardwood/conifer forest is the norm here, whether you take a day hike or a short backpacking excursion to one of the many lakes scattered throughout the area.

More than 10 miles of trails cover Sand Lakes' 2,500 acres of Pere Marquette State Forest land. Motorized traffic is barred, and hikers can back-country camp anywhere within the trail system. Several secluded lakes, with fine swimming and fishing, are especially good places to set up camp. Sites are also available at the Guernsey Lake State Forest Campground, on the eastern end of the Quiet Area off Guernsey Lake Road.

You can reach the trail system from several roads that border the Quiet Area. A large parking lot on Broomhead Road at the northeast corner, for example, provides easy access and is the only entry point in the winter for cross country skiers. You can also enter the area from a few pulloffs along Island Lake Road and from a parking lot at the state-forest campground.

Maps of the trail system are posted throughout the area or are available from any local DNR office.

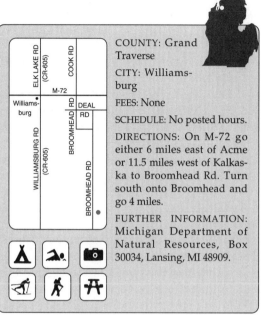

COUNTY: Grand Traverse

CITY: Williamsburg

FEES: None

SCHEDULE: No posted hours.

DIRECTIONS: On M-72 go either 6 miles east of Acme or 11.5 miles west of Kalkaska to Broomhead Rd. Turn south onto Broomhead and go 4 miles.

FURTHER INFORMATION: Michigan Department of Natural Resources, Box 30034, Lansing, MI 48909.

114 SKEGEMOG LAKE WILDLIFE AREA

Quicksand, Massasauga rattlesnakes, and the wet and wild terrain were enough to keep out 19th-century loggers and farmers but not 20th-century real-estate developers. So in the 1970s, private and public organizations, plus 900 individual contributors had to combine forces to save this uniquely beautiful 2,700 acres of marshes, quaking bogs, streams, cedar swamps, and ponds, all wrapped around the southeastern end of Lake Skegemog.

Through their efforts, much more than a unique and beautiful landscape was saved. The Lake Skegemog Wildlife Area, located partially within the Pere Marquette State Forest, is home to a wide variety of wildlife, including many rare and endangered species. Repeated sightings of two adult and two juvenile Bald Eagles, for example, is good evidence that those great birds nest in the area, as do osprey. Bobcats, otter, black bear, ruffled grouse, mink, beaver, weasels and badgers roam the marshes and forests, and some of the state's largest muskellunge prowl the shallow stump-infested waters of the lake.

For an outstanding panoramic view of not only the entire Skegemog Lake Wildlife Area, but also Elk Lake and the Torch River, drive to a scenic turnout off M-72 about eight miles west of Kalkaska. Good views also come from an observation platform reached from Rapid City Road (CR-597) on the park's north side near the mouth of the Torch River.

For a more intimate look at the Lake Skegemog area, walk an old railroad grade that cuts through the western edge of the preserve. This 4.5-mile hiking/skiing trail, closed to all motorized use, runs from the park's southern boundary at M-72 to the northern edge at Schneider Road. Don't wander off the trail; it's too easy to become lost in the trackless swamps and bogs that conceal quicksand and Massasauga rattlesnakes.

One of the best ways to appreciate this unique piece of wilderness area is to quietly coast along the shore of Lake Skegemog in a canoe. Boggs Road, on the south, and the Torch River, on the north, both have public access points.

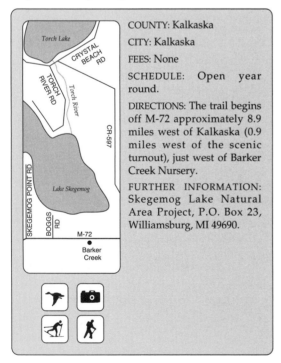

COUNTY: Kalkaska

CITY: Kalkaska

FEES: None

SCHEDULE: Open year round.

DIRECTIONS: The trail begins off M-72 approximately 8.9 miles west of Kalkaska (0.9 miles west of the scenic turnout), just west of Barker Creek Nursery.

FURTHER INFORMATION: Skegemog Lake Natural Area Project, P.O. Box 23, Williamsburg, MI 49690.

Elk Rapids County Park is as pretty a picnic spot as you can find on either arm of Grand Traverse Bay. Low, wooded dunes border a wide, sandy beach perfect for sunbathers, sand-castle architects, beachcombers and swimmers. You get pillow-soft sand, a gently shelving bottom, and a magnificent view of both the east arm of the long, narrow bay and the picturesque Old Mission Peninsula across the waters. And when children tire of wading, swimming and playing in the sand, they can make tracks to the playground equipment that edges the landward side of the beach.

Back from the beach, individual picnic tables and grills nestle in small openings in the dense evergreens, birch and hardwoods that cover the ridged dunes. Almost every picnic site offers seclusion and privacy. Some of the spots have a view of the beach through a screen of trees, while others are cut off from the shoreline by the low sand ridges and heavy woods.

A maze of sandy, paved and needle-strewn trails wind through the 13-acre park. The trails follow depressions between the interdunal ridges, cut through the dense woods, and continually climb and descend the closely spaced ridge lines. Even a short walk gives the pleasant illusion of traversing a much greater distance and, in spite of being in the middle of a picnic area, of walking through a quiet and little-visited woodland.

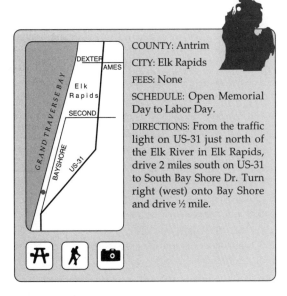

COUNTY: Antrim

CITY: Elk Rapids

FEES: None

SCHEDULE: Open Memorial Day to Labor Day.

DIRECTIONS: From the traffic light on US-31 just north of the Elk River in Elk Rapids, drive 2 miles south on US-31 to South Bay Shore Dr. Turn right (west) onto Bay Shore and drive ½ mile.

116 PALMER-WILCOX-GATES PRESERVE

Mother Nature never seems to tire of creating magical beauty from wind, sand and water along Lake Michigan's seemingly endless shoreline. The jaded may, after the umpteenth breathtaking view, remain unmoved by yet another striking expanse of blinding-white sand framed by green-and-brown-cloaked dunes on one side and emerald-blue water on the other. But even those most dulled by the constant beauty of Michigan's coastline can't help but pause and appreciate the setting of this Nature Conservancy preserve.

The long, narrow 15-acre preserve rests on the east shore of the east arm of Grand Traverse Bay. From anywhere on the beach, you have a memorable view of the picturesque bay and, four miles across the water, the equally beautiful Old Mission Peninsula, crowned by million-dollar homes, sprawling orchards and rolling hills.

From Bay Shore Road, which gives access to the preserve, low, wooded dunes hide the shoreline, but a short 30-yard walk from the road's shoulder reveals the glorious beach. The wide strip of sand gently slips toward the water from the low, sandy ridges anchored by hemlock, cedar, fir, pine, hardwoods and low-growing junipers. Hidden along the edges of the dunes and nestled in the woods are a bounty of rare wildflowers.

No trails, except the one leading to the beach, mar the fragile charm of the dunes, and visitors are urged to stay off the low, sandy ridges because even occasional foot traffic can threaten many of the plants' tenuous grip on life.

But the beach allows plenty of room for exploring. Beachcombers can build castles in the fine-grain sand or wade the surf that washes the pebble-strewn shore. Naturalists and birdwatchers will want to walk the shore close to the edge of the wooded dunes and search for the rare Lake Huron tansy and the many warblers that inhabit the area. Also be sure to keep an eye peeled for shorebirds and waterfowl.

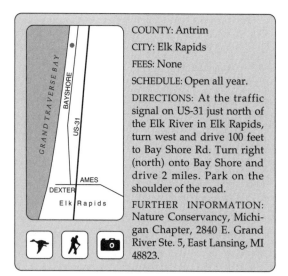

COUNTY: Antrim

CITY: Elk Rapids

FEES: None

SCHEDULE: Open all year.

DIRECTIONS: At the traffic signal on US-31 just north of the Elk River in Elk Rapids, turn west and drive 100 feet to Bay Shore Rd. Turn right (north) onto Bay Shore and drive 2 miles. Park on the shoulder of the road.

FURTHER INFORMATION: Nature Conservancy, Michigan Chapter, 2840 E. Grand River Ste. 5, East Lansing, MI 48823.

There are usually two ways into a natural area: on foot or by car. At the Grass River Natural Area you have a third choice: by boat. The preserve is located on the Grass River, which connects Lake Bellaire and Clam Lake, and boaters can reach the natural area from either lake and tie up at a dock large enough to accommodate two or three craft.

No matter how you get here, it's well worth the trip. More than a mile of boardwalks plus several bridges, benches and observation platforms guarantee easy access to and added enjoyment of this 965-acre area of upland forests, meadows, riverside marshes and cedar swamp, all ribboned by a creek and a river. And the manmade structures don't detract from the beauty of the natural setting.

Most of the trails here loop through the cedar swamp and marsh area bordering the Grass River, which cuts through the park's northern section just before flowing into Clam Lake. The bark- and wood-chip-covered paths are easy walking over level ground and vary in length from an eighth of a mile to a little more than a mile. Where the ground is not firm, boardwalks carry foot traffic (some are also wide enough for wheelchairs) over the swamp and marsh. The walkways — which seem to merge and become a part of the natural setting — also border and repeatedly cross scenic little Finch Creek as it splits into several channels before emptying into Grass River.

Several foot bridges and three platforms, too, are as pleasing in this natural setting as the view from them. Many of the bridges, for example, have incorporated benches into their design so that visitors can sit and enjoy the whispering creek or contemplate the beauty of the surrounding swamp. Panoramic views of the river, Clam Lake and the grassy

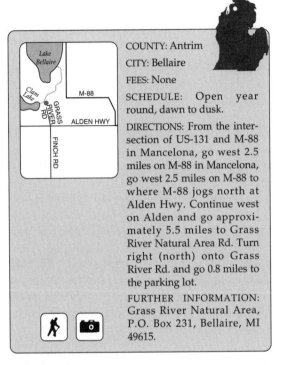

COUNTY: Antrim

CITY: Bellaire

FEES: None

SCHEDULE: Open year round, dawn to dusk.

DIRECTIONS: From the intersection of US-131 and M-88 in Mancelona, go west 2.5 miles on M-88 in Mancelona, go west 2.5 miles on M-88 to where M-88 jogs north at Alden Hwy. Continue west on Alden and go approximately 5.5 miles to Grass River Natural Area Rd. Turn right (north) onto Grass River Rd. and go 0.8 miles to the parking lot.

FURTHER INFORMATION: Grass River Natural Area, P.O. Box 231, Bellaire, MI 49615.

marsh bordering the riverbank come from two observation platforms located next to the Grass River on either side of the mouth of Finch Creek and a third set next to the creek about 100 yards back from the river.

Wildflowers proliferate in the Grass River Natural Area, and more than 300 species of plant life have been identified within its varied habitat and ecosystems. Forty species of mammals and 53 varied bird species also call the park home.

This Antrim County Park is funded by public donations and is managed by a volunteer organization. A guide to the natural area's trails is available for $2 at local businesses. Future plans call for the construction of an interpretive building.

118 BIG BEAR LAKE NATURE PATHWAY

The likely chance of spotting a beaver is the main attraction at this Mackinaw State Forest trail, but even without sighting North America's largest rodent, you'll leave with many pleasant memories.

The pathway's two loops total 2.2 miles and lead through a variety of landscape and habitats home to deer, porcupine, Ruffed Grouse, Woodcock, waterfowl and beaver. The shorter 0.8-mile Beaver Lodge Loop attracts the most attention because it circles a pond with an active beaver colony. The trail initially follows an abandoned railroad grade then edges a marsh-fringed pond and cuts through a stand of mature red pine. Once out of the pine, the trail circles the beaver pond and briefly follows the shoreline of Big Bear Lake before returning to the trailhead.

The longer Eagles Roost Trail carves a wide two-mile loop through country east of the Beaver Lodge Trail. During that approximately 40-minute walk, you'll thread your way through upland hardwoods, encounter a small pond and a dense stand of aspen, and pass through open areas carpeted with wildflowers. Occasional interpretive signs along both loops explain some of the natural and human history of this remote, out-of-the-way area.

Both trails begin and end at a large state forest campground that hugs the north shore of Big Bear Lake. An adjacent day-use area, including a picnic site, is a pleasant place to cool down after a hike.

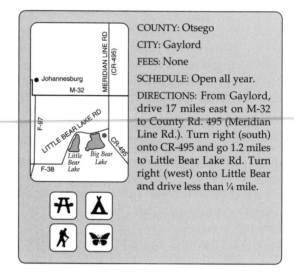

COUNTY: Otsego

CITY: Gaylord

FEES: None

SCHEDULE: Open all year.

DIRECTIONS: From Gaylord, drive 17 miles east on M-32 to County Rd. 495 (Meridian Line Rd.). Turn right (south) onto CR-495 and go 1.2 miles to Little Bear Lake Rd. Turn right (west) onto Little Bear and drive less than ¼ mile.

ASPEN PARK 119

Blindfold someone before taking them to Aspen Park, and they won't believe they are in a city park less than half a mile from a strip mall. The 100 acres of hilly, wooded and wild terrain seem more appropriate to the farther reaches of Otsego County rather than minutes away from downtown Gaylord.

The jumble of sharply rising hills is covered in a tangle of dense hardwoods, young white pine and low thickets. Deep depressions between the hills are wet with ponds and marshes. The broad assortment of habitats attracts numerous birds, and you'll have especially good chances of spotting warblers, upland game birds, and marsh and shore-birds.

Two-tracks and trails lead every which-way through the park and appear to have evolved through random wanderings by visitors rather than by systematic design. Narrow trails descend into the water-filled depressions between the hills, with some of the paths so steep that on the way back up, you'll find yourself negotiating the paths on hands and knees while still remaining nearly upright. Other easier-walked routes circle the highlands, shoulder their way through dense woodlots, and occasionally allow glimpses of homes near the park.

The park also contains a picnic area and accommodates cross country skiers in the winter.

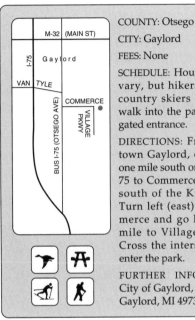

COUNTY: Otsego

CITY: Gaylord

FEES: None

SCHEDULE: Hours and days vary, but hikers and cross country skiers can always walk into the park from the gated entrance.

DIRECTIONS: From downtown Gaylord, drive about one mile south on Business I-75 to Commerce Blvd., just south of the Kmart store. Turn left (east) onto Commerce and go less than ½ mile to Village Parkway. Cross the intersection and enter the park.

FURTHER INFORMATION: City of Gaylord, 225 S. Main, Gaylord, MI 49735.

120 PIGEON RIVER COUNTRY STATE FOREST

At the mention of Pigeon River Country, two thoughts usually come to mind: elk and controversy.

The Pigeon River Country State Forest, a 97,000-acre parcel in the Mackinaw State Forest, is a good example of how the state attempts to balance land use between recreation and the harvesting of natural resources. That responsibility is awesome when you consider that nearly half of Michigan, more than 18 million acres, is wooded land and that nearly four million of those acres make up the largest dedicated state-forest system in the continental United States. That responsibility can also generate controversy, as evidenced by the public outcry and protest over the granting of carefully monitored oil and natural-gas drilling rights in the Pigeon River Country within range of Michigan's only elk herd. Most outdoor purists will find, however, that the drilling has, so far, had little impact on the area.

Oil and gas aren't the first natural resources to be removed from the Pigeon River Coun-

OUTDOOR IMAGES/TOM HUGGLER

try. Lumbermen ravaged the area between 1860 and 1900, and in their wake, the seemingly inevitable forest fires left the land scarred and barren. When farmers failed and left the land, the state, in 1919, created the Pigeon River State Forest.

And the state planted something other than just seedling trees. In 1918 seven elk — once numerous in Michigan but long gone with the destruction of their habitat — were released in the area. Today, the herd of over a thousand elk are without a doubt the forest's major tourist attraction.

According to the DNR, one of the best chances of seeing the imposing animals comes from an area near the corner of Osmun and Clark Bridge roads (see *Directions*). South of that intersection, a half-mile path leads from a parking lot on the west side of Osmun Road up gently rising ground to Inspiration Point, a high hill overlooking broad meadows and the Cornwall Creek Floodings. Elk often graze in the meadows spread around the bottom of the hill. A sweeping view of another large meadow where elk come to feed comes from a parking area on the east side of Osmun Road, just north of the same intersection with Clark Bridge Road. Early morning and early evening are the best times to spot the magnificent creatures.

And elk aren't the only wildlife that roams the area. Deer are so numerous they are often spotted along the roads. Bear, coyote, bobcat, beaver, otter, grouse, woodcock Turkey, Bald Eagle, Osprey, loons, Blue Heron and many other species also inhabit the forest, but most are more elusive and difficult to spot than deer and elk. Good chances of spotting wildlife come from the forest's many good dirt roads, which also make pleasant scenic drives.

Hiking trails, too, traverse some of the most beautiful parts of the country. The Shingle Mill Pathway, with five loops ranging in length from 0.75 miles to 11 miles, passes through deep woods, borders the Pigeon River, and on the longer northern loops, crosses rolling, hilly terrain. The Pathway begins at the Pigeon Bridge Forest Campground, just off Sturgeon Valley Road 10 miles east of Vanderbilt.

Ten heavily shaded sites at the Pigeon Bridge Forest Campground border the river, and 2.5 miles uptrail are 19 more sites at the Pigeon River Forest Campground. Hikers walking Shingle Mill Pathway's 6- 10- or 11-mile loops will pass the campground, which can also be reached by car from Twin Lakes Road.

The Pigeon River Country State Forest field office is a mile north of Sturgeon Valley Road on Twin Lakes Road. Maps of the Pigeon River Country are available there.

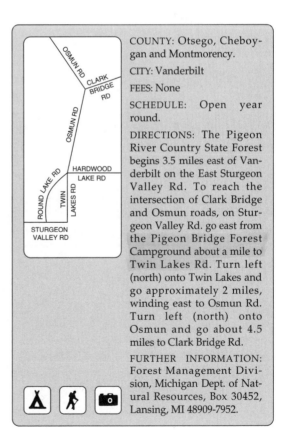

COUNTY: Otsego, Cheboygan and Montmorency.

CITY: Vanderbilt

FEES: None

SCHEDULE: Open year round.

DIRECTIONS: The Pigeon River Country State Forest begins 3.5 miles east of Vanderbilt on the East Sturgeon Valley Rd. To reach the intersection of Clark Bridge and Osmun roads, on Sturgeon Valley Rd. go east from the Pigeon Bridge Forest Campground about a mile to Twin Lakes Rd. Turn left (north) onto Twin Lakes and go approximately 2 miles, winding east to Osmun Rd. Turn left (north) onto Osmun and go about 4.5 miles to Clark Bridge Rd.

FURTHER INFORMATION: Forest Management Division, Michigan Dept. of Natural Resources, Box 30452, Lansing, MI 48909-7952.

121 WARNER CREEK PATHWAY

Deer tracks often outnumber the heel marks of hikers on the soft ground of this lightly used trail, which takes both hikers and cross country skiers through the picturesque Harwood Hills section of the Jordan River State Forest. The easily walked 3.8-mile-long single loop passes through stands of young pine and old maples and also skirts a swamp, the creek from which the trail takes its name, and at the halfway point, a large pond. Blue DNR trail markers lead from the parking lot on M-32 down a short access route to the main pathway, which circles through highlands overlooking the Jordan River Valley. Once

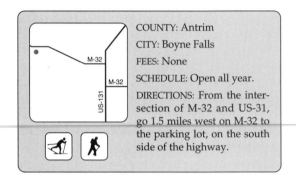

COUNTY: Antrim

CITY: Boyne Falls

FEES: None

SCHEDULE: Open all year.

DIRECTIONS: From the intersection of M-32 and US-31, go 1.5 miles west on M-32 to the parking lot, on the south side of the highway.

away from the highway, you are enveloped in beauty and a quiet broken only by the call of birds or the rattle of wind through the trees.

JORDAN RIVER PATHWAY 122

Catch even just a glimpse of the Jordan River, say from the top of Deadman's Hill or maybe from the river's edge just a few feet from Jordan River Road, and you will immediately understand why, in 1972, it was dedicated as Michigan's first Natural Scenic River. Even such quick images of this river — hurrying around small islands; twisting, turning and looping back on itself; lined by leaning pine and cedar that shelter wild iris and orchids; bed atumble with moss- and lichen-covered fallen trees; and all magnificently framed by sharply rising hills — are hard to forget.

For an indelible memory of the sublime beauty of the Jordan's setting in the Mackinaw State Forest, hike all or parts of two trails, one short, one long, and both of which begin and end at Deadman's Hill (so named because, in 1903, a Big Wheel — a huge single-axled device used to drag logs in the summer — broke loose, crashed down the hill and killed an unlucky lumberjack).

Panoramic views of the Jordan River Valley plus many intimate contacts with the river itself come from an 18-mile trail, which begins at the hill then passes over high hills, crosses countless small spring-fed streams, passes old logging railroad grades, skirts a beaver dam and cuts through deep woods. Several short sections of this trail are also accessible from county roads that cross it. For those who would like to hike the entire 18 miles (a two-day trip), an overnight stay at the Pinney Bridge Campground marks the halfway point. Facilities at this site of an old logging camp include pit toilets but no electricity.

A short three-mile loop, which only takes about two hours to hike, also begins at Deadman's Hill, descends into the valley (with

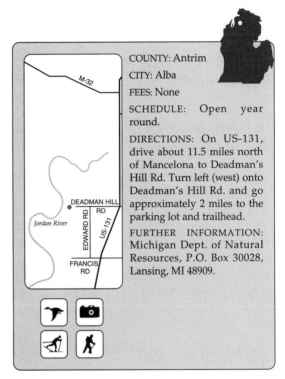

COUNTY: Antrim

CITY: Alba

FEES: None

SCHEDULE: Open year round.

DIRECTIONS: On US-131, drive about 11.5 miles north of Mancelona to Deadman's Hill Rd. Turn left (west) onto Deadman's Hill Rd. and go approximately 2 miles to the parking lot and trailhead.

FURTHER INFORMATION: Michigan Dept. of Natural Resources, P.O. Box 30028, Lansing, MI 48909.

brief glimpses of the river), then returns. Just before reclimbing Deadman's Hill, a quarter-mile side trip to the quiet beauty of an old beaver dam and pond is well worth the time and effort.

Section-by-section mileage plus historical and natural points of interest along both trails are included on a detailed map and brochure published by the Department of Natural Resources and available by mail from their Lansing offices.

Several scenic views that require virtually no walking come from pulloffs along the Jordan River Road, which descends into the valley from US-131 then borders the river for about 10 miles.

123 AVALANCHE PRESERVE

Avalanche Preserve, on the south side of Boyne City, offers the most spectacular view of Lake Charlevoix and the surrounding countryside to be had from any vantage point in Charlevoix County. But there is a price to pay. Barn Mountain looms over and dominates the 320-acre city park, and there is no easy way up the steep slope to the observation deck on the summit.

For traditionalists a trail begins on the right-hand side of the huge hill and curves up and around its western face. Along this route you'll pass through a second-growth hardwood forest on a loose-sand trail that makes for some hard slogging. The forest is so thick that there's no view or visual perspective by which to judge how high you have climbed. You don't know how much farther it is to the top until you get there.

A more direct route leads straight up the open face of the mountain on a long series of staircases that total 460 steps. This route is also more monotonous, but at least when you stop for a breather and look over your shoulder, you get a view that broadens the higher you climb.

Either way takes stamina, but the magnificent view of Lake Charlevoix, the surrounding hills that seem to cup the lake, and Boyne City, which looks like an HO-scale modeler's layout, is worth the effort. And during the color season, nature takes a paint brush to the vast canvas to create an even more vibrant landscape.

If you have any energy left after the climb, you can walk trails that depart from the summit of Barn Mountain and circle through the surrounding high, rolling country.

In winter, locals and tourists flock to the park for cross country skiing, to zoom down the slopes on sleds and toboggans, or for ice skating or hockey on two ice rinks.

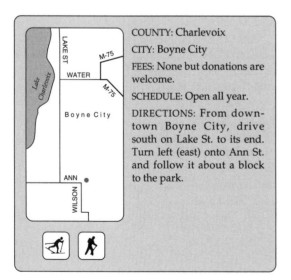

COUNTY: Charlevoix

CITY: Boyne City

FEES: None but donations are welcome.

SCHEDULE: Open all year.

DIRECTIONS: From downtown Boyne City, drive south on Lake St. to its end. Turn left (east) onto Ann St. and follow it about a block to the park.

Sportsmen's Park cozies up to the south arm of Lake Charlevoix and the Jordan River at the point where the stream enters the long, narrow fjord-like lake. There's not much room to stretch your legs, but the postcard-size area will certainly give your eyes a work-out. Only an Al Kaline throw away, at the opposite end of a bridge that carries M-32 traffic over the lake, is downtown East Jordan. From the small, grassy park and its half dozen picnic tables, you get a marvelous view of the quaint village, which hugs the lakeshore, and the low, wooded hills that ring the horizon and tumble down the picturesque body of water.

The vista is beautiful, but most nature lovers will be drawn to scenery closer at hand. A sluggish creek and marshy area make an indistinct border between the park and Lake Charlevoix. And on the park's south end, the Jordan River separates the picnic grounds from a large natural area that surrounds the southern tip of the lake. The broad, slow-moving river, the great expanse of marshy wetlands, and the open water all attract rafts of waterfowl and numerous shorebirds.

With patience, a pair of binoculars or spotting scope, and virtually no exercise, you stand an excellent chance of seeing a wide variety of ducks plus geese, swans and marsh birds. And on a good day, binoculars aren't even necessary, as the birds paddle about near shore or wing by close overhead. Many of the Canadian geese, mallards and swans have become so used to visitors that they panhandle for food. Several Osprey nesting platforms in the area increase your chances of seeing that majestic bird. And recently added eagle nesting platforms have attracted mature birds, often seen over the lake and wetland.

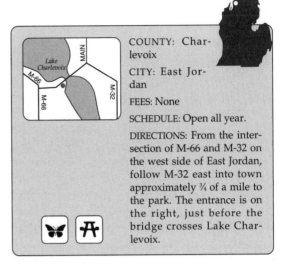

COUNTY: Charlevoix

CITY: East Jordan

FEES: None

SCHEDULE: Open all year.

DIRECTIONS: From the intersection of M-66 and M-32 on the west side of East Jordan, follow M-32 east into town approximately ¾ of a mile to the park. The entrance is on the right, just before the bridge crosses Lake Charlevoix.

125 NORTH POINT PRESERVE
126 MT. MCSAUBA RECREATION AREA

These two adjoining areas are prime examples of the unique and nearly indescribable beauty found only along the enchanted coastline of the Great Lakes. That this pair of natural wonderlands lie less than a mile from downtown Charlevoix, are easily accessible by car, and still have somehow escaped commercial development only adds to their special value as places to enjoy the gifts of nature. Together they total 79 acres of wooded dunes and more than a mile of gorgeous Lake Michigan shoreline.

North Point Preserve, the northernmost of the two parcels, is composed of 27 acres of low, wooded dunes and cedar swamps populated by world-class-size birch and cedar. The towering trees shade a thick understory of shrubby evergreens, vines that Tarzan would be proud to swing on, and a forest floor accented with wildflowers. A maze of trails meander every which-way through this other-worldly setting and give the impression that no matter how many times you visit, it would be impossible to duplicate an earlier walk. The dense cover, small clearings, and variety of plants, plus the nearness of open water suggest that the area could be excellent for birdwatching.

Fronting the maze of trails and deep, quiet woods is a rugged, rocky beach. The cobble, which extends for dozens of yards from tree line to water line, is not for barefoot beachcombers. But tennis-shoe-clad explorers and photographers can search for waterfowl, pretty or unusual rocks, and water-sculpted driftwood. About 50 yards south — that is, left, from the end of McSauba Road — you can get a commanding view of the point from a low observation platform nearly hidden in the tree line.

Just south of and sharing a property line with North Point Preserve is Mt. McSauba Recreation Area. Sawtooth-shaped dunes — indiscriminately interrupted by gullies, cuts and draws — characterize this 52-acre city park. A variety of unmarked but well-trod paths wind over and through tall dunes anchored against the wind by birch, beech and a smattering of pine and maple. If you like to search for the unusual, you can also find sassafras and mountain maple trees. The

soft, sandy trails and steep climbs are tiring, but the scenery — including a glimpse of Lake Michigan from atop the piles of sand — and the sense of adventure in exploring the dunes' hidden nooks and crannies draw you up one slope after another. Not surprisingly, the area is also popular with skiers and sledders in the winter.

A walk to the beach reveals another side of the park. In contrast to North Point Preserve, the shoreline here resembles a monstrous sandbox. A wide strip of down-soft sand separates the tree line from the water, and you'll find the urge to walk barefoot along the edge of the surf nearly irresistible. The view is spectacular. South down the beach, the port of Charlevoix is clearly visible, while to the west and north, nothing but the blue-green waters of Lake Michigan reach out to the horizon.

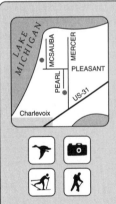

COUNTY: Charlevoix

CITY: Charlevoix

FEES: None

SCHEDULE: Open all year.

DIRECTIONS: Drive north, then east out of Charlevoix on US-31 approximately one mile to Mercer Rd. Turn left (north) onto Mercer and go one mile to Pleasant St. To reach North Point Preserve, turn left (west) onto Pleasant and drive 2 blocks to McSauba Rd. Turn right (north) onto McSauba and go 3 blocks to the parking lot.

To reach Mt. McSauba Recreation Area, turn left (west) onto Pleasant from Mercer and go one block to Pearl St. turn left (south) onto Pearl and drive ½ mile to the parking area.

FURTHER INFORMATION: City of Charlevoix, Recreation Dept., 210 State, Charlevoix, MI 49720.

127 CHARLES A. RANSOM PRESERVE

On clear days from this 80-acre preserve perched 320 feet above Lake Michigan, you can see more than 20 miles in either direction — south to the Leelanau Peninsula and north to Beaver Island. On just about any day, you will not be disappointed with the panoramic view of Lake Michigan plus the city of and lake Charlevoix. And you don't even have to leave the parking lot — or, if you're handicapped, the car — to enjoy the view.

But those who are able should leave their vehicles and take a mile-long nature trail down the hill, through woods and a small forest clearing, back up the moderately steep banks and along the edge of a large meadow. Or, hike an even shorter path that loops for less than half a mile through the woods before crossing the big meadow and returning to the parking area. In spring, the large meadow is blanketed with wildflowers. The forest floor, too, before its leafy canopy restricts the sunlight, comes to life with wildflowers. In summer, ferns replace wildflowers in the shade of impressive specimens of birch, beech, sugar maple and aspen. Maps to both trails are included in a numbered self-guiding interpretive pamphlet, available from a box just inside the tree line near the trailhead.

The Charles A. Ransom preserve is one of 20 owned and managed by the Little Traverse Conservancy, a private, non-profit organization devoted to protecting and preserving natural areas in northern Michigan.

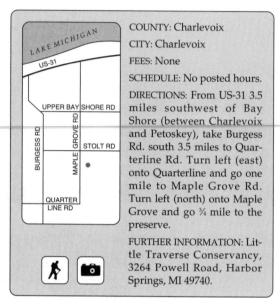

COUNTY: Charlevoix

CITY: Charlevoix

FEES: None

SCHEDULE: No posted hours.

DIRECTIONS: From US-31 3.5 miles southwest of Bay Shore (between Charlevoix and Petoskey), take Burgess Rd. south 3.5 miles to Quarterline Rd. Turn left (east) onto Quarterline and go one mile to Maple Grove Rd. Turn left (north) onto Maple Grove and go ¾ mile to the preserve.

FURTHER INFORMATION: Little Traverse Conservancy, 3264 Powell Road, Harbor Springs, MI 49740.

COVERT WILDLIFE SANCTUARY 128

This 62-acre preserve — perched near the tip of a blunt peninsula that juts out into Walloon Lake — serves up a veritable smorgasbord of natural habitats. A dense pine plantation, open meadows and glens, hardwood-covered hills, berry patches, marshy wetlands, a secluded pond, and an abandoned orchard favored by deer, grouse and songbirds all grace this Little Traverse Conservancy wildlife sanctuary.

The land was donated to the conservancy in 1980 with the stipulation that it remain in an entirely natural state. The lush diversity of untouched habitats attracts an abundance of wildlife, and the sanctuary has become a favorite of local nature photographers and birdwatchers.

No established or formal trails mar the landscape, and the Conservancy requests that visitors make only light use of the preserve.

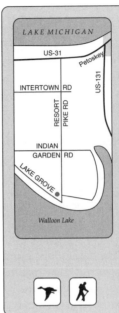

COUNTY: Emmet

CITY: Petoskey

FEES: None

SCHEDULE: Open all year.

DIRECTIONS: From the intersection of US-131 and US-31 in Petoskey, drive west on US-31 one mile to Resort Pike Rd. turn left (south) onto Resort Pike and drive approximately 6 miles to where it deadends at Lake Grove Dr., at the small township park at the end of the road. Access to the preserve is across Lake Grove Rd. from the parking lot.

FURTHER INFORMATION: Little Traverse Conservancy, 3264 Powell Rd., Harbor Springs, MI 49740.

129 BEAR RIVER VALLEY RECREATION AREA

This 36-acre city-owned park traces a long, narrow ribbon of natural beauty through the center of Petoskey, yet hundreds of vacation-bound tourists pass over it daily without even knowing of its existence. In downtown Petoskey just before northbound US-31 bends left to follow the Lake Michigan coastline, the highway crosses an old concrete bridge. Below that bridge, hidden in a steep-sided valley cut by the Bear River, the park offers what many vacationers are searching for but are passing by — a chance to enjoy a picturesque outing in a natural setting.

The park follows the river valley for more than a mile back inland from the point where the Bear River joins Lake Michigan. In many spots, except for an occasional power line and an infrequent glimpse of a house, you can almost imagine that you are in the wilderness. Once you're away from the bridge, the murmur of traffic is nearly drowned out by the rushing waters of the Bear River. The trail stays close to the banks of the river and pass-

es mature birch, maple and white pine. Farther inland the trail climbs to a small waterfall and a pedestrian bridge across the river.

The open woods, areas of tall grass, dense thickets lining the river, shrub-studded hillsides and moving water attract numerous birds. Adding to the chances of good birding is the fact that the park is a natural oasis for wildlife in a busy and heavily populated urban area.

At the park entrance, on Lake Street directly across from City Hall, a small, pleasant picnic area edges the river just above a final dam before the river loses itself in Lake Michigan. In the fall you can be held spellbound at the sight of salmon trying to jump the dam as they attempt to swim upriver and spawn. The picnic grounds contains a shelter, grills and tables, and there is plenty of room to spread a blanket and enjoy the surroundings.

In the winter, cross country skiers find the park an easily accessible and beautiful area for enjoying their sport.

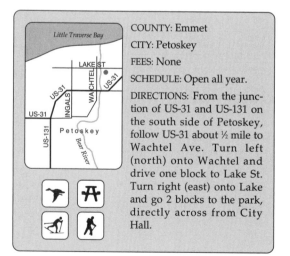

COUNTY: Emmet

CITY: Petoskey

FEES: None

SCHEDULE: Open all year.

DIRECTIONS: From the junction of US-31 and US-131 on the south side of Petoskey, follow US-31 about ½ mile to Wachtel Ave. Turn left (north) onto Wachtel and drive one block to Lake St. Turn right (east) onto Lake and go 2 blocks to the park, directly across from City Hall.

Orchis Fen is a naturalist's dream and a hiker's nightmare. The 38-acre fen — a low-lying land wholly or partially covered by water — harbors a number of striking plants. Sundew, bladderwort, pitcher plant and 19 varieties of orchids grow here. But this Little Traverse Conservancy preserve does not reveal its beauty or give up its secrets easily.

Plant life literally chokes the sanctuary. Moss and sedge cover the wet ground, and stands of tamarack, cedar and black spruce grow so thick that at times the preserve seems almost impenetrable.

Deer tracks score the soft ground everywhere you look, and game trails are also about the only routes for people into the riot of vegetation. Best access comes from a small meadow on the northeast corner of the property. A compass, a good sense of direction, waterproof hiking boots, and plenty of insect repellent are necessities for exploring this area, which at best is difficult to walk.

Because of the fragile nature of the preserve, the conservancy requests that visits be limited to individuals or very small groups.

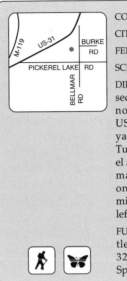

COUNTY: Emmet

CITY: Petoskey

FEES: None

SCHEDULE: Open all year.

DIRECTIONS: From the intersection of M-119 and US-31 north of Petoskey, take US-31 northeast about 200 yards to Pickerel Lake Rd. Turn right (east) onto Pickerel and drive 1.9 miles to Bellmar Rd. Turn left (north) onto Bellmar and drive ½ mile to the preserve, on the left-hand side of the road.

FURTHER INFORMATION: Little Traverse Conservancy, 3264 Powell Rd., Harbor Springs, MI 49740.

131 McCUNE NATURE PRESERVE

Out of the way, strikingly beautiful, and lightly used yet easily accessible, this 168-acre Little Traverse Conservancy nature preserve has just the right mix of elements for a perfect outing in northern Michigan's wooded environment. And an added plus: You can match your outdoor experience to your skill and endurance.

From the parking lot just off a paved but little-used road, McCune's gently rolling and wooded terrain descends to the east branch of Minnehaha Creek, which cuts the sanctuary into two unequal sections. You can easily access the eastern parcel via a well-worn and comfortably walked nature trail. But exploring the west section requires the fording of at least one, and possibly both, of the creek's two branches and bushwhacking your own trail. You can walk the east side without fear of getting lost or wet, but if you want to head into the far reaches of the western section, a compass, a sense of direction and some basic outdoor skills are necessities.

The three-quarter-mile-long Hemlock Trail, on the preserve's east side, is a great introduction to the northern woods and will be a more-than-sufficient outdoor experience for most visitors. The trail, shaped like an old-fashioned rug beater, begins at the parking lot, next to a pine plantation. The first third of the trail, the handle of the beater, edges an open field then, just as it plunges into a forest of hardwoods, splits into a long oval that takes you to the banks of Minnehaha Creek.

After entering the forest, the trail makes a sharp four- or five-foot drop to the creek's flood plain, where the trees are so old and big that you are in perpetual shadow. You wind your way around some truly impressive hardwoods and evergreens before you meet the shallow, picturesque east branch of the stream. The fallen trees dipping into the stream, the dark and swiftly moving water, and the simmering reflection of the forest above is mesmerizing. After following the creek for a few dozen yards, the trail loops around to meet the handle and return you to the parking lot. The route also takes you past a variety of flora and through a great wildlife area where bear, beaver, deer, fox, rabbit, coyote, porcupine and numerous birds have either left signs or been spotted.

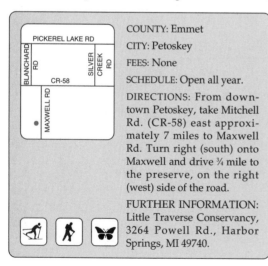

COUNTY: Emmet

CITY: Petoskey

FEES: None

SCHEDULE: Open all year.

DIRECTIONS: From downtown Petoskey, take Mitchell Rd. (CR-58) east approximately 7 miles to Maxwell Rd. Turn right (south) onto Maxwell and drive ¾ mile to the preserve, on the right (west) side of the road.

FURTHER INFORMATION: Little Traverse Conservancy, 3264 Powell Rd., Harbor Springs, MI 49740.

Bay View, a picturesque community of Victorian summer homes and cottages that overlook Little Traverse Bay, deserves to be as famous for its nature preserve as for its unique collection of houses. Hidden away at the back of the labyrinth of winding roads that web the enchanting picture-book homes, Bay View Woods encompasses some of the most memorable natural beauty in the northern Lower Peninsula. The diverse habitat, cover and food attract plenty of birds, and bring your camera because the area almost begs to be photographed.

The beguiling mixture of scenery and ecosystems is easily accessible via four inter-

pretive trails and several other paths that crisscross the area. A cedar/hemlock swamp, wooded ridges, lowland hardwoods, natural springs, wooded uplands, and steep bluffs that mark the former shoreline of a prehistoric lake give just a hint of the constant variety and beauty of Bay View Woods.

For an in-depth examination of the area, pick up a detailed, illustrated 16-page brochure and map at one of the preserve's two trailheads. The booklet — with numbered paragraphs that correspond to markers along the four interpretive trails — lists, for example, many varieties of ferns found here, including horsetail, ostrich, cinnamon, wood and regal. You can also use the brochure to search out numerous wildflowers, fungi, lichen and moss and help identify white and yellow birch, beech, hemlock, ash, sugar maple, striped maple, cedar, dogwood, wild cherry, balsam fir and basswood.

Easy access to the sanctuary comes from a small parking area at Richards and Knapp streets. From there the half-mile-long Old Indian Trail loops into the preserve and connects to all the other trails. Initially it follows the crest of a wooded ridge studded with imposing trees. When the trail leaves the ridge, it circles to the right and edges the bottom of a bluff, where numerous small springs trickle from the hillside, cross the path, and eventually become lost in a swamp bisected by the trail on its return to the trailhead.

Also on Knapp Street, two blocks west of the Old Indian trailhead, the Gateway Trail enters the sanctuary. This half-mile-long path circles through a stand of mixed hardwoods, many of which bear identifying labels, and also crosses a pretty stream that empties the swamp.

Another half-mile-long path, Deer Trail, connects the Gateway Trail and the Old Indian Trail, and you can only reach it by hiking one of the latter trails. While threading its way between the base of a bluff and low, swampy ground, Deer Trail meets several more rivulets that spring from the hillside and flow into the swamp.

The fourth interpretive route, the mile-plus Algonquin Trail, penetrates the far reaches of the preserve. Beginning at the south end of Gateway Trail, it climbs a steep bluff that used to form the shoreline of ancient Lake Algonquin, which covered much of the present-day Great Lakes and Michigan during the last ice age. While following the edge of the bluff and weaving through a wooded highland, you get a few glimpses of Little Traverse Bay plus a good look at the effects of the last ice age and erosion on the surrounding landscape.

If you don't get enough walking on the interpretive trails, you can take any of several other informal paths that wind through the preserve.

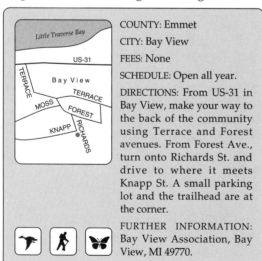

COUNTY: Emmet

CITY: Bay View

FEES: None

SCHEDULE: Open all year.

DIRECTIONS: From US-31 in Bay View, make your way to the back of the community using Terrace and Forest avenues. From Forest Ave., turn onto Richards St. and drive to where it meets Knapp St. A small parking lot and the trailhead are at the corner.

FURTHER INFORMATION: Bay View Association, Bay View, MI 49770.

ROUND LAKE NATURE PRESERVE 133

"Double your pleasure, double your fun," as the commercial goes, pretty accurately describes what awaits visitors to the Round Lake Nature Preserve. Complementing the preserve and located directly across M-119 is Petoskey State Park. So simply by crossing the highway from either place, hikers can nearly double trail mileage and birdwatchers and wildflower enthusiasts can explore a larger variety of habitat.

The habitat at Round Lake Nature Preserve is composed of a mixed hardwood/conifer forest, swamp, dense vegetation and 500 feet of frontage on the northwest corner of the lake from which the preserve takes its name. Under the canopy of some fine white pine, red maple, cedar and hemlock specimens is dense vegetation, especially near the lakeshore and swampy area. Marsh marigolds and trillium are among the many spring wildflowers native to the preserve,. and the good cover and variety of habitats attract numerous birds and other animal life.

A well-trodden path cuts through the heart of the preserve; a side trail branches off toward the lakeshore.

The office of the Little Traverse Conservancy, which owns Round Lake Nature Preserve, is on the northern edge of the property. Information — including pamphlets, brochures and maps — on this and more than 70 other preserves owned by the organization is available at that building.

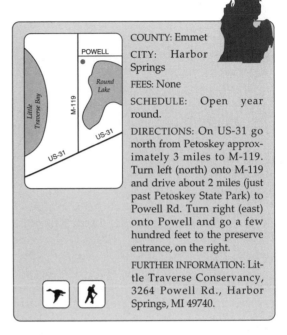

COUNTY: Emmet

CITY: Harbor Springs

FEES: None

SCHEDULE: Open year round.

DIRECTIONS: On US-31 go north from Petoskey approximately 3 miles to M-119. Turn left (north) onto M-119 and drive about 2 miles (just past Petoskey State Park) to Powell Rd. Turn right (east) onto Powell and go a few hundred feet to the preserve entrance, on the right.

FURTHER INFORMATION: Little Traverse Conservancy, 3264 Powell Rd., Harbor Springs, MI 49740.

134 BISSELL, (135) FISCHER and (136) JAMES NATURE PRESERVES

This trio of Little Traverse Conservancy Nature preserves, just east of Harbor Springs, totals more than 55 acres of pristine natural beauty. Composed of upland woods, cedar swamps, a free-flowing well, a small stream, dense pines and evergreens, and downed, moss-covered trees, the preserves serve as reminders and examples of what the area must have looked like before Harbor Springs felt the presence of man.

Because the terrain of this small pocket of wilderness is so rugged, most visitors opt to view the area from Beach Road, a two-lane stretch of pavement that backs the three preserves. For the adventurous, a few access points and faint trails do allow close-at-hand exploration of the lush vegetation, bountiful wildflowers, and delicate ferns, plus a chance to seek out the numerous birds that inhabit the area.

The 3.5-acre pie-shaped S.A. Bissell Preserve is the westernmost of the three sanctuaries. On its east edge not more than 25 yards from the road, an artesian well springs from the ground and flows into a 55-year-old hand-built fieldstone reflecting pool. Adding to the charm of the setting, a tiny stream slips from the pool and winds its way to nearby Lake Michigan

Also leading from the pool is a faint, seldom-trod footpath that, just a few steps directly east, crosses into the 50-acre A.C. Fischer Preserve's quiet world of lowland conifers and wetlands. The trail, however, is often wet, and walking can be difficult.

The smallest of the trio, the Dan and Ruby James Nature Preserve, lies across Beach Road from Bissell and Fischer. If the other preserves make for difficult walking, this two-plus acres of very wet cedar swamp is next to impossible to traverse, except on an old railroad bed that crosses the property. As with its larger counterparts across the road, James Preserve is rife with spring wildflowers and packed with untouched natural beauty.

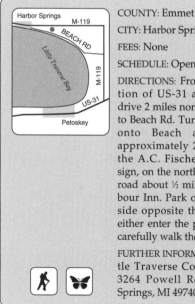

COUNTY: Emmet

CITY: Harbor Springs

FEES: None

SCHEDULE: Open all year.

DIRECTIONS: From the junction of US-31 and M-119, drive 2 miles north on M-119 to Beach Rd. Turn left (west) onto Beach and drive approximately 2.5 miles to the A.C. Fischer Preserve sign, on the north side of the road about ½ mile past Harbour Inn. Park on the roadside opposite the sign and either enter the preserves or carefully walk the road.

FURTHER INFORMATION: Little Traverse Conservancy, 3264 Powell Rd., Harbor Springs, MI 49740.

MEADOWGATE (137) and SANDFORD 138 NATURE PRESERVES

These two adjoining Little Traverse Conservancy nature preserves are a study in contrasting ecosystems.

Just one-tenth of an acre shy of 10 acres, the Meadowgate Preserve is an old farm field that is slowly being reclaimed by nature. The Conservancy acquired the property in 1978, just as it appeared that a huge condominium complex would forever alter the landscape. But instead of buildings and asphalt, a colorful mosaic of tall grass dotted with staghorn sumac, apple trees, lilac bushes, and mature sugar maple covers the field. During the past 10 years, at least one bear and a Great Grey Owl have paid a visit. There are no trails, but you are free to traipse anywhere over the pleasant meadow.

Bordering the west edge of Meadowgate and standing in sharp contrast to it is Sandford Nature Preserve's one-acre parcel of picturesque hardwoods. Inside the dead-level tract, mature hemlock, beech and maple shoulder their way to the sky in competition for the sunlight. Below their thick canopy, the leaf-strewn forest floor stays in perpetual shadow during the summer. There are no trails, but there also is no dense understory. So walking is easy, and you will find the area carpeted with wildflowers in the spring and cool and secluded in the summer.

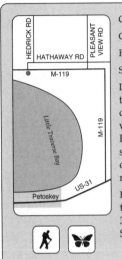

COUNTY: Emmet

CITY: Harbor Springs

FEES: None

SCHEDULE: Open all year.

DIRECTIONS: From the junction of M-119 and US-31, drive 4.5 miles north then west on M-119 to Hedrick Rd. The preserves are on the south side of the highway, opposite where Hedrick Rd. meets M-119.

FURTHER INFORMATION: Little Traverse Conservancy, 3264 Powell Rd., Harbor Springs, MI 49740.

139 RAUNECKER NATURE PRESERVE

Though located within a few blocks of the swank, expensive and trendy gift shops of Harbor Springs and nearly surrounded by some of the most expensive resort property in northern Michigan, Raunecker Nature Preserve appears all but untouched by man.

No trails mark this 40-acre Little Traverse Conservancy preserve, but you can gain access from Fourth Street, which borders the tract's northern boundary. From there the land falls away to a low, wet cedar swamp. The hillside holds a stand of tall maples, and the lowland is studded with equally impressive cedars. In the heart of the preserve, downed trees, dense undergrowth, and wet ground in the lower reaches add up to rugged terrain and, at best, difficult walking. The sanctuary also features a pond, a creek and a naturally flowing well. The wild and untamed area shelters a wide variety of bird and animal life plus a pleasing number of wildflowers.

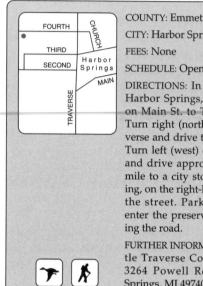

COUNTY: Emmet

CITY: Harbor Springs

FEES: None

SCHEDULE: Open all year.

DIRECTIONS: In downtown Harbor Springs, drive west on Main St. to Traverse St. Turn right (north) onto Traverse and drive to Fourth St. Turn left (west) onto Fourth and drive approximately ¼ mile to a city storage building, on the right-hand side of the street. Park there and enter the preserve by crossing the road.

FURTHER INFORMATION: Little Traverse Conservancy, 3264 Powell Rd., Harbor Springs, MI 49740.

A cedar swamp even Steven Spielberg would have trouble re-creating and a picture-postcard view of Lake Michigan shoreline are two very good scenic reasons to visit the Thorne Swift Nature Preserve.

The shallow-rooted, sweet-smelling cedars in the swamp here are easily toppled and, as a result, become crazily canted in all directions. Even after being completely blown over, the trees seem to defy destruction, and their trunks make bends contortionists would envy as they strain to reach for sunlight and life. Wildflowers and ferns color this eerie, unworldly landscape, and birds add surrealistic charm.

Three short nature trails, some with extensive sections of boardwalks, lead into the swamp area as well as through an evergreen woodland, around a pond and to the beach.

The preserve's nearly 1,000-foot-long sandy Lake Michigan beach and low dunes are divided into two areas. The largest section, about two-thirds of the shoreline, is off limits to foot traffic. One of the trails, however, leads to an observation platform that extends from the edge of the restricted area out onto a low dune. From the dune, a grand panorama of water and shoreline stretches for several miles in both directions. The platform also allows close-up inspection of the untrammeled dune and the plants trying to colonize the barren sand. At the smaller public-use shoreline area, also reached by the trails, a 300-foot-long swimming beach is a fine alternative to crowded public Lake Michigan beaches in the area.

The 30-acre preserve is home to a wide variety of plant and animal life. The abundance of wildflowers includes orchids and two of Michigan's threatened plant species, pitcher's thistle and Lake Huron tansy. The

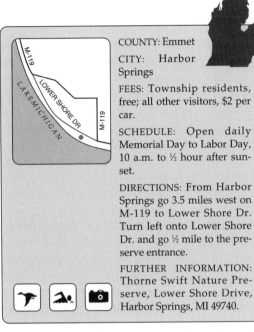

COUNTY: Emmet

CITY: Harbor Springs

FEES: Township residents, free; all other visitors, $2 per car.

SCHEDULE: Open daily Memorial Day to Labor Day, 10 a.m. to ½ hour after sunset.

DIRECTIONS: From Harbor Springs go 3.5 miles west on M-119 to Lower Shore Dr. Turn left onto Lower Shore Dr. and go ½ mile to the preserve entrance.

FURTHER INFORMATION: Thorne Swift Nature Preserve, Lower Shore Drive, Harbor Springs, MI 49740.

park's birdwatchers' checklist identifies 74 species, including 19 varieties of warblers and five different kinds of woodpeckers (including Pileated).

Guided walks begin at the preserve's nature center, which houses interpretive displays and exhibits. A park naturalist is usually on duty to welcome visitors, answer questions, and highlight seasonal points of interest.

The Little Traverse Conservancy and West Traverse Township cooperatively developed this small but singularly beautiful natural area.

141 M-119

Drive every other mile of blacktop in the Lower Peninsula and you still won't find a more beautiful or scenic 20 miles of Michigan highway south of Big Mac than the narrow, twisting ribbon of asphalt that connects Harbor Springs to Cross Village. The route, highway M-119, follows an old Indian trail and, with its several historical markers, is as rich in history as it is in scenery.

In the course of 200 years, countless moccasin-clad feet wore a narrow path along the edge of the high bluffs that guard this remote section of Lake Michigan coastline. Ottawa and Chippewa, on journeys to and from their villages in the vicinity of present-day Cross Village, stayed close to the edge of the bluffs, and M-119 follows the same path. While twisting through hairpin turns, the road tunnels through a magnificent forest of giant beech, sugar maple and eye-grabbing white birch. And for most of its length, the highway rarely strays more than a few feet from the edge of the towering headlands that rise from the lakeshore.

Just driving through the forest is memorable, but through numerous gaps in the wall of trees, you are also treated to some stunning views of Lake Michigan, the Beaver Island archipelago and Waugoshance Point. Spectacular at any time of the year, the drive is absolutely breathtaking at the peak of the color season, when a virtual caravan of cars

and bicyclists stream up and down the highway.

Actually, the term "highway" is rather generous in describing this road. The 16-foot-wide snaking pavement is devoid of a centerline or shoulders. Huge trees stand within a foot or two of the roadbed and for long stretches it is impossible to find room to pull off the blacktop. Drivers have to spend so much time watching the road, they have little chance to soak up the scenery.

COUNTY: Emmet

CITY: Harbor Springs

FEES: None

SCHEDULE: None

DIRECTIONS: Drive north out of Harbor Springs on M-119.

Elmer Johnston Nature Preserve, owned by the Little Traverse Conservancy, is one of those rare private nature sanctuaries that you can enjoy either on foot or from your car. The preserve sits atop a line of high, heavily wooded hills almost a mile back from the Lake Michigan shoreline near Good Hart. From several clearings scattered throughout its 220 acres, you get spectacular, panoramic views of the great lake and the Beaver Island archipelago, strewn across the surface nearly 20 miles offshore.

A wide-two-track ambles through open meadows and into the heart of a hardwood forest thick with giant maple and birch and scattered with boulders by the glacier that sculpted these hills. In the spring, wildflowers carpet the forest floor, and deer, fox and other wildlife are plentiful throughout the year.

Except for some moderately steep hills, the primitive road makes for easy walking and cross country skiing.

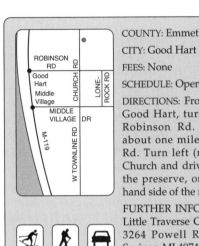

COUNTY: Emmet

CITY: Good Hart

FEES: None

SCHEDULE: Open all year.

DIRECTIONS: From M-119 in Good Hart, turn east onto Robinson Rd. and drive about one mile to Church Rd. Turn left (north) onto Church and drive ½ mile to the preserve, on the right-hand side of the road.

FURTHER INFORMATION: Little Traverse Conservancy, 3264 Powell Rd., Harbor Springs, MI 49740.

143 BEAVER ISLAND

At many places in Michigan, relaxation, seclusion and a chance to enjoy nature are options. On Beaver Island they're forced on you. This, the most remote inhabited island in the Great Lakes, is a detox center for compulsive workaholics and urban dwellers. Counted among the pleasures here is what you don't find — no fast-food outlets, no four-lane highways, no crowds, no fudge shops, no convenience stores and no pretense.

What you will find on this 12-mile-long, 6-mile-wide island includes almost unlimited stretches of deserted beaches, excellent backpacking opportunities, and beautiful scenery that includes deep woods, seascapes, seven inland lakes, small streams, cedar swamps, bogs, and abandoned homesteads and cleared fields left by early settlers.

The natural world here seems more sharply defined and intimate. That's not to say man's presence is not felt; the island is not a nature preserve. Yet rabbits overrun the land, it's unusual to take an evening drive without seeing numerous, deer, and an active beaver colony thrives in the heart of the island. Coyotes, otter, fox and raccoon also roam freely, and 300 species of birds have been documented here over the years.

Two designated campgrounds plus the

opportunity to pitch a tent anywhere on the state forest land that covers a third of the island add up to a perfect setting for some great backpacking. St. James Township Campground, on the north shore, is only a one-mile walk west from Beaver Island's lone town, St. James. The Jordan River State Forest Campground — on the east side of the island, adjacent to the largest tract of state land — is about seven miles south of the town's ferry dock. Camping at both is $5 per day (no reservations accepted) and primitive, meaning no electricity or flush toilets.

The island is usually less than overrun by tourists, and for good reason. During most of the summer, only two ferries arrive daily, after a two-hour-plus voyage from Charlevoix. (The only other way to get to the island — unless you have your own yacht or airplane — is via Welke Flying Service from Charlevoix.) The total combined auto capacity for both ferries doesn't exceed 30 vehicles. Many visitors arrive without cars, either to backpack or just to leave another vestige of urban life behind.

If you don't bring your own car and don't want to walk everywhere, you can rent a vehicle at one of four agencies, and taxi service is also available. Island Sports and Rentals leases boats and bikes, and as a last resort, hitchhiking is acceptable.

Whatever method you choose, you can take hours or even days to fully explore the vaguely tear-drop-shaped island. One hundred miles of little-traveled, scenic roads lace the land, and many more miles of secluded, sometimes-faint foot trails lead into the most-remote corners. From the small village of St. James, at the north end of the island, East Side Drive heads south and follows the sunrise shoreline past many of the island's summer homes on its way to the Jordan River State Forest Campground.

Across the road from the campground, a short trail system barely penetrates the

approximately 15-square-mile main portion of state land that blankets the interior of the southern half of the island. This large tract of forest is the most inaccessible and undisturbed land on the island. A good gravel road circles it, with numerous faint trails heading off from it into the woods and swamp. The trails border many beaver floodings, and if you're quiet, you may be lucky enough to see one, in addition to deer, fox, or even rarer, an otter or coyote. Berry pickers will find strawberries, blackberries, blueberries cranberries and raspberries.

East Side Drive continues south from the campground to Beaver Head Lighthouse and beautiful Iron Ore Bay, on the island's south end. The Coast Guard abandoned the light in 1962, and it slowly fell into disrepair until 1979, when Charlevoix Public Schools personnel began restoring it for use as a summer education center. You can climb up an old spiral staircase to the top of the 50-foot-tower for an unforgettable view of the nearby beaches and the Fox Islands, 15 miles to the south. Just west of the lighthouse, the road borders Iron Ore Bay. This sweeping arch of

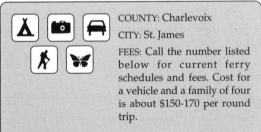

COUNTY: Charlevoix

CITY: St. James

FEES: Call the number listed below for current ferry schedules and fees. Cost for a vehicle and a family of four is about $150-170 per round trip.

SCHEDULE: You can get to the island all year, but winter storms and bad weather can cut off ferry service.

DIRECTIONS: Ferries to the island depart from a municipal parking lot next to the drawbridge in downtown Charlevoix.

FURTHER INFORMATION: You can get ferry schedules and current costs, plus a list of accommodations from the Beaver Island Chamber of Commerce, P.O. Box 5, Beaver Island, St. James, MI 49782; (616) 448-2505.

fine sand is one of the most beautiful and accessible beaches on the island.

Once past the bay, the road turns north and winds through deep woods as it heads up the west side of the island. Known there as West Side Drive, it rarely passes closer than a mile to Lake Michigan, but several dirt roads and less-passable two-tracks lead to within a half mile of the lake. From the end of any of them, a short walk will take you to miles of deserted surf-swept beaches. For a truly memorable day, pack a picnic lunch, grab a map, head to one of those many beach areas, and swim, beachcomb, sunbathe and hunt for wildflowers, all while out of sight of another human being.

The northern third of the island is webbed with roads that pass through more-open landscape. There, the haunting beauty of the fields, old orchards, abandoned farmhouses and decaying log cabins of the early settlers attract the lens of any passing camera.

An early evening trip to the Bonner's Bluff section of public land, on the island's west shore, is a must. Natives and visitors both flock to the spot — easily reached by bicycle or car from St. James and then a short walk down a steep bluff that ridges the whole western side of the island — to watch the sun set over Lake Michigan.

Virtually all the island's businesses and services are concentrated at St. James, which

hugs the shore of picturesque Beaver Harbor. Two general stores attend to the basic needs of both vacationers and natives, and if you can't bear to cook, you have your choice of five restaurants. Several motels scattered around town provide clean, pleasant rooms. Also, housekeeping units and a wide variety of cottages and houses throughout the island are let on a weekly basis. You can get a complete accommodations list from the Beaver Island Chamber of Commerce (address in *Further Information*). And you can make any room reservation with almost certain assurance that upon arrival you will find neat, clean and comfortable quarters.

But — either as a reassurance or a warning — just because you take a room in town, you shouldn't jump to the conclusion that you will be at the center of what's happening (nothing) or be bothered by the daily commerce of the island's capitol. In fact, it's just as easy to wile away the day undisturbed by cars, noise and busy goings-on in the center of this tranquil village as it is on some of the deserted beaches to the south. The high point of the day in town may be watching the ferry arrive or deciding whether to walk down to one of the two general stores to buy a Detroit paper. (That is if, after a day or two, you even care about what's going on in the outside world.) And one more cautionary note. If you live to shop, you'll have a life expectancy of less than three hours.

Beaver Island's unique ambiance is matched by its unusual history. In the 1840s James Jesse Strang led a band of heretical Mormons to the island and, once there, announced to his faithful that he was Vice Regent of God on Earth. He made himself ruler of the Kingdom of St. James and turned Beaver Island into the only self-proclaimed kingdom in the United States. But Strang's reign was brief, and little remains of his rule except the Mormon Print Shop, which serves as the island's museum.

BOIS BLANC ISLAND 144

As you clear Cheboygan Harbor aboard the small ferry, the low, green outline of the island that appears near the edge of the horizon seems to belie its name. French explorers called it Bois Blanc (white wood) for the great birch forest that ringed the island with its palisade of white trunks.

That birch forest, which blanketed the entire island, is long gone, but Bois Blanc remains an undeveloped natural wonderland that is overshadowed by the most famous island in the Great Lakes. While ferries crammed with sightseers depart every few minutes to and from Mackinac Island, the Plaunt Transportation ferry at the height of the tourist season makes three trips a day to Bob-lo (as the natives call Bois Blanc), usually carrying only a dozen passengers and three or four cars. While Mackinac is crowned by the Grand Hotel and dotted with huge Victorian summer homes, Bois Blanc, except for a few small cottages, sits silent and green, appearing all but untouched by humans, even from only a mile off shore. In fact, the most striking view from the ferry as it crosses Lake Huron is not Bois Blanc but the Mackinac Bridge 15 miles to the north.

Once on the island, you may begin to think this might be the spot where the classic question, "If a tree fell in a forest and nobody was there to hear it fall, did it make a noise?' was first asked. A thick forest of spruce, fir, pine, beech, oak, maple and cedar covers the 23,000-acre isle. Sixty percent of the land is state-owned, and buildings occupy considerably less than 10 percent of the remaining property. The year-round population hovers at about 40 or so, with summer swelling the number to 1,000. The comforts of home and concessions to the tourist trade amount to a combination tavern/restaurant and a couple of cottages for rent. The one hotel on the island went out of business years ago.

In short, Bois Blanc is a quiet, lush, very special place to go to experience nature and the out-of-doors close at hand without anyone serving as an intermediary. You can beachcomb miles of deserted shoreline, find a secluded swimming beach, hope for a glimpse of a Bald Eagle or Osprey, and from the island's northwest tip, take in the most stunning view of Mackinac Island from anywhere in the Straits area. You can search for and identify 200 varieties of trees, flowers, and shrubs, including several of the state's threatened plant species that have found sanctuary here. Stands of old-growth red and white pine cover the center of the island, which has been undisturbed by settlement.

The 45 miles of roads that lace Bois Blanc vary from good gravel and soft sand to barely discernible two-tracks. They tunnel through dense forests, border Lake Huron for miles, and cut across the center of the island. They are seldom traveled by cars, however, which makes the island a great place for mountain bikers and backpackers. You can backcountry camp almost anywhere on state land, but you must get permission from the Cheboygan DNR office (see *Further Information*).

COUNTY: Cheboygan

CITY: Cheboygan

FEES & SCHEDULE: Contact the Cheboygan Chamber of Commerce (address and phone number below) for current ferry schedule and rates.

DIRECTIONS: The ferry dock is in downtown Cheboygan, on Water St. just south of the bridge.

FURTHER INFORMATION: Cheboygan Area Chamber of Commerce, P.O. Box 69, Cheboygan, MI 49721. Or DNR Cheboygan Field Office, P.O. Box 117, Cheboygan, MI 49721.

145 GORDON TURNER PARK

Gordon Turner Park proves that you are known by the company you keep. It's only 4.6 acres in size — most of which appears to be parking lot — and a large wetlands area makes its western boundary both indistinct and impassable.

But marking the park's eastern end is the busy Cheboygan River, and Lake Huron laps at its northern limits. From almost anywhere in the park you can see the Mackinac Bridge rising above the water 15 miles to the northwest. Directly north, 10 miles across the lake, Bois Blanc Island cuts off the horizon. And the park, which is only three blocks from downtown Cheboygan, also provides a ringside seat to the busy little harbor, where pleasure boats constantly come and go and, less frequently, a ferry journeys back and forth to Bois Blanc Island.

You get the best view of the scenery and all the water-borne activity from a small picnic grounds laid out on a narrow strip of green between the parking lot and the lakeshore. East of the picnic tables and grills, a sandy swimming beach extends along the shore to a breakwater that marks the entrance to the Cheboygan River. The concrete pier reaches far out into the harbor and is a favorite spot of fishermen.

West of the picnic grounds, a boardwalk crosses a cattail marsh and ends at an observation deck overlooking a vast wetlands that borders Lake Huron. Open pools of water surrounded by acres of dense cattails and waving marsh grass attract numerous birds. With a pair of binoculars, patience and luck, it's possible to spot a wide variety of waterfowl and shorebirds without any exertion other than raising and lowering the glasses.

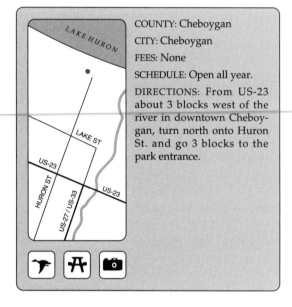

COUNTY: Cheboygan

CITY: Cheboygan

FEES: None

SCHEDULE: Open all year.

DIRECTIONS: From US-23 about 3 blocks west of the river in downtown Cheboygan, turn north onto Huron St. and go 3 blocks to the park entrance.

GRASS BAY PRESERVE 146

Grass Bay Preserve is one of the finest examples of original Great Lakes interdunal wetland habitat — characterized by beach pools, marshes, flats and wetlands, all separated from the lakes by low dunes — found anywhere around the five Great Lakes.

This delicate ecosystem hosts an extraordinary diversity of plant life, including more than 300 species of vascular plants, 25 species of orchids and 11 types of conifers. Four of the plants — dwarf lake iris, Lake Huron tansy, pitcher's thistle and Houghton's goldenrod — grow only on the shores of lakes Huron and Michigan. Five plants included on a federally threatened species list and two on a similar state list also thrive here.

From May to September, wildflowers of every description and size literally grow underfoot in the sanctuary. Grass Bay is particularly noted for its abundance of carnivorous plants, including yellow bladderworts, pitcher plants and sundews. Other interesting flowers here include ram's head, lady's-slipper, showy lady's-slipper, Indian paintbrush, blue harebell and orange hawkweed.

The best way to view them is from one or both of the park's two short trails. One descends from US-23 for a half mile through an aspen/birch forest and across a succession of old shoreline ridges to the beach. The other parallels the shoreline. While the walk to the beach and back can easily be accomplished in 45 minutes, it's just as easy to get distracted for half a day.

The Nature Conservancy, a private, non-profit organization dedicated to the preservation of natural areas nationwide, considers Grass Bay the creme de la creme of the Michigan areas they own. The group's original 80-acre purchase here has — through the generous support of the Federated Garden Clubs of

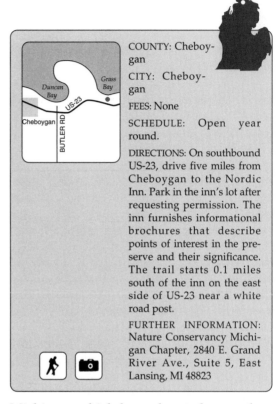

COUNTY: Cheboygan

CITY: Cheboygan

FEES: None

SCHEDULE: Open year round.

DIRECTIONS: On southbound US-23, drive five miles from Cheboygan to the Nordic Inn. Park in the inn's lot after requesting permission. The inn furnishes informational brochures that describe points of interest in the preserve and their significance. The trail starts 0.1 miles south of the inn on the east side of US-23 near a white road post.

FURTHER INFORMATION: Nature Conservancy Michigan Chapter, 2840 E. Grand River Ave., Suite 5, East Lansing, MI 48823

Michigan, which have donated more than $100,000 — grown to 400 acres, including a mile of Lake Huron shoreline.

Visitors should be aware that, although they are welcome, this is not only private, but also fragile land. For those reasons the Conservancy asks all visitors to adhere to the following suggestions when visiting this or any other of their preserves:

1. Use trails, where present, to avoid trampling vegetation.

2. Avoid walking in boggy areas due to their sensitivity.

3. Do not remove any poles, stakes, signs or other objects; they may be part of a research project.

147 COLONIAL POINT PATHWAY

Somehow by chance and luck over the last century and a half, both loggers and forest fires spared heavily wooded Colonial Point. As a result, this peninsula, which protrudes into Burt Lake like an old witch's nose, embraces a valuable and unique natural treasure: a 100- to 150-year-old hardwood forest that includes the largest stand of old-growth red oaks south of the Straits. Scattered among these telephone-pole-straight, towering oaks are equally impressive specimens of maple, beech, white pine, basswood, white ash and black cherry.

This unique piece of Michigan's natural heritage did almost run out of luck in the 1980s, however. A sawmill purchased the tract from its long-time owner, a family trust, then scheduled the area for harvesting.

Fortunately, the Little Traverse Conservancy, the Nature Conservancy, and the University of Michigan Biological Station joined forces to save the 283-acre tract. The sawmill agreed to stay the harvesting while the nature organizations, with the help of public donations, began raising the $1.25 million required to buy all of the land. The purchase agreement allowed the groups to obtain 13 separate parcels over a 36-month period.

The immediacy of this near disaster is forcefully brought home when you wander through the forest and see the great trees tagged for cutting. The logging of these regal giants would have been especially tragic because, for all their imposing size, they are relatively young. Forestry experts, in fact, estimate that many of the trees could live another 200 years.

A walk into this peaceful, beautiful woodland is just about guaranteed to leave you with a feeling of awe and reverence. Though no designated trails mark the area, hikers can use a two-track that cuts through the heart of the preserve from north to south or a foot path that crosses it from east to west. From Lathers Road (itself a two-track that marks part of the preserve's western boundary), both a footpath and another two-track angle east to the area of the largest oaks.

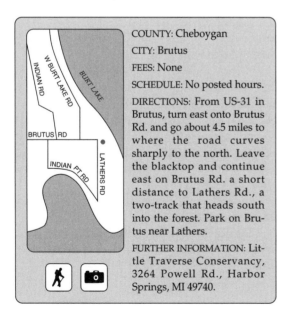

COUNTY: Cheboygan

CITY: Brutus

FEES: None

SCHEDULE: No posted hours.

DIRECTIONS: From US-31 in Brutus, turn east onto Brutus Rd. and go about 4.5 miles to where the road curves sharply to the north. Leave the blacktop and continue east on Brutus Rd. a short distance to Lathers Rd., a two-track that heads south into the forest. Park on Brutus near Lathers.

FURTHER INFORMATION: Little Traverse Conservancy, 3264 Powell Rd., Harbor Springs, MI 49740.

WILDWOOD HILLS PATHWAY 148

Wildwood Hills Pathway's three well-marked, easily followed trails take hikers and skiers into the heart of a northern Michigan second-growth forest. Ranging from four to more than nine miles in length, three interconnected loops — stacked one on top of the other like a snowman — cross high, rolling hills in the Mackinac State Forest just a few miles south of Burt Lake.

From either of two trailheads on Wildwood Road, you plunge into a forest of hardwoods and evergreens marked by an understory of shrubs and ferns so dense that it's almost impossible to leave the trail in some places. The quiet woods give the sense of complete isolation, with the wind through the trees, an occasional bird call, and your own soft footfalls the only sounds you may hear.

Although long, the trails are easy walking, and you can bypass the few steep hills. Trail system maps, which include mile markers, are located at the trailheads and most major trail intersections.

The pathway is regularly groomed in the winter for cross country skiing.

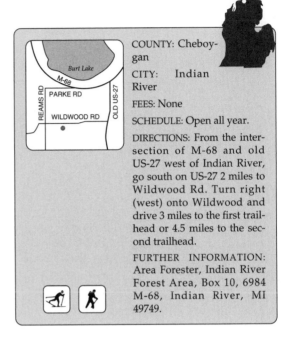

COUNTY: Cheboygan

CITY: Indian River

FEES: None

SCHEDULE: Open all year.

DIRECTIONS: From the intersection of M-68 and old US-27 west of Indian River, go south on US-27 2 miles to Wildwood Rd. Turn right (west) onto Wildwood and drive 3 miles to the first trailhead or 4.5 miles to the second trailhead.

FURTHER INFORMATION: Area Forester, Indian River Forest Area, Box 10, 6984 M-68, Indian River, MI 49749.

149 AGNES ANDREAE NATURE PRESERVE

Two thousand feet of frontage on the swift and turbulent Pigeon River is the main attraction to this beautiful, secluded 27-acre preserve. Ten to 15 feet above the state-designated Wild Scenic River, a picturesque suspension bridge reaches from bluff to bluff to connect wild and untamed preserve property on both banks.

On the west side of the river, where the great majority of the preserve property is located, lowland stands of cedar bordering the riverbank rise to high bluffs covered by dense hardwoods and conifers — many of imposing size — which eventually give way to a blueberry plain. No designated trails probe the area, but a well-worn two-track leads from the parking area to a large, old log cabin that overlooks the bridge and the fast-moving water. Other faint trails border the river both upstream and downstream.

The much smaller eastern section of the preserve covers a densely wooded high bluff.

The Little Traverse Conservancy, which acquired this small but picturesque preserve in 1983, encourages visitors to roam the entire area but not trespass on neighboring private property, which is well-marked. Cross country skiers are welcome in the winter.

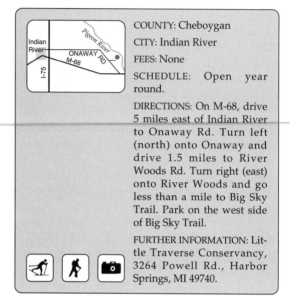

COUNTY: Cheboygan

CITY: Indian River

FEES: None

SCHEDULE: Open year round.

DIRECTIONS: On M-68, drive 5 miles east of Indian River to Onaway Rd. Turn left (north) onto Onaway and drive 1.5 miles to River Woods Rd. Turn right (east) onto River Woods and go less than a mile to Big Sky Trail. Park on the west side of Big Sky Trail.

FURTHER INFORMATION: Little Traverse Conservancy, 3264 Powell Rd., Harbor Springs, MI 49740.

SINKHOLES PATHWAY 150

"The bottom dropped right out from under him," is more than just a figurative expression in certain areas of Presque Isle County and other sections of the northeastern Lower Peninsula. There, the insidiously slow action of underground water on the highly porous, easily dissolvable limestone bedrock gradually creates subterranean caves. When the erosion gets close enough to the thin layer of glacial drift above the rock, the bottom (if you were standing on it) does literally drop out, that is collapse, to form "sinkholes," conical depressions up to several hundred feet across and more than a hundred feet deep.

A 1.5-mile trail in the Sinkholes Pathway circles five major sinkholes; a shorter 0.75-mile loop circles just the first two. The trail passes through jack pine, red pine, aspen and the still-visible signs of a 1939 forest fire as it follows the lip of the holes. For an unusual view, one that you won't get at any of the other areas in this book, peer over the edge of one of the giant thimble-shaped depressions and look down at the tops of the large (10- to 30-foot) trees that have grown in the glacial drift that lines the holes.

Sinkholes drain off water and usually remain dry. But when a creek or stream carries silt or clay into a hole, it can become plugged and form a lake. Across the road from the Pathway trailhead, Shoepac Lake is such a body of water, its shoreline being more than 100 feet above the bone-dry bottom of the trail's first sinkhole, just a quarter mile to the east.

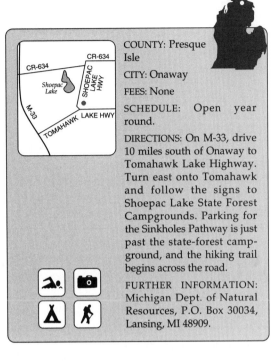

COUNTY: Presque Isle

CITY: Onaway

FEES: None

SCHEDULE: Open year round.

DIRECTIONS: On M-33, drive 10 miles south of Onaway to Tomahawk Lake Highway. Turn east onto Tomahawk and follow the signs to Shoepac Lake State Forest Campgrounds. Parking for the Sinkholes Pathway is just past the state-forest campground, and the hiking trail begins across the road.

FURTHER INFORMATION: Michigan Dept. of Natural Resources, P.O. Box 30034, Lansing, MI 48909.

151 OCQUEOC FALLS BICENTENNIAL PATHWAY

The Lower Peninsula's only major waterfall cascades over a series of two- to six-foot drops and ledges just a few hundred yards from the beginning of the pathway bearing its name.

The Pathway, made up of three loops, winds through the deep woods and over the gently rolling hills of this section of Presque Isle County and the Mackinaw State Forest. all three loops — which measure 3, 4 and 6.5 miles — border the Ocqueoc (meaning "sacred water") River, and the middle loop bridges the Little Ocqueoc River.

Across M-68 from the trailhead and parking area is a state-forest campground. An appealing picnic grounds adjacent to the Pathway parking area is heavily used. Many people also picnic, relax and sunbathe on

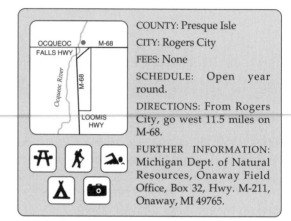

COUNTY: Presque Isle

CITY: Rogers City

FEES: None

SCHEDULE: Open year round.

DIRECTIONS: From Rogers City, go west 11.5 miles on M-68.

FURTHER INFORMATION: Michigan Dept. of Natural Resources, Onaway Field Office, Box 32, Hwy. M-211, Onaway, MI 49765.

blankets spread on the grassy riverbank next to the falls, which also appear to be a favorite swimming hole for many local residents as well as campers.

GARY W. BARFKNECHT

158

PRESQUE ISLE COUNTY 152
LIGHTHOUSE PARK

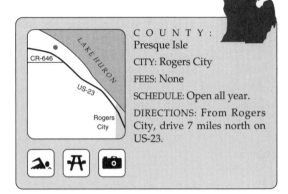

Although Huron ranks as the third-largest of the Great Lakes, in many people's minds it just doesn't have the same mystical or legendary fascination as lakes Michigan and Superior. It you're one who holds that view, stop at Presque Isle County Lighthouse Park and take in the limitless expanse of blue water that extends in a 180-degree arc to the horizon. No islands interrupt the immense sweep of water, and no headlands in either direction frame the view. You'll discover that lakes Superior and Michigan don't have a lock on size, beauty and mood.

A sandy, gently sloping beach — just right for wading, sand castle building, beachcombing and swimming — runs the length of the park. Forty Mile Point Lighthouse stands guard over this section of the lake as a reminder that Huron can and does turn ugly and dangerous.

COUNTY: Presque Isle

CITY: Rogers City

FEES: None

SCHEDULE: Open all year.

DIRECTIONS: From Rogers City, drive 7 miles north on US-23.

South of the lighthouse, which is not open to the public, a picnic area in a stand of birch and pine lines the back of the beach. Many tables and grills, although in full shade, are only a few steps away from the sun and sand. The light's foghorn building has been converted into a one-of-a-kind picnic pavilion.

153 SEAGULL POINT PARK

Curved like a scimitar, the three-quarter-mile-plus beach at Seagull Point Park is the main draw for most visitors. The Lake Huron coastline here is undeniably beautiful. The soft sand runs in a wide band along the shore before gently dipping into the lake and is reason enough for beachcombers, sunbathers and waders to make the short drive from Rogers City.

But there's more.

Behind the lightly used beach lies a series of low dunes that, although not as dramatic as the shoreline, entreat you to enjoy their fragile and subtle beauty. Spreading junipers, sand cherries, stunted pine and other shrubs creep down the foreslopes of the sandy hillocks and fight to retain a foothold on the easily eroded ground. On the inland side, small trees give way to larger ones.

A two-mile interpretive trail, which winds back and forth between the beach and the sparsely wooded dunes, crosses a small stream and is seldom out of sight of the lake. Interpretive signs along the route tell of the area's natural history and identify the flora. Crossing wide patches of soft sand slows the pace, and the trail takes at least an hour to walk, twice as long if you pause to enjoy the many striking views and investigate the complex and interesting dunal environment.

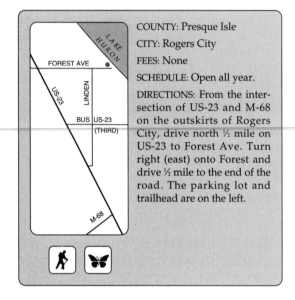

COUNTY: Presque Isle

CITY: Rogers City

FEES: None

SCHEDULE: Open all year.

DIRECTIONS: From the intersection of US-23 and M-68 on the outskirts of Rogers City, drive north ½ mile on US-23 to Forest Ave. Turn right (east) onto Forest and drive ½ mile to the end of the road. The parking lot and trailhead are on the left.

PRESQUE ISLE LIGHTHOUSE 154

There are two jewels in the crown of the Presque Isle Peninsula, and either one is worth driving out of your way to experience. A 90-acre park caps the very end of the strangely shaped peninsula — which, on a map, looks like a beckoning finger — and near the center of the park rises the tallest lighthouse on the Great Lakes.

The 109-foot-tall tower was put into service in 1870 as a replacement for an older, smaller light a mile to the south. (You'll pass it on your way to the top of the peninsula.) Set in front of the tall, white column is a carefully restored lightkeeper's house that, except for the cars parked outside, looks much as it did a hundred years ago. Inside, exhibits and displays relate the history of shipping and light-

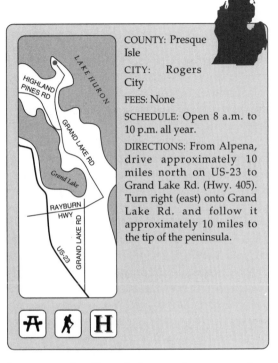

COUNTY: Presque Isle

CITY: Rogers City

FEES: None

SCHEDULE: Open 8 a.m. to 10 p.m. all year.

DIRECTIONS: From Alpena, drive approximately 10 miles north on US-23 to Grand Lake Rd. (Hwy. 405). Turn right (east) onto Grand Lake Rd. and follow it approximately 10 miles to the tip of the peninsula.

houses on the Great Lakes, and one room furnished with artifacts and antiques looks so authentic that a lightkeeper from a hundred years ago could step inside and not feel out of place.

Several short nature trails, totaling more than a mile, begin at the lighthouse and circle the tip of the peninsula. Using a map that hangs in a small shed across the park drive from the lighthouse, you can choose walks from less than a quarter mile to any combination of routes up to 1.2 miles long. The trails border the rugged shoreline and weave in and out of evergreens and hardwoods. Trees along the way are labeled, and you can rest and enjoy views from strategically located benches. At the very tip of the peninsula, which is accessible either on foot or by car, a small picnic grounds and pavilion edges the rocky beach and looks out over Lake Huron.

155 BESSER NATURAL AREA

Nearly a mile of wild, undeveloped Lake Huron shoreline, a ghost town, a sunken ship in a small lagoon, and one of the few remaining stands of virgin white pine left in the state are attractions to this 137-acre preserve.

A stone pier that reaches out into Lake Huron and the name "Bell" (which is still listed on some county maps) are the only reminders of the school, sawmill, store, saloon and several houses that covered the area during the 1880s. Bell was born to serve the lumbering industry, and Bell died along with the lumbering industry.

A one-mile self-guiding trail leads through a magnificent stand of virgin white pine and past the ghost town, a tract of red pine, and a tiny inland lagoon, which serves as the graveyard for an unnamed small vessel, whose date and cause of sinking have long been forgotten. A bronze plaque halfway along the trail honors Jesse Besser who, in 1966, donated this land to the state as a memorial to Michigan's lumbermen.

Just a short, easy walk from the parking area is the area's 4,500 feet of Lake Huron frontage, including 500 feet of sandy beach.

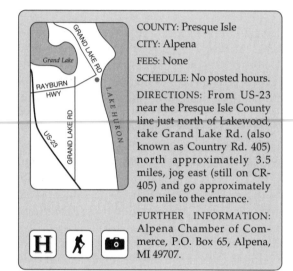

COUNTY: Presque Isle

CITY: Alpena

FEES: None

SCHEDULE: No posted hours.

DIRECTIONS: From US-23 near the Presque Isle County line just north of Lakewood, take Grand Lake Rd. (also known as Country Rd. 405) north approximately 3.5 miles, jog east (still on CR-405) and go approximately one mile to the entrance.

FURTHER INFORMATION: Alpena Chamber of Commerce, P.O. Box 65, Alpena, MI 49707.

ALPENA WILDLIFE SANCTUARY 156

For a "natural" area, the Alpena Wildlife Sanctuary has a rich human history. Prehistoric man, for example, walked here as early as 2000 B.C. Some 3,500 years later, Indians camped along the riverbanks until the coming of the Europeans. And shortly after the Civil War, lumbermen floated white-pine logs down the river to sawmills.

Today, nature lovers, hikers, canoeists and fishermen all seek refuge in this 500-acre sanctuary bordering the Thunder Bay River within the limits of northeast lower Michigan's largest city. A dam, constructed during the logging era, created a reservoir and, behind it, the sanctuary's large expanse of wetlands. Within the sanctuary, two large islands interrupt the river, which forms most of the sanctuary's border.

A bridge, closed to all but foot or wheelchair traffic, connects the mainland to several trails that traverse or circle the shoreline of the larger island, known as Island Park. Several scattered fishing platforms also jut out from the shoreline of this recently acquired 17.5-acre addition to the sanctuary, and a viewing platform for the handicapped overlooks the river.

The Michigan Conservation Department first released ducks, geese and swans and also began a feeding program in 1938, the same year the agency, at the urging of local citizens, officially designated this area a wildlife sanctuary. Today, according to the Thunder Bay Audubon Society, 128 different birds have been spotted in the sanctuary. Year-round residents now include Mute Swans, Canadian Geese and Mallards, and spring migration brings Common Goldeneye, Bufflehead, Scaup, Canvasback, Redhead, Pintail, Gadwall, Widgeon, Black Ducks, Coots and Whistling Swans.

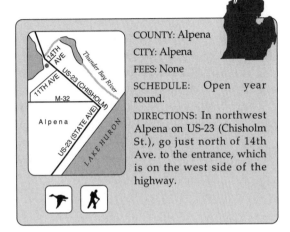

COUNTY: Alpena

CITY: Alpena

FEES: None

SCHEDULE: Open year round.

DIRECTIONS: In northwest Alpena on US-23 (Chisholm St.), go just north of 14th Ave. to the entrance, which is on the west side of the highway.

157 CHIPPEWA HILLS PATHWAY

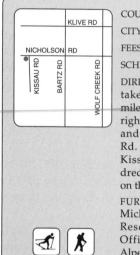

No matter what your mood, energy level or ability, when you arrive at the Chippewa Hills Pathway you should be able to find a hike to match. Your choice of four trails — 0.5, 1.3, 2.5 or 4.5 miles long — pass over the hilly, rolling terrain and through the pine-covered valleys of the Mackinaw State Forest in Alpena County. The longest trail also skirts a cedar grove and cuts across an old logging trail.

The trails are open in the winter and offer a wide variety — with difficulty ranging from novice to expert — of cross country skiing opportunities. A trail map is available at any local DNR office or the Alpena Visitors Bureau (call 1-800-4-ALPENA to receive one by mail).

COUNTY: Alpena

CITY: Alpena

FEES: None

SCHEDULE: No posted hours.

DIRECTIONS: From Alpena, take US-23 south about 12 miles to Nicholson Rd. Turn right (west) onto Nicholson and go 11 miles to Kissau Rd. Turn left (south) onto Kissau and go a few hundred feet to a parking area on the west side of the road.

FURTHER INFORMATION: Michigan Dept. of Natural Resources, Alpena Field Office, 4343 M-32 West, Alpena, MI 49707.

REID LAKE FOOT TRAVEL AREA 158

Both novice and veteran backpackers will find the Reid Lake Foot Travel Area a good place to gain experience or test equipment. Here, in the Huron National Forest, you can set up camp in anything from fairly civilized to wilderness conditions. Walk-in camping is permitted anywhere along the 6.1-mile trail system with only one restriction: camps must not be set up within 200 feet of water or trails. Other rustic campsites, marked by benches, are scattered around Reid Lake itself. An on the northwestern edge of the lake are developed sites, which include pit toilets, fire rings and a well.

The area, opened in 1975, is also an excellent destination for a day hike and picnic. Hiking begins with a single trail that leads southwest from the parking area at M-72 for about a mile to Reid Lake. There, it splits into three adjacent loops. One circles the lake; the other two reach to the east and west around marshes, bogs and a beaver pond. Maps are posted at all loop intersections.

The old fields and open meadows that make up part of the trail system mark the boundaries of an old farm that was worked until it was purchased by the U.S. Forest Service and incorporated into the Huron National Forest in the mid-1960s. Surrounding the farm fields are some of the most imposing hardwoods in the area.

The trails are open in the winter for cross country skiing.

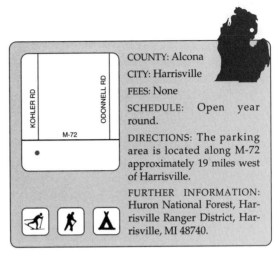

COUNTY: Alcona

CITY: Harrisville

FEES: None

SCHEDULE: Open year round.

DIRECTIONS: The parking area is located along M-72 approximately 19 miles west of Harrisville.

FURTHER INFORMATION: Huron National Forest, Harrisville Ranger District, Harrisville, MI 48740.

159 HOIST LAKES FOOT TRAVEL AREA

Lower Peninsula backpackers who don't want to drive most of the day to find a wilderness camping experience will want to visit the Hoist Lakes Trail system in the Huron National Forest. Backcountry camping, with a few restrictions, is allowed just about anywhere in this large, rugged area, but it's a good idea to carry a compass and a map of the region if you venture very far from either of the two parking areas.

Such freedom does carry with it some responsibilities, however. To minimize man's impact on this wilderness area, camping parties are limited to a maximum of 10 people and must set up no closer than 200 feet to any water or trail. Backpackers are also asked to carry out, not bury, all refuse.

Campers and hikers have a lot of territory to choose from in this more than 10,000-acre parcel. Almost 20 miles of trails wander through second-growth forest, over gently rolling wooded terrain, around marshes, past beaver floodings and across streams. Hikers can also use several two-tracks — barred to motorized traffic — which crisscross the area. Plans call for even more trails and campsites to be developed in the future.

Another added plus for campers and hikers: This section of the Huron National Forest teems with deer, bear, coyote, fox, owls, hawks and songbirds, plus turkey, grouse, woodcock and other gamebirds.

Fishing, too, is rated good on the several lakes within the trail system. Bass and panfish are taken in good numbers from Carp, Byron and North Hoist lakes; rainbows have been stocked in South Hoist Lake. Fishermen may carry in light boats or canoes, but motors are banned on all of the lakes.

Originally developed as a place to cross country ski, the area was later opened up to hikers because of the growing demand for places in which to backpack.

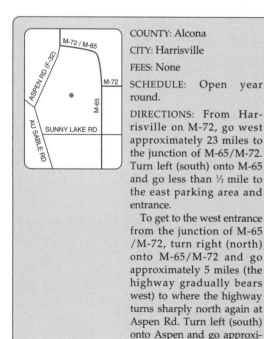

COUNTY: Alcona

CITY: Harrisville

FEES: None

SCHEDULE: Open year round.

DIRECTIONS: From Harrisville on M-72, go west approximately 23 miles to the junction of M-65/M-72. Turn left (south) onto M-65 and go less than ½ mile to the east parking area and entrance.

To get to the west entrance from the junction of M-65/M-72, turn right (north) onto M-65/M-72 and go approximately 5 miles (the highway gradually bears west) to where the highway turns sharply north again at Aspen Rd. Turn left (south) onto Aspen and go approximately 4 miles to the parking area.

FURTHER INFORMATION: Huron Ranger District, Harrisville Ranger District, Harrisville, MI 48740.

JEWELL LAKE TRAIL 160

This lightly visited and out-of-the-way recreation area in the Huron National Forest certainly lives up to its name. You won't find any precious stones here, but the lake, campground, and especially the trail make up a gem of a spot for the quiet enjoyment of some positively serene natural beauty.

Jewell Lake, almost smack dab in the middle of Alcona County, is a crystal-clear pool in a sea of forest-green trees. The rustic national forest campground, on the south shore, contains 32 spacious sites that are well-shaded by a leafy canopy. A small, sandy beach and shallow swimming area are only a few steps away. Day-users will find a small two-table picnic area snuggled up to the lake at the boat launching ramp, east of the campground.

Capping off this delightful recreation area is the Jewell Lake Trail, which begins at the west side of the beach area. Only a few yards down the trail, a rustic footbridge spans a slow-moving stream edged by a picturesque cedar swamp. Across the bridge, the path makes a hard right and hugs the shoreline of Jewell Lake for almost half the trail's one-mile length. Cedar, birch and pine line the water's edge, while inland the forest floor is thick with ferns and an understory of young trees and shrubs. Eventually and almost regrettably, the trail turns inland and loops through a stand of birch and aspen before returning to the lake and the footbridge. Birds and wildflowers abound along the easy-walking path, which was constructed in 1974 by the Youth Conservation Corps. Two benches strategically placed along the route allow you to prolong your stay in this treasured corner of the national forest.

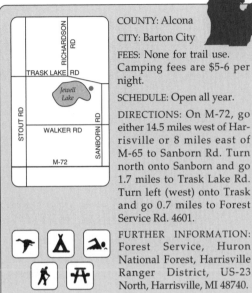

COUNTY: Alcona

CITY: Barton City

FEES: None for trail use. Camping fees are $5-6 per night.

SCHEDULE: Open all year.

DIRECTIONS: On M-72, go either 14.5 miles west of Harrisville or 8 miles east of M-65 to Sanborn Rd. Turn north onto Sanborn and go 1.7 miles to Trask Lake Rd. Turn left (west) onto Trask and go 0.7 miles to Forest Service Rd. 4601.

FURTHER INFORMATION: Forest Service, Huron National Forest, Harrisville Ranger District, US-23 North, Harrisville, MI 48740.

161-164 RIVER ROAD NATIONAL FOREST SCENIC BYWAY

The River Road National Forest Scenic Byway is 22 miles of two-lane blacktop highway that you can drive in less than half an hour. But don't bet on it. The 4.3 miles of state highway M-65 and 17.7 miles of a county road known as River Road that together make up the byway pass some of the most spectacular scenery in the eastern Lower Peninsula.

The byway borders the south bank of the AuSable River atop highlands that rise 150 to 200 feet from the water. A series of four dams along this stretch of the historic trout stream create large impoundments, and a map of the AuSable looks more like either a series of long, narrow lakes or a single long serpentine body of water that has been corseted in four spots. The bordering highlands do not gently roll down to the river. Rather, the impoundments lap at the very edge of the sheer banks — or, more accurately, wooded cliffs — that rise up almost perpendicular to the water. When you stand at the lip of the banks, you get a breathtaking view of a water-filled valley dotted with marshy wetlands; flooded areas with old trunks protruding from the

water; the steep, forested banks on the opposite shore; and, surprisingly, a towering sand dune nearly the equal of Sleeping Bear Dunes.

The catch at this scenic drive is that you can't appreciate or even observe most of the beauty and points of interest from your car. In fact, most of the byway is just a tunnel through lush, green forest. To truly enjoy this unusual and beautiful natural attraction necessitates exercise, some of it strenuous.

Four major facilities are strung out along the byway, and almost all are barrier-free. To explore all four will take the better part of a day, yet each in its own right is worth a trip to the AuSable.

161 EAGLE RUN
SKI AND NATURE TRAIL

Located two miles west of Oscoda on River Road across from Oscoda High School, Eagle Run holds 6.9 miles of the most-level cross country ski and hiking trails in the area. The broad paths burrow through the dense foliage of second-growth forest on the highlands that overlook the valley. Skiing and hiking are easy here, but this is also the least-scenic of the byway's five major attractions. The trails don't lead to the breathtaking views you'll find at the other spots, but you can enjoy a walk through the quiet solitude only a deep woods can offer. You can choose from three loops — which measure 1.0, 4.8 and 6.9 miles — and you can use a large map in the parking lot at the trailhead to help plan your outing.

162 LUMBERMAN'S MONUMENT

The largest tourist attraction and, arguably, the prettiest stop along the scenic byway is Lumberman's Monument, 15 miles west of Oscoda. The centerpiece here is a nine-foot-tall bronze statue that has become a landmark in Michigan. Composed of three figures — a sawyer with an axe and a saw, a river driver with a pivey, and a timber cruiser with a compass — the statue was completed in 1932 and dedicated as a tribute to the memory of Michigan lumbermen.

Surrounding the statue is a modest display of lumberjack memorabilia, a giant pile of logs tumbled as if in a game of pickup sticks, and exhibits and displays that depict the lumbermen's work and lifestyle. A visitor center next to the monument is the focal point for a summer-long series of interpretive programs, which range from lumbering-era stories to presentations on Bald Eagles, Kirtland's Warblers, and the life of a forest firefighter. Books, stationery, and other gift shop items are sold at the center.

A short walk from the statue takes you to the edge of a cliff that plummets in a near-vertical 160-foot dive to the AuSable River. The spot not only presents a stunning view of the valley but also is the steeping-off point for the most unusual interpretive nature trail in Michigan. The Stairway to Discovery, which descends 260 steps to the edge of the river, may be the only interpretive nature trail in the U.S. perched in its entirety on a staircase.

Signs at 10 stops along the way explain the area's unique natural history, and you can also pick up a printed guide at the visitor cen-

COUNTY: Iosco

CITY: Oscoda

FEES: None for day use. Fee for camping.

SCHEDULE: Open Memorial Day weekend through Labor Day.

DIRECTIONS: From the stop light on US-23 in Oscoda, turn west onto River Road and drive 18 miles to Iargo Springs and another 5 miles to Rollways.

FURTHER INFORMATION: Tawas Ranger District, P.O. Box 472, East Tawas, MI 48730.

ter. Hint: Plan to stop at the interpretive points on your way back up because, unless you're in incredibly good shape, you're going to have to stop for rests during the return trip anyway.

If you're not too tired from the stairway, or after a rest you can also take a 20-minute brisk walk down a paved walkway that begins to the right of the visitor center, edges the rim of the cliff, then climbs to a deck with another impressive view of the surrounding landscape.

Lumberman's Monument is also a lovely setting for a leisurely picnic in the woods. Grills and picnic tables invitingly rest amid a stand of red pine near the parking lot. Next to the day-use area is a 19-site primitive campground.

Less than a mile west of the monument area, a turnout on River Road leads to another sweeping look at the valley from the

Canoers' Memorial site. But unlike the rigors at Lumberman's Monument, you only have to take a few short steps before the valley opens up at your feet.

163 IARGO SPRINGS

From a platform built out over the bluff edge at Iargo Springs, about two miles west of Lumberman's Monument, you get probably the most-panoramic view of the river from any spot on the byway. The river here has a slightly different character. Grass and sedge border much of the riverbank and soften the shoreline. And the AuSable gives no sense of moving or that it's even a river.

At the bottom of a long flight of stairs that starts at the overlook, Iargo Springs virtually pours out of the hillside. The creek's two forks seemingly materialize from the side of the hill, meet about 30 yards later, then flow only a short distance before joining the Au Sable. It is a decidedly unusual sight, and the Chippewa Indians believed that the "magical" appearance of water held mystical and curative powers. Twelve hundred feet of boardwalk, with four small observation decks, meanders through the spring area.

Take your time fully exploring and investigating the picture-perfect setting, because the long climb back will leave you breathless from more than just the beauty.

164 ROLLWAYS

The last stop on the scenic byway is six miles west of Iargo Springs on highway M-65. There, a small picnic area borders the bluff and overlooks the backed-up river. The tables and grills are scattered among shade trees only a few steps from the steep bank, which drops off to Loud Pond. Across Rollways road from the picnic area, 19 pull-through camping sites are arranged in a loop along the bluff's edge.

Tuttle Marsh is a Hyatt Regency for waterfowl. And for birdwatchers it's one of those rare areas where observing can be as productive from a car as on foot.

In spring 1990 as a result of a cooperative effort of the United States Forest Service, Michigan Department of Natural Resources and Ducks Unlimited, construction was completed of an earthen dam and water control system that created a shallow 380-acre impoundment and wetland in this small section of the Huron-Manistee National Forest. Previously, only shrub land, scattered areas of grass and sedge, and very little open water covered the area. To further increase nesting capacity, 35 earthen nesting islands were constructed, and future plans call for upland nesting enhancement.

Birding is good now, and as marsh vegetation colonizes the wetlands, it can only get better. The wetlands are expected to attract large numbers of migrating waterfowl, significant numbers of shorebirds and Sandhill Cranes, plus muskrats, mink, beaver and even Bald Eagles. Most important, an area that formerly produced an estimated 10 duck and only three goose broods annually is expected to yield 65 and 10 respectively. The species most likely to benefit from the impoundment are Mallard, Wood Duck, blue-winged Teal, Canada Goose, and the relatively scarce Black Duck.

All this potential for finding birds can come from the inside of your car or only a few steps from the roadside. Tuttle Marsh Road borders the impoundment area and, in fact, the earthen dam runs along the west shoulder of the gravel road for almost a mile. At many places the dam is just high enough to obscure views of the wetlands, but you only have to climb a

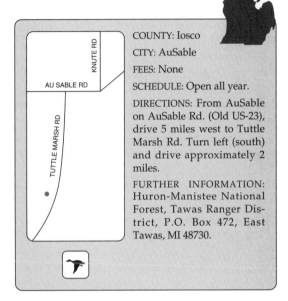

COUNTY: Iosco

CITY: AuSable

FEES: None

SCHEDULE: Open all year.

DIRECTIONS: From AuSable on AuSable Rd. (Old US-23), drive 5 miles west to Tuttle Marsh Rd. Turn left (south) and drive approximately 2 miles.

FURTHER INFORMATION: Huron-Manistee National Forest, Tawas Ranger District, P.O. Box 472, East Tawas, MI 48730.

few steps up the low dike to be able to sweep your binoculars across the broad expanse of water and marsh. An elevated observation platform is also scheduled for construction. On the east side of the road, marshy areas and small pools of quiet, grass-fringed water skirt the road.

166 CORSAIR TRAIL SYSTEM

Situated in a lovely valley in the Huron-Manistee National Forest, the Corsair Trail System bills itself as Michigan's Cross Country Ski Capital. And for good reason. More than 15 loops totaling 27 miles of well-marked trails make up this sprawling complex, and a map of the system looks like a web spun by a spider high on LSD. From the center, where the parking lot sits, loops and trails of varying lengths head out, connect with other trails, and eventually wind their erratic way back to the hub.

Groomed in winter, the trail complex is one of the longest and finest in the state for cross country skiing. And during the summer, both day-hikers and backpackers can wear down boot leather on the countless paths. It would take an Einstein to calculate all the possible trail combinations, but it's easy to plan a hike to suit your exact wishes, from a short walk alongside Silver Creek to a two-day trek around the entire system.

At the trailhead a large map of the system, etched on a tabletop-size board, will help you plan your adventure, and smaller maps with "you are here" markers are placed at all trail intersections. Trails in the valley floor border fast-moving creeks and streams. Others pass over rolling hills that in some places become chest pounders because of their steepness.

You can backwoods camp anywhere within the area, but you must set up at least 200 feet from lakes and streams and a minimum of 100 feet from trails. Day-hikers can stoke up before or ease hunger pains after their treks at a small picnic area at the trailhead.

This entire area was the hunting grounds of the Chippewa and Ottawa Indians until nature delivered a one-two punch. A great storm flattened the forest, and years later a forest fire turned the fallen timber to ash. As a result, the first white visitors considered the area a wasteland. The lush forest the trails wind through today are the result of reforestation by the Civilian Conservation Corps.

COUNTY: Iosco

CITY: East Tawas

FEES: None

SCHEDULE: Open all year.

DIRECTIONS: From US-23 in downtown East Tawas, turn north onto Newman St. and drive 2 blocks to State St. Turn left (west) onto State and go about ½ mile to where the road bears right, onto Bridge St. Just after Bridge crosses the Tawas River, the road forks. Take the right-hand fork, Monument Rd., about 7 miles.

FURTHER INFORMATION: Huron-Manistee National Forest, Tawas Ranger District, P.O. Box 472, East Tawas, MI 48730.

ISLAND LAKE RECREATION AREA 167

Framed on the north and south by the shores of Loon and Island lakes, Island Lake Recreation Area — with its rolling morainal hills, deep glacial potholes, and beautiful hardwood forest — is a quiet and beautiful alternative to the more heavily used state and county parks in the region. This unit of the Huron National Forest may be out of the way, little-known and relatively small, but it still offers a full complement of outdoor activities.

A pleasant picnic grounds and small swimming beach at Loon Lake make up the day-use section. On the southern end of the area, a neat 17-site campground hugs the north shore of Island Lake. Each of the widely spaced sites has a paved slip, and a small swimming beach and picnic area are only a few steps away from any point in the rustic campground. The 65-acre lake supports good fishing for perch, bluegills, and large and small-mouth bass.

Connecting the two lakes and their facilities are two loops that make up the self-guiding Island Lake Nature Trail. The well-marked paths wander through a hilly, forested landscape carved by the glaciers of the last ice age. Twenty numbered stops along the route correspond to coded paragraphs in a brochure available at either the Mio Ranger Station or from a box at the campgrounds fee station. The brochure explains the natural history of the area and notes points of interest along the trail. From the trailhead at the campground, a round trip between the two lakes totals 1.2 miles on the short route or 1.6 miles on the larger loop.

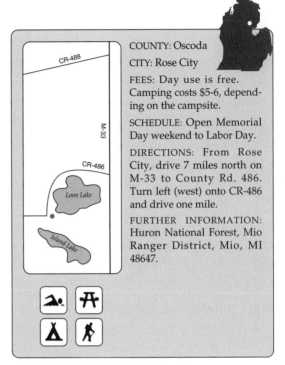

COUNTY: Oscoda

CITY: Rose City

FEES: Day use is free. Camping costs $5-6, depending on the campsite.

SCHEDULE: Open Memorial Day weekend to Labor Day.

DIRECTIONS: From Rose City, drive 7 miles north on M-33 to County Rd. 486. Turn left (west) onto CR-486 and drive one mile.

FURTHER INFORMATION: Huron National Forest, Mio Ranger District, Mio, MI 48647.

168 KIRTLAND'S WARBLER BREEDING GROUNDS

Kirtland's Warbler — a small bluish-gray bird sporting a yellow vest streaked with black — is Michigan's most unique inhabitant. The species wasn't discovered until 1851, and it took another 52 years to pinpoint that its only breeding grounds on earth were in northern lower Michigan. In 1903 Norman A. Wood found the world's first breeding pair in Oscoda County about a half mile from the Crawford County line and a mile north of the AuSable River. Every nest or breeding pair found since has been within 60 miles of the nest Wood discovered. But it's not like the tiny bird is overrunning the area. From the late 1960s to the late 1980s, the *world* population of Kirtland's Warbler averaged under 500. The population since has steadily increased to a 1994 all-time high of 633 pairs.

The little bird's precarious hold on existence stems from its specialization. It will only set up housekeeping in jack pine stands that are from eight to 20 years old and usually more than 80 acres in size. Although it winters in the Bahamas and nearby islands, it will or can breed only under very specific conditions found in 12 Michigan counties.

Given the rarity of the bird, its unusual natural history, and the fact that its very existence as a species depends on managed jack pine plantations and wildfire-produced habitat in Michigan, Kirtland's Warbler draws curiosity seekers and devoted birders from around the globe, all of whom want a glimpse of one of the world's rarest creatures.

But to ensure, as much as possible, the continued viability of the species, the U.S. Forest Service and Michigan Department of Natural Resources has closed the birds' nesting areas to public entry. You can view them by taking guided tours conducted by the U.S. Fish and Wildlife Service from Grayling or the U.S. Forest Service from Mio. The free tours usually run twice a day at 7 a.m. and 11 a.m. from mid-May through July 4. The exact days, dates and times may vary slightly from year to year so write for details before planning a trip. Late May and early to mid-June present the best chances for seeing the birds, and you should, of course, bring binoculars or spotting scope.

Kirtland's Warbler sightings can never be guaranteed, so a trip north for the sole purpose of viewing one can turn out to be a monumental goose chase. But if you *are* lucky enough to spot a bird, you'll join one of the most exclusive clubs in the world.

COUNTY: Oscoda/Crawford

CITY: Mio/Grayling

FEES: None

SCHEDULE: Write for details.

DIRECTIONS: Write for details.

FURTHER INFORMATION: U.S. Fish and Wildlife Service, c/o Michigan DNR Grayling Field Office, P.O. Box 507, Grayling, MI 49738. Or U.S. Forest Service District Ranger Office, Huron National Forest, 401 Court St., Mio, MI 48647.

169 WAKELEY LAKE FOOT TRAVEL AREA

A picture-perfect lake undisturbed by any development is the focal point of this 1,415-acre natural area. Cupped in low, wooded hills and fringed by quiet marshes and whispering trees, Wakeley Lake is so pristine that loons nest here and eagles are a common sight.

The federal government purchased the area in 1986 to manage it as a sanctuary for wildlife, with emphasis on protecting the eagles and loons. To help preserve the natural setting, motorized traffic is not allowed, and the loon nesting area, on the north end of the lake, is closed to the public from March 1 through July 15.

The eagles and loons are enough to draw both serious and occasional birdwatchers, but this small corner of the Huron National Forest offers a lot more to birders. More than 100 species have been spotted here, including Wild Turkey, Great Horned Owl, Great Grey Owl, Red-eyed Vireo, Northern Goshawk, Virginia Rail, two species of grosbeak, numerous warblers, and the rare Northern Shrike. A bird checklist is posted next to a detailed trail map at the area's single entry point, on M-72.

From that lone trailhead, a wide, level, easily walked path cuts through an aspen and pine forest for a half mile, then breaks out of the trees at a small picnic area on the east side of Wakeley Lake. Beyond the open meadow and its pleasing view of the lake, a network of abandoned two-tracks and foot trails head off into the farther reaches of the preserve. The paths circle the lake, skirt swamps and marshes, and cross an upland forest of jack pine and oak in which young white pine are securing a toehold.

This is an ideal area for novice backpackers to test their stamina and skills. You can back-country camp throughout the foot-traffic

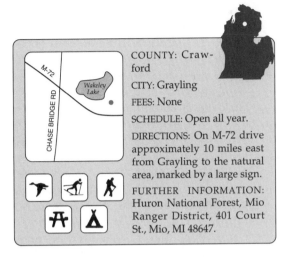

COUNTY: Crawford

CITY: Grayling

FEES: None

SCHEDULE: Open all year.

DIRECTIONS: On M-72 drive approximately 10 miles east from Grayling to the natural area, marked by a large sign.

FURTHER INFORMATION: Huron National Forest, Mio Ranger District, 401 Court St., Mio, MI 48647.

area, with two restrictions: You must set up camp at least 200 feet from the lake and, of course, can't camp in the loon nesting area during the restricted period.

You can fish from June 19 through August 31 but must release all catches for the benefit of the eagles and loons.

The trails are open, but not groomed, for cross country skiing.

170 RED PINE NATURAL AREA

At one time, as DNR Area Forest Manager Don Torchia tells it, the Red Pine Natural Area "contained the (single) largest red pine in Michigan. But several years ago, a larger one was documented, and at the same time, the monarch red pine died. It is now the largest dead red pine in Michigan."

Though the old giant died — maybe even of chagrin after learning it was no longer the biggest of its species in the state — there are so many other pines of imposing size and magnificence that the area has been designated a National Natural Landmark. The old-growth stand of red pine and jack pine is even more impressive because the area has been undisturbed by man — and never will be. The DNR will intervene in the case of wildfire, but because the purpose of the preserve is to study the trees' natural changes, no other human influence is permitted.

A half-mile-long path that winds through the grove's flat terrain makes for a pleasant, even inspiring, walk. The scent of pine permeates the air, and old needles soften your footfalls on most of the hike. The majestic, old trees tower above the fern-covered forest floor, and you can spot them at every point on the compass, with some of the giants even crowding the trail. Interpretive signs scattered along the route explain the natural history of the forest.

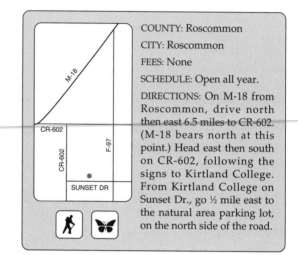

COUNTY: Roscommon

CITY: Roscommon

FEES: None

SCHEDULE: Open all year.

DIRECTIONS: On M-18 from Roscommon, drive north then east 6.5 miles to CR-602. (M-18 bears north at this point.) Head east then south on CR-602, following the signs to Kirtland College. From Kirtland College on Sunset Dr., go ½ mile east to the natural area parking lot, on the north side of the road.

Dog-hair-thick white cedar liberally mixed with balsam fir and black spruce coats the Dead Stream Swamp, which at 30 square miles is the largest roadless parcel of real estate south of the Straits. Occasionally interrupting and accenting the wide sweep of evergreens in this seemingly endless expanse of the swamp spread across two counties are pockets or red maple, aspen, black ash, birch and tag alder.

No roads or even two-tracks completely traverse the heart of the Dead Stream Swamp. You can get a brief, albeit antiseptic, glimpse of this unique ecosystem by driving on US-27, which cuts for two miles through the eastern edge of the swamp just north of Houghton Lake. Several county roads follow the edges, and here and there a two-track penetrates the swamp for a mile or two. Access is also possible from oil-drilling areas on the fringes of the swamp. Several two-tracks and oil-well access roads lead to the very edge of the wilderness from Boynton Road, reached by going 4.5 miles west of US-27 on M-55. This gravel road, which changes names at almost every curve, heads more or less north for about five miles, then turns in a westerly direction and parallels the southern edge of the swamp. The Addis Creek Trail begins at this road with a dozen names and penetrates the deepest — two miles — into the heart of the swamp, before ending at the Dead Stream. Best access on the north side of the area comes from the Norwich Oil Field Headquarters Road.

You can explore the backwaters and miles of flooded, timber-lined shore by either hiking or launching a boat from the Reedsburg Dam Forest Campground, located in the Pere Marquette State Forest. There, 42 well-shaded sites dot a small peninsula that nudges into a 2,000-acre manmade lake created by the Reedsburg Dam on the Muskegon River. The marshy pond stretches upstream for three miles where it touches the southeastern edge of the swamp. Also, an extensive system of unmapped, unposted, and unblazed but well-worn trails follow the banks of the river upstream and downstream from the dam, head off into the surrounding forest or follow the curving banks of the impoundment.

Several prominent birdwatchers have included the impoundment, forest and swamp in their list of favorite locations. During fall and spring migrations, birds nest and feed in the area in great numbers. At any time, you are likely to see a wide variety of species ranging from songbirds and waterfowl to herons, Osprey, Bald Eagles, bitterns, rails, gallinules and Black Terns.

Bear, coyote, otter, deer, bobcat, mink, fox and raccoon are among the wide variety of wildlife that inhabit the swamp, and anglers report good catches of bass, perch, bluegill and pike in the backwaters.

Other facilities at the campground include a day-use picnic area that overlooks the dam.

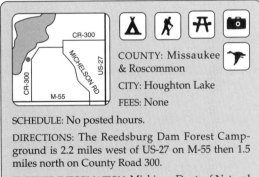

COUNTY: Missaukee & Roscommon

CITY: Houghton Lake

FEES: None

SCHEDULE: No posted hours.

DIRECTIONS: The Reedsburg Dam Forest Campground is 2.2 miles west of US-27 on M-55 then 1.5 miles north on County Road 300.

FURTHER INFORMATION: Michigan Dept. of Natural Resources, Box 30034, Lansing, MI 48909.

172 NEITHERCUT WOODLAND

There are four ways to have a meaningful experience at Neithercut Woodland. One: do what thousands of elementary through college-age students, plus hundreds of teachers and naturalists have done — enroll in one of the many classes that are conducted at the 252-acre site, owned and operated by Central Michigan University. Two: attend regularly scheduled monthly outdoor programs. Three: pick up a fistful of helpful interpretive brochures, walk the many trails and informally increase your environmental education. Or, four: just walk the trails with no particular goal or thoughts in mind and simply enjoy the out-of-doors.

Three trails, totaling 3.25 miles, wander through a varied landscape of hardwood forests, cedar swamps, fields, pine plantations, seasonal spring ponds and marshes. The ¾-mile-long self-guiding Brookwood Trail, for example, passes through a beech/maple forest, crosses a creek and wanders beside spring ponds and cedar swamps. An excellent trail guide, available at the beginning of the path, not only interprets the natural setting and phenomena found along this 45-minute walk, but also includes a partial checklist of the preserve's flora and fauna.

Branching off from the Brookwood Trail, the 2.1 mile Arborvitae Trail passes through a quiet, secluded forest. This trail is also open in the winter for cross country skiing.

Designed specially for the handicapped, a 1,325-foot-long elevated boardwalk and paved path called the Freedom Trail leads in a round-about way from the parking lot across a swamp to the interpretive building.

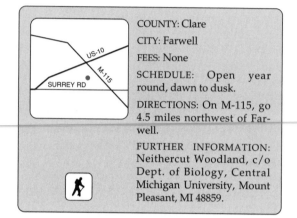

COUNTY: Clare

CITY: Farwell

FEES: None

SCHEDULE: Open year round, dawn to dusk.

DIRECTIONS: On M-115, go 4.5 miles northwest of Farwell.

FURTHER INFORMATION: Neithercut Woodland, c/o Dept. of Biology, Central Michigan University, Mount Pleasant, MI 48859.

GREEN PINE LAKE PATHWAY 173

Experienced hikers and greenhorn back-packers alike have several options to choose from at this trail system that cuts through the AuSable State Forest. The Pathway — which totals 11 miles and includes three loops, measuring 1.0, 2.5 and 5 miles — connects Pike Lake State Forest Campground on the east to Mud Lake State Forest campground, on the west. You can plan hikes that range from short, pleasant walks to a two-day round trip with overnight stays at the campgrounds.

On the Pathway's eastern side, a 5-mile loop circles a large swamp. Stacked on top of that large loop on its north side at Green Pine Lake is a smaller 2.5-mile loop, and perched at its "top," its northernmost point, is the 30-site Pike Lake State Forest Campground. On the system's extreme west edge, a single one-mile trail loops east from the small eight-site Mud Lake State Forest Campground. A 2.5-mile trail that links the small loops at either end of the pathway curves around numerous bogs filled with delicate and unusual flora ranging from tamarack trees to carnivorous plants and exquisite orchids.

Although both campgrounds cozy up to lakes, neither offers good swimming. But fishermen might like to take a break from hiking to go after bluegills, perch, bass and pike in both lakes.

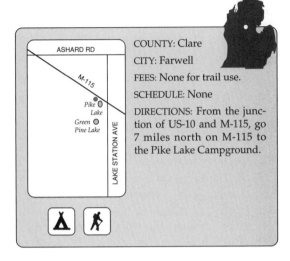

ASHARD RD

M-115

Pike Lake

Green Pine Lake

LAKE STATION AVE

COUNTY: Clare

CITY: Farwell

FEES: None for trail use.

SCHEDULE: None

DIRECTIONS: From the junction of US-10 and M-115, go 7 miles north on M-115 to the Pike Lake Campground.

174 DEERFIELD NATURE PARK

The focal point of this 591-acre park is the beautiful, clear and swift-moving Chippewa River which, like a piece of discarded ribbon, twists and turns for three miles through the heavily wooded landscape. Other draws to this flagship of the Isabella County park system include two suspension footbridges that connect to a scenic and extensive trail system, a covered bridge open only to foot traffic, several picturesque picnic areas, an interpretive nature trail, good fishing, a swimming beach, rustic and uncrowded campgrounds, and groomed cross country ski trails.

Two swaybacked suspension footbridges mark the north and south trailheads to the park's seven-mile-plus network of wide, well-marked footpaths, and crossing either of the spans is the only way onto the system. Three named routes pass through the gently rolling, wooded terrain on the east side of the river. The River Loop trail sticks close to the

Chippewa, and you'll catch several glimpses of the hurrying water from atop the high banks. That loop also crosses a covered bridge, from which you can usually see fish hovering in the crystal-clear water. The Wildwood Pathway takes a more direct route, over hillier and more-remote landscape, between the two cable-hung bridges. Several small cutoffs run between the Wildwood and River loops, which allows you to choose jaunts of varying lengths and scenery.

A sandy swimming beach is cupped in the backwaters of the river, and the park is loaded with choice picnic areas. Along the main entrance road, you can stake claims to tables at three different areas: at the beach, well back from the river in the Elm Branch Picnic Area, or in the shadow of the north suspension bridge. For a mini-adventure you can lug picnic basket and blankets across the span and spread out on the shore of the Chippewa where it broadens into a large pool before sweeping under the bridge. An even more out-of-the-way picnic spot borders the river at the south entrance of the park off Winn Road.

A small, primitive campground (no flush toilets or showers) covers part of the north bank of the river only a short walk from either the swimming beach or the north trailhead bridge. A backcountry campground, accessible only by canoeing the river or hiking the River Loop Trail, sits on the east bank about halfway between the two trailheads. Its remoteness ensures a degree of privacy not usually found in downstate campgrounds, and it's also a good testing ground for backpackers who are planning more ambitious trips into the wilds of northern Michigan.

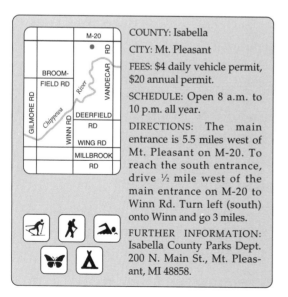

COUNTY: Isabella

CITY: Mt. Pleasant

FEES: $4 daily vehicle permit, $20 annual permit.

SCHEDULE: Open 8 a.m. to 10 p.m. all year.

DIRECTIONS: The main entrance is 5.5 miles west of Mt. Pleasant on M-20. To reach the south entrance, drive ½ mile west of the main entrance on M-20 to Winn Rd. Turn left (south) onto Winn and go 3 miles.

FURTHER INFORMATION: Isabella County Parks Dept. 200 N. Main St., Mt. Pleasant, MI 48858.

Every September the Pine Haven Recreation Area hosts the Mud Creek Crawl, a foot race that Runner's World magazine lists as one of the nation's top 13 Out-of-the-Way Races. So what does that have to do with nature and nature lovers? The reason the magazine rates the race so highly is because of its beautiful and unusual surroundings, and that's of definite interest to hikers and cross country skiers.

Eight wooded trails — with intriguing names like Logger's Flats, Mud Creek Loop, Riverside Ravine, and Oxbow Flats — cut through the dense upland forest of second-growth pine, birch and hardwoods that covers this 325-acre Midland County Park. The generally flat landscape is interrupted by low sand ridges that mark the shoreline of an ancient great lake and also by the narrow flood plain valley of the Salt River and Mud Creek, both of which flow through the park.

The wide, well-marked trails, which range in length from 0.7 to 2.3 miles, are beautiful year round. Wildflowers mat the forest floor in the spring and give way to feathery ferns dappled by shadows in the summer. In the fall the trails are dark lines drawn through an avant-garde canvas of bright color formed by fallen leaves. And in winter, dark, leafless trunks rise out of the snow in sharp contrast to the blanket of white.

With a little imagination, you can combine the eight miles of interconnected pathways into an outing tailored to your skill and stamina. Trail markers indicate degree of difficulty to cross country skiers, and hikers can also use them to determine the amount of exertion required to traverse the various routes. For skiers, green circles identify beginning trails, blue squares mark ones of intermediate level, and black diamonds indicate

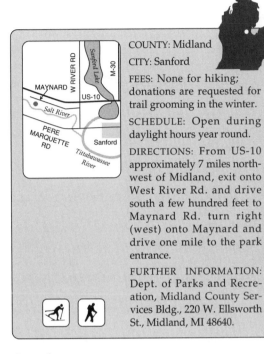

COUNTY: Midland

CITY: Sanford

FEES: None for hiking; donations are requested for trail grooming in the winter.

SCHEDULE: Open during daylight hours year round.

DIRECTIONS: From US-10 approximately 7 miles northwest of Midland, exit onto West River Rd. and drive south a few hundred feet to Maynard Rd. turn right (west) onto Maynard and drive one mile to the park entrance.

FURTHER INFORMATION: Dept. of Parks and Recreation, Midland County Services Bldg., 220 W. Ellsworth St., Midland, MI 48640.

those for experts.

A descriptive brochure that includes a trail map is usually available at the trailhead. A map of the entire system is also posted at the trailhead and at all trail intersections.

176 VETERANS MEMORIAL PARK

Hiding in a small corner of this sprawling Midland County park is one of the state's rarest and most precious natural treasures — one of only four known stands of virgin white pine in the Lower Peninsula. An added plus : It takes little effort to walk among the majestic, awe-inspiring giants that have been reaching for the sky since the presidency of James Monroe.

Just steps from the park entrance, the quarter-mile-long Veterans Memorial Trail plunges into a world untouched by man. The circular, bark-covered path crosses a creek, then borders a deep, narrow ravine. It is on the edge of this ravine that the huge 170-year-old white pine and virgin red pine rise from the needle-strewn ground and punch through a green canopy spread by lesser trees. It's a unique piece of natural architecture, as though the leafy roof is being supported by huge Greek columns. You could walk the trail non-stop in 10 minutes, but that's nearly impossibly once you're amidst the jaw-dropping splendor.

The mile-long Upland Trail, though it bypasses the dramatic virgin pines, does lead to a variety of other interesting natural features as it loops through the park's lower half. The easily walked path crosses a pretty stream, skirts vernal ponds (pools created by melting winter snow and spring rain that dry up in the summer), tunnels through deep woods, and climbs over low sand ridges that mark the shoreline of a prehistoric great lake that preceded present-day Lake Huron.

A self-guiding brochure to both trails is available at the park entrance. Numbered stops along the routes correspond to numbered paragraphs that describe the park's natural features, identify various trees and vegetation, tell the natural history of the area, and explain how man and nature interact. The Veterans Trail has eight stops, and the Upland Trail, with 30 stops, can easily take an hour to walk. You are also free to bushwhack into the completely undeveloped wilderness that makes up the park's northern half.

Picnic tables and grills are widely scattered amid stately hardwoods and pines in the southern half of the park. It's only a short walk from almost any of the picnic sites to the trailheads or also to a canoe launch on the Salt River, which crosses the park's eastern boundary. From that put-in it's only a quarter-mile float to the Salt's juncture with the Tittabawassee River and from there a scenic four-hour paddle to downtown Midland.

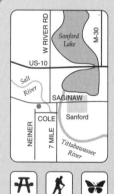

COUNTY: Midland

CITY: Midland

FEES: None

SCHEDULE: Memorial Day to Labor Day, 7 a.m. to dusk; rest of the year, 8 a.m. to dusk.

DIRECTIONS: From US-10 approximately 7 miles northwest of Midland, take the West River Rd. exit and go south on West River Rd. one mile to Saginaw Rd. Turn left (east) onto Saginaw and drive ¼ mile to Seven Mile Rd. Turn right (south) onto Seven Mile and drive ¼ mile to Cole Rd. turn right (west) onto Cole and drive ½ mile to Neiner Rd. turn right (north) onto Neiner and drive one block to the park entrance.

FURTHER INFORMATION: Dept. of Parks and Recreation, Midland County Services Bldg., 220 W. Ellsworth St., Midland, MI 48640.

BULLOCK CREEK NATURE SANCTUARY 177

If you like the freedom to find your own way and not travel the usual well-marked trail, you will enjoy Bullock Creek Nature Sanctuary. Except for a faint path that enters from the east boundary and quickly disappears, no roads or groomed hiking trails scar this 80-acre parcel, and the owner and caretaker, the Michigan Nature Association, cautions that no one should walk here without a compass.

But a careful exploration of this interesting and varied terrain usually will pay dividends. Michigan lily, tufted loosestrife, trillium, bloodroot, buttercup, violets and cardinal flower are just a few of the wildflowers you might see. This is also a good birding area; grosbeaks, flycatchers orioles and warblers are regular nesters. And according to the M.N.A., most of the common Michigan mammals, including badger and beaver, roam the Bullock Creek area.

Bullock Creek itself cuts across the southeastern corner of the sanctuary, and sandy ridges — once part of the shoreline of ancient Saginaw Bay — alternate with low marshy areas throughout the property. All support a wide variety of plant life including burr oak, swamp white oak, hickory, basswood, cottonwood, red maple, black gum, white birch and sassafras. One substantial wet area in the center of the property supports a blueberry/cranberry marsh. You probably will encounter heavy brush and young woods as you enter the sanctuary, and prickly ash seems to be everywhere here, so wear heavy clothing.

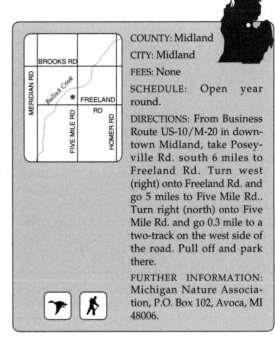

COUNTY: Midland

CITY: Midland

FEES: None

SCHEDULE: Open year round.

DIRECTIONS: From Business Route US-10/M-20 in downtown Midland, take Poseyville Rd. south 6 miles to Freeland Rd. Turn west (right) onto Freeland Rd. and go 5 miles to Five Mile Rd.. Turn right (north) onto Five Mile Rd. and go 0.3 mile to a two-track on the west side of the road. Pull off and park there.

FURTHER INFORMATION: Michigan Nature Association, P.O. Box 102, Avoca, MI 48006.

178 CHIPPEWA NATURE CENTER

The Chippewa Nature Center is the "Cadillac" of Michigan nature centers. In fact, this complex is "one of the finest — if not *the* finest — private nature centers in the *world*," according to a vice-president of the National Audubon Society who visited in the 1970s. Since then the Center has done even more to enhance that reputation.

The Visitor Center alone is worth a visit. Midland's Alden B. Dow, the first Architect Laureate of Michigan, designed the structure, and his influence can certainly be seen and felt in the beautiful brick building, dedicated in 1975. The most striking feature is the River Overlook, a 60-foot-long, glass-walled room that is cantilevered over the Pine River. A fascinating and informative hands-on nature exhibit fills the Naturalist's Challenge, and a museum area features dioramas and displays of the natural and human history of the Saginaw Valley, including Woodland Indian artifacts discovered during archaeological digs on the Center's property. Other facilities include an auditorium, a library, classrooms and a gift shop.

But seclusion, peace and beauty are the hallmarks of Michigan's premier nature center. To fully experience, enjoy and appreciate the 900-acre area, pick up a map at the Visitor Center and take one or more of the well-marked trails, totaling 14 miles, that wind through many and varied habitats. But don't plan to see them all in one day. You'll want to pay return visits to completely appreciate and explore the 700 acres of woodlands, ponds, marshes, and open fields, plus three miles of river frontage along the Pine and Chippewa rivers and their confluence on the Center's northern boundary (visible from the River Overlook). A paved half-mile trail skirts the Pine River, passes a small pond and meanders through pine woods.

Other attractions include a Wetlands Area with three marsh basins, a remnant bog, and two miles of trails to explore. Three carefully and accurately restored log buildings — the 1870 Homestead Farm cabin, schoolhouse and maple sugar house — are open seasonally.

A lineup of more than a dozen standard programs for school groups, weekend and weekday programs for families, adults and children, and a Nature Day Camp summer program for children are just a few of the reasons the National Park Service has cited the Chippewa Nature Center for its outstanding educational accomplishments and designated it as a National Environmental Study Area.

COUNTY: Midland

CITY: Midland

FEES: Free admission to trails, Visitor Center and most programs, except during major festivals.

SCHEDULE: The Visitor Center is open Monday through Friday, 8 a.m. - 5 p.m.; Saturday, 9 a.m. - 5 p.m.; and Sunday 1 p.m. - 5 p.m. The trails are open dawn to dusk daily. The Center is closed Thanksgiving and Christmas.

DIRECTIONS: From Business Rte. US-10 in Midland, take Cronkright St. southwest across the bridge to Poseyville Rd. and follow Poseyville to Ashby Rd. Turn right (west) onto Ashby and drive to Badour Rd. Turn right (north) onto Badour and follow it to its end at the nature center entrance.

Or from M-20, turn south onto Homer Rd. and go one mile to Prairie Rd. Turn left (east) onto Prairie and drive 2 miles.

FURTHER INFORMATION: Chippewa Nature Center, 400 S. Badour Rd. Route 9, Midland, MI 48640.

A wealthy industrialist's home garden has grown to become one of Michigan's most beautiful natural attractions.

In 1899 Herbert H. Dow, founder of the Dow Chemical Company, began Dow Gardens as a hobby in what essentially was his backyard: 10 acres of sandy soil covered by jack pine. Dow approached his hobby seriously. He corresponded with Luther Burbank and other leading horticulturists of his era and, during his lifetime, planted 5,000 fruit trees, including 40 varieties of plums.

After Herbert Dow's death in 1930, his family, through the Hubert H. and Grace A. Dow Foundation, not only cared for but expanded the gardens to its present 110 acres of trees, shrubs, flowering plants, streams, ponds, waterfalls, small footbridges, paths and greenhouse.

Paved paths, including a Sensory Trail for the handicapped or young elementary students, lead through this place of natural beauty and charm. But visitors are encouraged to walk anywhere, including on the grass.

No matter where you walk, you can't help but be impressed with the spectacular variety and number of plantings. Each year, for example, Dow Gardens' staff plants some 15,000 annuals representing more than 450 varieties. A collection of more than 105 different kinds of flowering crab apple trees reflects Herbert Dow's original interest in fruit trees. In mid-May when these crab apples — along with dogwood, lilacs, rhododendrons, azaleas and viburnum — all burst into bloom, the show is dazzling. All plant materials in Dow Gardens are identified for visitors by both common and scientific names.

Because the varied habitat is good for both feeding and nesting, Dow Gardens is also a good birdwatching area.

CALENDAR
OF OUTSTANDING DISPLAYS

JANUARY - FEBRUARY: Witch hazel

MARCH: Spring bulbs

APRIL: Magnolia, spring bulbs

MAY: Crab apples, spring bulbs, rhododendrons, azaleas, viburnum, lilacs

JUNE: Rhododendrons, azaleas, perennials, viburnum, lilacs

JULY: Vegetable gardens, rhododendrons, azaleas, perennials

SEPTEMBER: Perennials

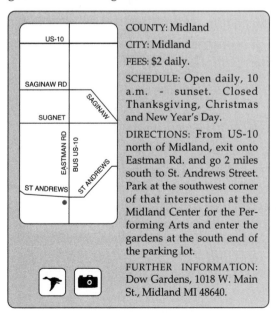

COUNTY: Midland

CITY: Midland

FEES: $2 daily.

SCHEDULE: Open daily, 10 a.m. - sunset. Closed Thanksgiving, Christmas and New Year's Day.

DIRECTIONS: From US-10 north of Midland, exit onto Eastman Rd. and go 2 miles south to St. Andrews Street. Park at the southwest corner of that intersection at the Midland Center for the Performing Arts and enter the gardens at the south end of the parking lot.

FURTHER INFORMATION: Dow Gardens, 1018 W. Main St., Midland MI 48640.

180 NAYANQUING POINT WILDLIFE AREA

The Nayanquing Point Wildlife Area is nearly in the center of a long chain of great birdwatching spots that ring Saginaw Bay in a stretch from Port Crescent to Tawas Point. The exceedingly flat landscape of diked and ditched farm fields, plus marshland, lagoons and the open waters of Saginaw Bay make this an excellent area to observe both shorebirds and waterfowl. Spring and fall migrations are the best time. But in addition to the many migrates that pass through, several species stay here to breed, so birdwatchers are usually rewarded at any time of year. Among the sandpipers, ducks, gulls, hawks and terns, the lucky observer might spot a Dunlin, a Black-bellied Plover, a Tundra Swan or a Black Skimmer.

Parking areas at the end of both Kitchen and Tower Beach roads lead to the area's extensive dike system. You can walk for several miles along these dikes and, in the company of songbirds that continually flit through the bordering thickets, enjoy the sights of gulls soaring overhead, terns hovering then plunging into ditches to retrieve fish, and several different species of heron silently fishing from the dike edges.

Other parking areas are located along both Erickson and Coggins roads.

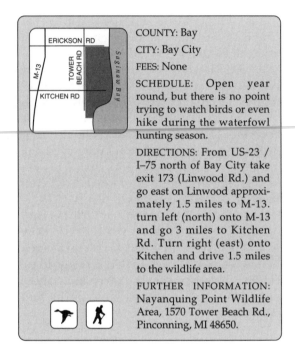

COUNTY: Bay

CITY: Bay City

FEES: None

SCHEDULE: Open year round, but there is no point trying to watch birds or even hike during the waterfowl hunting season.

DIRECTIONS: From US-23 / I–75 north of Bay City take exit 173 (Linwood Rd.) and go east on Linwood approximately 1.5 miles to M-13. turn left (north) onto M-13 and go 3 miles to Kitchen Rd. Turn right (east) onto Kitchen and drive 1.5 miles to the wildlife area.

FURTHER INFORMATION: Nayanquing Point Wildlife Area, 1570 Tower Beach Rd., Pinconning, MI 48650.

FISH POINT WILDLIFE AREA 181

Every spring and fall, migrating waterfowl nearly blacken the skies over the Fish Point Wildlife Area. Another reason this state game area and refuge, on Saginaw Bay just west of Sebewaing, has earned its reputation as one of the state's premier birding spots is that you don't even have to leave your car to enjoy and marvel at the staggering number of birds. In fact, remaining in your vehicle often is an advantage. A slow-moving car does not alarm birds here, whereas walking along the road usually produces the opposite results.

Ringle Road, which marks the western edge of the refuge, is an outstanding spot to observe shorebirds and waterfowl from a moving vehicle at close range. A variety of species communally congregate in a marshy area that hugs the roadside, plus geese and ducks swoop overhead before landing in the open waters a few hundred yards away. The shallow waters of Saginaw Bay adjacent to Fish Point provide other good spots, which are accessible from several roads joining the two areas.

But you don't have to stay in your car to enjoy the area. A 1.1-mile nature trail, cosponsored by the Saginaw Bay Chapter of the Michigan Duck Hunters Association and the DNR, begins at a parking area 0.6 miles north of the headquarters building, follows a dike bordering the Wisconsin Drain, which marks the southern boundary of the refuge, then circles through a cattail marsh.

Waterfowl commonly seen at Fish Point include geese, ducks, grebes and cormorants. Pintails, Redheads, Canvasbacks, Blue- and Green-winged Teal and Northern Shovelers make up most of the duck population, but the area also holds good chances for spotting rare Tundra Swans, Surf Scoters and Oldsquaw Ducks. Shorebirds and songbirds are also

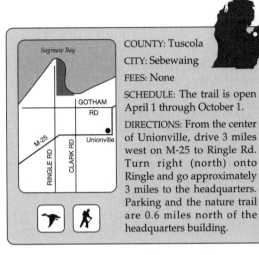

COUNTY: Tuscola

CITY: Sebewaing

FEES: None

SCHEDULE: The trail is open April 1 through October 1.

DIRECTIONS: From the center of Unionville, drive 3 miles west on M-25 to Ringle Rd. Turn right (north) onto Ringle and go approximately 3 miles to the headquarters. Parking and the nature trail are 0.6 miles north of the headquarters building.

plentiful through the area.

Fish Point Wildlife Area, begun with small purchases of land by the state in the 1950s, today totals over 2,000 diked, ditched and flooded acres divided almost equally between refuge and game area.

182 WILDFOWL BAY WILDLIFE AREA

At the Wildfowl Bay Wildlife Area, it almost appears as if man and nature conspired to fashion a near-perfect area to view water and wading birds.

The shallow waters fringing Saginaw Bay have from time immemorial been a gathering place for waterfowl on their annual migrations and provided nesting sites for countless ducks, geese and other waders and waterfowl. But the very habitat that makes the area so attractive for birds — the vast expanse of shallow water and weedy marshes — usually makes for hard and damp slogging for birdwatchers.

But at Wildfowl Bay you can literally drive your car out over the saucer shallow waters of Saginaw Bay and park high and dry in a prime birdwatching area. And if you don't give a hoot for birding, it's still worth a trip for the serene and sublime beauty created by the sometimes indistinct intersection of water and land.

Geiger Road, the route into the area, doesn't end at the shore of Saginaw Bay but continues at least a hundred yards out into the bay on a causeway where it finally comes to a halt at a large DNR parking area and small boat ramp. There, you are virtually surrounded by water. To the west the bay stretches out to where the sky dips to meet the water, with the blue horizon constantly interrupted by lush, green barrier islands. To the north a jumble of islands that are hardly distinct from the marshes crowding their shores cuts off the view of the bay. More open water is visible to the south, and back east down Geiger Road, marshes, small openings of water and wetlands greet the eye. It's not only beautiful, it's waterfowl heaven.

Early October and mid-March through the end of April are the best times for viewing, but a trip here anytime during open water and out-of-hunting season will be rewarding. Coots, terns, geese, ducks (including all three species of mergansers), Black-crowned Night Herons, Common Snipe, Common Gallinules, and grebes all frequent the area. And a lucky few have spotted King Eiders, Bald Eagles, and Brant, White-winged and Black scoters.

Not too shabby a list to spot from the comfort of your car or, if you insist on stretching your legs, a walk of a few dozen steps. Binoculars and a birding book are a must, and a spotting scope will greatly increase your enjoyment. Also bring along a lunch even if you plan on stopping for only a short time, because the birds and the beauty of the surroundings can easily seduce you into spending several hours here.

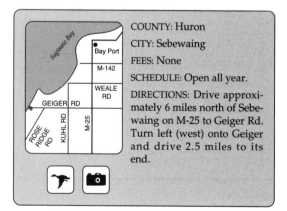

COUNTY: Huron

CITY: Sebewaing

FEES: None

SCHEDULE: Open all year.

DIRECTIONS: Drive approximately 6 miles north of Sebewaing on M-25 to Geiger Rd. Turn left (west) onto Geiger and drive 2.5 miles to its end.

A beech/maple forest untouched for more than 200 years plus a creek, open fields, and a small area of wetlands make up the 173-acre Price Nature Center.

The best way to explore the area is to pick up self-guiding maps and helpful brochures at the information center near the park's entrance, then hike three trails totaling 3.5 miles. Hikers taking the White Oak Trail, named for a nearly 300-year-old tree that towers over the trailhead, have the option of walking a short 0.8-mile or slightly longer one-mile loop through the heart of the park. A trail shelter marks the halfway point of the longer loop.

An elevated boardwalk along the Cottonwood Trail, which branches off the White Oak Trail, crosses the park's wetlands. Portions of this mile-long trail pass through stands of cottonwood and, as on the White Oak Trail, a shelter has been constructed at the halfway point. An observation platform a few hundred yards up a 0.7-mile-long extension of the Cottonwood Trail, known as the Deer Run Trail, is an excellent spot to search for wildlife along the forest edges. Also along Deer Run on spring evenings, woodcocks can sometimes be seen in their courtship-display flights.

Cross country skiers and snowshoers are welcome on all trails in the winter.

Other facilities within the park, operated by the Saginaw County Parks and Recreation Commission, include picnic grounds, a play area and public restrooms.

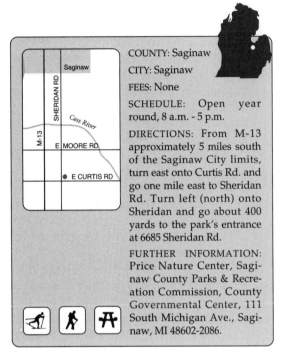

COUNTY: Saginaw

CITY: Saginaw

FEES: None

SCHEDULE: Open year round, 8 a.m. - 5 p.m.

DIRECTIONS: From M-13 approximately 5 miles south of the Saginaw City limits, turn east onto Curtis Rd. and go one mile east to Sheridan Rd. Turn left (north) onto Sheridan and go about 400 yards to the park's entrance at 6685 Sheridan Rd.

FURTHER INFORMATION: Price Nature Center, Saginaw County Parks & Recreation Commission, County Governmental Center, 111 South Michigan Ave., Saginaw, MI 48602-2086.

184 CROW ISLAND STATE GAME AREA

Each year thousands of amateur and hundreds of dedicated birders literally drive right over this excellent birdwatching area without realizing it's there. The high retaining walls of the new Zilwaukee Bridge, which carries I-75/US-23 over the Saginaw River, barely allows a glimpse of the more than 1,000-acre state game area that stretches along the river from the foot of the bridge to Bay City. But the last exit before crossing the bridge from the south leads to a 1.5-mile-long strip of highway M-13, from which you can potentially spot thousands of birds.

The entire Crow Island State Game Area serves as a giant overflow basin for Michigan's largest watershed, and what's not perpetually covered with water is usually wet at some time during the year. M-13 runs along the east bank of the Saginaw River, which divides the preserve into east and west sections. An immense dike circles the 300-plus-acre east unit, which consists mostly of a huge cattail sedge, marsh and occasional open ponds. Public access is not permitted in that area, which is just as well since walking there would be impossible. But the wide

shoulders of M-13 make a great platform for birding. And don't direct all your attention to the marsh, because the river attracts more than its fair share of birds.

An astonishing number of waterfowl and shorebirds stop over, feed and nest in the state game area. Gulls and terns seem ever-present, and you can often spot ducks and geese by the hundreds. Wood ducks, American Black ducks, Mallards, Blue-winged Teal, Northern Pintails, Gadwall, Canvasbacks, Green-winged Teal, and Redhead, Bufflehead and Ruddy ducks are all commonly sighted. Tundra Swans make biannual stops in spring and fall, and Ospreys Bald Eagles, Northern Harriers and Red-shouldered Hawks pay occasional visits. Among the shorebirds that frequent the marshy fringes are Black-crowned Night Herons, American Bitterns, Great Egrets, Great Blue Herons, Green Herons, Willets, Snowy Egrets, Soras and Virginia Rails.

That's not a bad day of birding without ever having to leave your car. The best times, of course, for spotting the greatest number and variety are during spring and fall migrations.

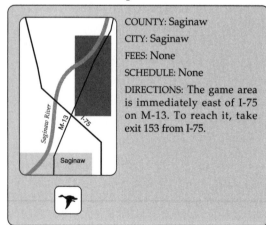

COUNTY: Saginaw

CITY: Saginaw

FEES: None

SCHEDULE: None

DIRECTIONS: The game area is immediately east of I-75 on M-13. To reach it, take exit 153 from I-75.

IMERMAN MEMORIAL PARK 185

Imerman Memorial Park combines the best features of an old-fashioned county park with those of a new multifacility recreation area. And what's more, it's a great place for nature lovers.

Its clean, well-maintained picnic grounds are the kind that city folks have chosen for generations as a place to enjoy an outdoor meal. Tables and grills are widely spaced across a sprawling, sun-drenched lawn, and families and other large groups can spread out around a chosen spot without crowding others or being crowded.

Those who want more than a traditional summer picnic have an almost unlimited choice of year-round facilities including baseball diamonds, a large children's playground, basketball courts, canoe rentals, a boat launching ramp, a fishing dock, a volleyball court, shuffleboard courts, tennis courts, horseshoe pits and cross country ski trails.

You can also enjoy a quiet, solitary experience with nature by walking the Floodplain Forest Trail, a 1.25-mile self-guiding nature/hiking path that circles the entire park. Eight stops along the route are keyed to an interpretive booklet, available at the park entrance, that explains how forest regeneration, wildlife, and the work of natural forces all affect the park's landscape. For instance, the entire trail lies in the flood plain of the Tittabawassee River, and seasonal floods in spring and fall occasionally place the trail and park at the bottom of a suddenly expanded river.

For more than half its distance, the trail borders the historic Tittabawassee. In the 1800s, this river, which flowed through an area rich in pine forests, served as a water highway for transporting millions of logs to sawmills that line the Saginaw River. Old pil-

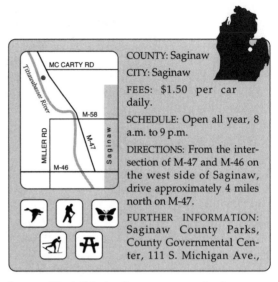

COUNTY: Saginaw

CITY: Saginaw

FEES: $1.50 per car daily.

SCHEDULE: Open all year, 8 a.m. to 9 p.m.

DIRECTIONS: From the intersection of M-47 and M-46 on the west side of Saginaw, drive approximately 4 miles north on M-47.

FURTHER INFORMATION: Saginaw County Parks, County Governmental Center, 111 S. Michigan Ave.,

ings, still visible in the water, are the last remnants of massive booms that collected the logs before they were floated to the mills and turned into lumber.

The park's variety of habitat and cover — which includes open meadows, a grove of giant cottonwoods, dense brush, moving water, and many areas of transition from woods to fields — attracts numerous birds and should prove fruitful to birdwatchers.

The river's water quality has improved in recent years and so has the fishing. Spring and fall anglers pull walleyes from the water, and white bass, channel catfish and bullheads provide the majority of the action the rest of the year.

Cross country skiers glide around the park on two trails in the winter, and recreation and nature programs are conducted at Imerman throughout the year.

186 SHIAWASSEE NATIONAL WILDLIFE REFUGE

A staggering number of birds visit the Shiawassee National Wildlife Refuge every spring and fall. Twenty-five thousand Canada geese (including Snow and Blue geese), 30,000 ducks (including Mallards, Teal, Wigeons, Mergansers, and Black, Pintail and Wood ducks), plus upwards of 500 Tundra Swans annually stop over here. A bird checklist available at the headquarters lists 246 species — including hawks, shorebirds, warblers and sparrows — that frequent or nest in the 9,000-acre area. An additional 29 species are listed as rare or accidental visitors, and most summers the refuge is home to a pair of nesting eagles.

Peak migration times for waterfowl are March, April, and September through November. Many, however, arrive as early as February on their way north and pass through on their return journey as late as December. The earlier you arrive in the spring, the better your chances are of seeing larger concentrations.

Located at the confluence of four rivers that drain one-sixth of the Lower Peninsula and form the Saginaw River, the area has always been a gathering place for waterfowl. To preserve and protect them from the surrounding, rapidly encroaching heavy agricultural and industrial development, the U.S. Fish and Wildlife Service formally established the Shiawassee National Wildlife Refuge in 1953.

The hand of man is still very much evident in preserving and maintaining this haven. Diked pools are mechanically flooded to add to the natural habitat of bayous, flood plains, shallow marshes, bottomland hardwoods and grasses. And local farmers — who raise corn, wheat, barley and soybeans on 1,200 acres of refuge land — by agreement leave a third of their crops standing as food for the wildlife.

The same conditions that attract hordes of birds also appeal to other wildlife. It's rare, for example, not to see white-tail deer, muskrats and woodchucks during a hike. Red fox and raccoons are also common but not so easily spotted. And though you probably won't see the reclusive beaver, many conically cut saplings and small stumps along the bayous and ponds confirms its presence here.

Access to the refuge comes from the Ferguson Bayou and Woodland nature trails. The Ferguson Bayou Trail (the most heavily used) begins at the end of Curtis Road and loops for 4.5 miles alongside large pools and extensive swamps atop a system of dikes. (Even the dikes, however, have been under water some springs). At the halfway point an observation tower equipped with a 10X spotting scope overlooks a vast panorama of farm units, pools and marshes. In spring and fall, the number of birds within view from this deck boggles the mind. Both good birding and scenery also come from a shorter 1.5-mile

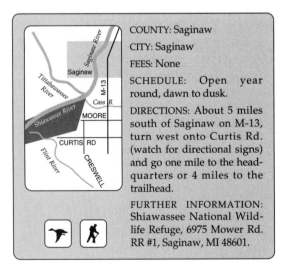

COUNTY: Saginaw

CITY: Saginaw

FEES: None

SCHEDULE: Open year round, dawn to dusk.

DIRECTIONS: About 5 miles south of Saginaw on M-13, turn west onto Curtis Rd. (watch for directional signs) and go one mile to the headquarters or 4 miles to the trailhead.

FURTHER INFORMATION: Shiawassee National Wildlife Refuge, 6975 Mower Rd. RR #1, Saginaw, MI 48601.

Hikers who arrive at the Green Point Environmental Learning Center in the spring might discover a feature unique to this 76-acre area. Because it lies in the flood plain of the Tittabawassee River, its entire trail system is occasionally under water. Though you can't hike during those brief spring periods, you still can observe the Center's interesting ecosystem from the comfort of an interpretive building constructed well above the highest flood level. While inside, also take a look at the exhibits, live animals, and a wildlife feeding station.

Green Point is home to a variety of animals (including a large number of mosquitoes during the summer, so bring insect repellent) and plants. The periodic floodings ensure a nutrient-rich soil for vegetation and determine what kinds of plants grow here. Plants that can stand wet conditions thrive. Common trees such as white pine and paper birch, on the other hand, are absent because they cannot tolerate standing for long periods in two-foot-deep water.

The Shiawassee National Wildlife Refuge, which operates Green Point, is located just across the river to the south and no doubt contributes to the 133 species of birds that appear on the Center's checklist available at the interpretive building. For best birding, visit during spring and fall migrations.

Seven trails, totaling 2.5 miles, are as varied as the habitat — including two ponds, a marsh, open fields, a young forest, and riverbanks — they wander through. An excellent view of the marsh's wildlife comes from a blind built along another path. Maps are available at the interpretive building, and during the winter months, the trails are open for cross country skiing.

Green Point also hosts a wide variety of nature classes for children.

loop along the inner dike system. The trailhead for both loops is about 200 yards north of the parking lot, and an informative guide and map are usually available there.

The Woodland Trail lies on the north side of the refuge. (To reach it, drive west out of Saginaw on M-46 to Center Road. Turn south onto Center and drive approximately two miles to Stroebel Road. Turn left onto Stroebel and enter the refuge parking lot.) Most of this four-mile-long trail passes through bottom and forest-type habitat and has a different "look" than the Ferguson Bayou Trail. This route is excellent for songbird observations and also has a 1.5-mile short loop.

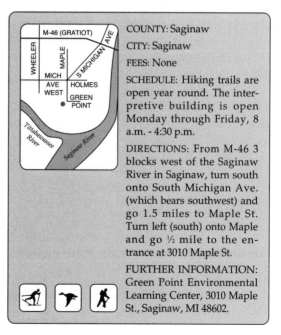

COUNTY: Saginaw

CITY: Saginaw

FEES: None

SCHEDULE: Hiking trails are open year round. The interpretive building is open Monday through Friday, 8 a.m. - 4:30 p.m.

DIRECTIONS: From M-46 3 blocks west of the Saginaw River in Saginaw, turn south onto South Michigan Ave. (which bears southwest) and go 1.5 miles to Maple St. Turn left (south) onto Maple and go ½ mile to the entrance at 3010 Maple St.

FURTHER INFORMATION: Green Point Environmental Learning Center, 3010 Maple St., Saginaw, MI 48602.

188 HARTLEY OUTDOOR EDUCATION CENTER

Although this 200-acre Saginaw Intermediate School District nature center's primary function is to serve as an outdoor classroom and learning center for students, the general public is also more than welcome to stop by and explore this beautiful facility on weekends.

From the central activities building — which houses four classrooms, a dining room and a student dormitory — nearly a dozen trails fan out through the marshes, lowland forests, ponds, creek, open meadows and upland forest that make up the preserve. A combination of asphalt, woodchip, cinder, and bare-earth trails plus extensive boardwalks lead to virtually every corner of the sanctuary. The lengthy routes make for a variety of beautiful and enjoyable walks. One winding asphalt route is handicap accessible.

The area, which shelters a wide variety of flora and fauna, is also rich in human history, and along the trails you'll see a coal mine that operated from 1896 to 1936, an authentic reproduction of an Indian village, and a 100-year-old pioneer cabin.

The diversity of habitat plus spillover from a huge wetlands that rings the preserve are reasons that an estimated 200-plus species of birds have been sighted in the area. Spotting, photographing and detailed study of the birds is easy and comfortable from four blinds that have been strategically placed along the trails to overlook a pond, a creek, a woods and a meadow.

Guided tours, including a Bluebird walk, are available but must be scheduled in advance. Phone (517) 865-6295.

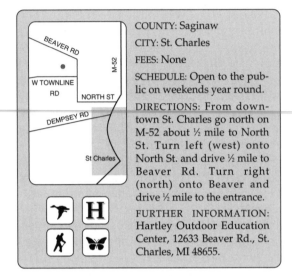

COUNTY: Saginaw

CITY: St. Charles

FEES: None

SCHEDULE: Open to the public on weekends year round.

DIRECTIONS: From downtown St. Charles go north on M-52 about ½ mile to North St. Turn left (west) onto North St. and drive ½ mile to Beaver Rd. Turn right (north) onto Beaver and drive ½ mile to the entrance.

FURTHER INFORMATION: Hartley Outdoor Education Center, 12633 Beaver Rd., St. Charles, MI 48655.

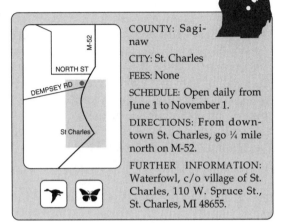

Waterfowl are some of Michigan's most beautiful birds, and their exquisite form, color and markings breed two insatiable obsessions. Once you get hooked on pursuing them with binoculars, you want to see more of them, and you want to see them up close. At the St. Charles Waterfowl Observatory, you can satisfy those passions.

There, from a 50-foot-diameter gazebo that encloses a small circular pond fed by a waterfall and surrounded by a covered walkway, you can sketch, photograph and study some of nature's most beautiful handiwork only a few feet away. Attached to the gazebo is a large, fenced-in breeding area where up to 30 pairs of waterfowl — including Canada Geese, Northern Shovelers, Wood Ducks, Green-wing Teal, and Pintail and Harlequin ducks — move among small pools and native Michigan plants. An especially interesting time to visit is during the spring breeding season, when the males preen and strut their stuff before the females. Decoy carvers find the observatory especially helpful in capturing the small details of waterfowl in wood.

The observatory, which sits on the west bank of the Bad River near downtown St. Charles, is surrounded by a vest-pocket-size area that is managed as a demonstration project for improving a wildlife habitat. A short wood-chip-covered trail slips past the gazebo through that parcel of natural plantings to the river's edge.

COUNTY: Saginaw

CITY: St. Charles

FEES: None

SCHEDULE: Open daily from June 1 to November 1.

DIRECTIONS: From downtown St. Charles, go ¼ mile north on M-52.

FURTHER INFORMATION: Waterfowl, c/o village of St. Charles, 110 W. Spruce St., St. Charles, MI 48655.

190 RINGWOOD FOREST

Man and nature forged a unique alliance to present us with unforgettable beauty at this 160-acre Saginaw County park. Like much of the Saginaw Valley, this tract of land along the south branch of the Bad River was denuded of trees during the heyday of the lumbering era. But the children of the loggers who clear-cut the land here must have mourned the passing of the great trees, because in 1883 they began replanting the area. The result of this unusual love of land and foresight (it was one of the first reforestation projects in the state) is a lush, dark and almost mystical woods laced with miles of winding trails.

You can pick from six routes, which range from a gentle 0.4-mile round-trip stroll to 3.5 miles of up and down walking over the entire system. All trails start at the park's tree-shrouded picnic area.

Easily the most memorable trail is Spruce Alley, which follows a logging road through a virtual canyon formed by rows of giant spruce that line the path. Planted in 1883 by the son of Eleazer J. Ring, who first cleared the land, the trees are now among the oldest of their kind in Michigan.

Spruce Alley leads to Lumberjack Loop, a 1.1-mile trail that circles through the heart of the park. The route passes two scenic overlooks of the Bad River, and 14 numbered posts along the trail correspond to numbered paragraphs in an interpretive brochure that details the area's rich natural and human history. The pamphlet, available at the picnic grounds, also includes a handy identification key to 22 kinds of trees found in the park.

Other trails meander through the far reaches of the park. The longest route, the 1.8-mile Witch Hazel Trail, slips through a vast swamp and river flood plain before crossing the Bad River and climbing to higher ground.

At the picnic grounds, a stand of towering pines looms over the small pavilion, grills and tables, and the trees' fragrance will mix with the aroma of almost anything you cook.

A canoe launch site and bank fishing spots on the Bad River are only a short walk from the picnic area.

When snow flies, the trails here turn into some of the most demanding and beautiful cross country ski routes in the area.

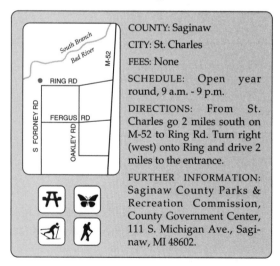

COUNTY: Saginaw

CITY: St. Charles

FEES: None

SCHEDULE: Open year round, 9 a.m. - 9 p.m.

DIRECTIONS: From St. Charles go 2 miles south on M-52 to Ring Rd. Turn right (west) onto Ring and drive 2 miles to the entrance.

FURTHER INFORMATION: Saginaw County Parks & Recreation Commission, County Government Center, 111 S. Michigan Ave., Saginaw, MI 48602.

UPPER PENINSULA

HORSESHOE BAY WILDERNESS 191

Only minutes away from the hoopla and hype of the tourist attractions of Mackinaw City, St. Ignace and Mackinac Island is one of the best kept secrets of the Straits area. The Horseshoe Bay Wilderness Area lies within hailing distance of I-75 just six miles north of St. Ignace, but this section of the Hiawatha National Forest — with its seven miles of pristine Lake Huron beach and thousands of acres of swamp and forest — appears much as it did during the era of explorers and fur trappers. Though parts of the area were logged near the turn of the century, little evidence remains of the lumberjacks' efforts, and the land has been virtually untouched since their passing.

Inland, the area is marked by low, forested ridges and dense cedar swamps, where deer like to winter. While the forest and swamps are pretty, the lakeshore is stunning. From the edge of the tree line on the southern third of the seven miles of lake frontage, the soft, brown sand extends for as much as 50 yards before it dips into Lake Huron. Driftwood lies scattered, there are a few stretches of cobblestone, and except for a lone house visible far to the south on Rabbit Back Point, the beach is a limitless expanse of sand devoid of human intrusion. The northern two-thirds of the lakefront varies from marshy to rocky, and the entire beach is frequently backed by shallow interdunal ponds.

Access into the area is on the one-mile-long Horseshoe Bay Hiking Trail, which begins at the north end of Foley Creek National Forest Campground and breaks out of the woods onto the two-mile stretch of sandy beach. It's a long way to lug a cooler and beach chairs, but day-hikers can tote a small backpack and set off for a memorable day of exploring, beachcombing and playing in the surf. The easily walked trail crosses the cedar swamps on long strings of railroad ties and passes over low ridges, where young evergreens crowd the path. Moss and unusual ferns cover much of the ground, morel mushrooms peek out from the forest floor in spring, and if you look closely, you might see insect-eating pitcher plants. Though the old trail has been well-worn by many years of use, you'll still usually see more deer tracks than human footprints.

The undisturbed wilderness also shelters bear, coyote, otter, mink, eagles, osprey, Great Blue Herons, gulls, shorebirds and numerous ducks.

The rustic (no flush toilets or electricity) Foley Creek Campground, on the southern edge of the wilderness tract, is one of the finest camping spots in the entire Straits area. All sites are heavily shaded, widely spaced, and screened by trees and shrubs.

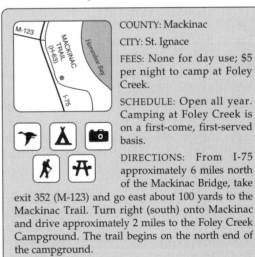

COUNTY: Mackinac

CITY: St. Ignace

FEES: None for day use; $5 per night to camp at Foley Creek.

SCHEDULE: Open all year. Camping at Foley Creek is on a first-come, first-served basis.

DIRECTIONS: From I-75 approximately 6 miles north of the Mackinac Bridge, take exit 352 (M-123) and go east about 100 yards to the Mackinac Trail. Turn right (south) onto Mackinac and drive approximately 2 miles to the Foley Creek Campground. The trail begins on the north end of the campground.

FURTHER INFORMATION: Hiawatha National Forest, St. Ignace Ranger District. St. Ignace, MI 49781.

192 SAND DUNES CROSS COUNTRY SKI TRAIL

This trail — a network of seven loops, which fit together like pieces of a jigsaw puzzle — is best known for its great cross country skiing on its regularly groomed tracks. But if you like to hike paths that are not compacted to the hardness of concrete by countless footfalls, you should set foot on this seldom-used complex of trails in the Hiawatha National Forest.

The hiking possibilities seem endless. Twenty hikers could start from the trailhead, which in the 1930s was the site of a Civilian Conservation Corps camp, and not follow the same route. Or better yet, one hiker could return 20 times and not follow his or her same footsteps.

The loops, ranging in length from 1.5 to 12.3 miles, wind through and across a series of old, wooded dunes. The trails pass under hushed hardwood forests thick with an understory of young trees and ferns, cut through a stand of red pines planted by the CCC in 1935, climb steep hills, follow old two-tracks, and cross open country. The trail's light summer use is especially apparent where it knifes through knee-high weeds and grasses, with only a thin fold in the foliage showing where others have passed. For that reason and the constant company of mosquitoes, you should wear long pants. Blue trail markers plus maps posted at every trail intersection help keep you oriented.

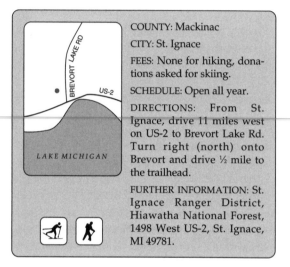

COUNTY: Mackinac

CITY: St. Ignace

FEES: None for hiking, donations asked for skiing.

SCHEDULE: Open all year.

DIRECTIONS: From St. Ignace, drive 11 miles west on US-2 to Brevort Lake Rd. Turn right (north) onto Brevort and drive ½ mile to the trailhead.

FURTHER INFORMATION: St. Ignace Ranger District, Hiawatha National Forest, 1498 West US-2, St. Ignace, MI 49781.

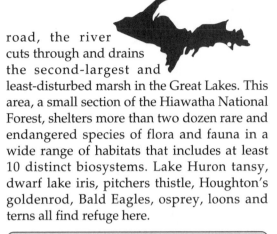

For 11 miles northwest of the Straits of Mackinac, US-2 and Lake Michigan flirt with motorists. The highway borders the northern reaches of Lake Michigan, and the great lake and its magnificent shoreline tease westbound traffic with peek-a-boo glimpses of stunning scenery. For brief stretches the highway runs alongside the beach, but before you can get your fill of the view, the road coyly strays inland or the lake hides behind tree lines or low dunes. When the highway cuts across the tip of Pointe Aux Chenes, about 10 miles west of the Straits, the lake is lost to view for over a mile as US-2 sets motorists up for a spectacular unveiling. The highway curves north along the west side of the stubby headland and then stretches out almost as straight as a guywire. For the next five glorious miles, US-2 borders one of the most beautiful and accessible beaches on Lake Michigan.

The blond ribbon of sand and limitless expanse of emerald-blue water compels even the hurried 55-mph traveler to stop, and there's plenty of room on the wide shoulder to safely pull off the highway. The wide, sandy beach begins at the very shoulder of the road and gently slopes down to the wave-lapped shore, where you can stake out a claim to a piece of sand as a base for beachcombing, sunbathing, and wading in the surf.

Across the road from the beach, low dunes rise toward the interior. Next to the road there, wildflowers and dune grasses sprinkle the sand, and stunted birches and evergreens cover the upper foreslopes of the dunes.

And there is more in this area than readily meets the eye. At about the halfway point on the five-mile beach, the Pointe Aux Chenes River flows into the big lake through a series of tortuous curves. On the inland side of the

road, the river cuts through and drains the second-largest and least-disturbed marsh in the Great Lakes. This area, a small section of the Hiawatha National Forest, shelters more than two dozen rare and endangered species of flora and fauna in a wide range of habitats that includes at least 10 distinct biosystems. Lake Huron tansy, dwarf lake iris, pitchers thistle, Houghton's goldenrod, Bald Eagles, osprey, loons and terns all find refuge here.

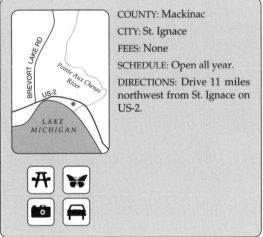

COUNTY: Mackinac

CITY: St. Ignace

FEES: None

SCHEDULE: Open all year.

DIRECTIONS: Drive 11 miles northwest from St. Ignace on US-2.

194 CARP RIVER

The 10,000-acre Carp River Wilderness Area (sometimes called the Mackinac Wilderness Area) is not for the faint-hearted or first-time outdoorsman. There are no marked trails into the area and no potable water. And don't even think about setting foot in the woods here unless you have excellent orientation skills, a compass and a topographical map. Depending on your enthusiasm, or lack of same, for exploring wild areas, Carp River is either that good or that bad.

Around the turn of the century, loggers stripped the area, and fires turned to cinder what little the lumberjacks left. But since then nature has reclaimed the land with a vengeance, and a dense 60- to 80-year-old second-growth forest now blankets a terrain of low sand ridges and wetlands. The Carp River, which dominates the wilderness here, flows in tight curves through the center of the tract, and numerous small trout streams lace the entire area.

Northern hardwoods dotted with stands of birch and aspen cover the generally higher ground of the parcel's north half. The south half is nearly impenetrable due to marshes and bogs. Several beaver dams have flooded even more acreage.

Though inhospitable to man, animals thrive in the area. Osprey, Sandhill Cranes, Great Blue Herons, Pine Martins, Pileated Woodpeckers, mink, muskrats, Ruffed Grouse, raccoons, deer and black bear all reside here.

Except by canoeing the Carp River, the only way into the area is on foot over old roads, faint two-tracks and narrow trails. None of the routes are marked or posted, but some are shown on a topographical map available from the U.S. Forest Service in Escanaba for $3. The easiest access is via a trail that heads east from M-123 a half mile north of where the highway crosses the Carp River. This trail also allows the tenderfoot a taste of the wilderness, because for the first mile or so, the overgrown two-track is easy to follow and no other trails branch off. The track cuts through a dense forest with vegetation sometimes so thick you can't see 20 feet into the woods. Majestic clumps of white birch line the footway, and once away from the highway, the only sound you'll hear is your own passage through the forest. Other access points into the wilderness are widely scattered along forest roads 3450, 3119 and 3122, which border the area's south, east and north sides.

You can backcountry camp here, but you are asked to follow low-impact, no-trace practices. That means setting up at least 100 feet from any trail or water, preferably using a self-contained gas or sterno stove, and packing out all garbage that you can't burn.

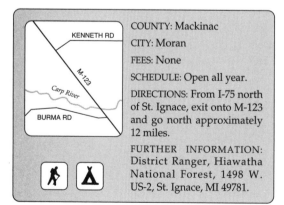

COUNTY: Mackinac

CITY: Moran

FEES: None

SCHEDULE: Open all year.

DIRECTIONS: From I-75 north of St. Ignace, exit onto M-123 and go north approximately 12 miles.

FURTHER INFORMATION: District Ranger, Hiawatha National Forest, 1498 W. US-2, St. Ignace, MI 49781.

PURPLE CONEFLOWER 195
PLANT PRESERVE

On a seemingly insignificant clearing surrounded by the Hiawatha National Forest is one of Michigan's most-puzzling botanical mysteries. North from Moran on highway M-123, the forest crowds both sides of the road for mile after mile. Then, on the site of the old ghost town of Kenneth, about halfway between Moran and Trout Lake, the forest draws back about 150 yards from the road for a half-mile stretch. The ghost town isn't a mystery. But the plant that blooms there late every summer — the purple coneflower — sure is.

By all rhyme and reason of nature, the purple coneflower should not survive in the inhospitable environment of the Upper Peninsula, some 25 miles north of the Mackinac Bridge. It is native to the Great Plains and thrives in Texas, Oklahoma, Kansas, and in a few spots in the dry grass plains of Illinois and Minnesota. Yet from late summer to first frost, this 21-acre clearing owned by the Michigan Nature Association is covered by a blanket of royal purple. The large, daisy-like blooms feature a deep-purple center, with swept-back rays or petals that vary in color intensity and hue from rosy brown to reddish purple. The flowers are at their peak of brilliance during the first two weeks of August.

A wide variety of other wildflowers and grasses dot the area, and the sanctuary is worth a stop any time of the year. In June, for instance, yellow lady's slippers put on an impressive display in the meadow that once held a town. Old foundations of a saloon and general store lurk at the northern end of the property. And rising from the flowers in the southwest corner, a rock the size of a car stands lonely vigil over the spot where the babies of Kenneth were buried.

No foot trails crease the meadow, and you are free to roam at will. But watch where you step, to cause as little harm as possible to both the plant life and yourself. Bedrock nudges out of the ground throughout the preserve where the thin layer of topsoil has eroded away. The low, flat expanse of rock shows the effects of centuries of erosion. Cracks and crevasses as large as a foot wide and four feet deep run through the stone, and you could easily twist an ankle with a wrong step.

The bedrock, only a couple of inches to a couple of feet under the topsoil, further compounds the coneflower mystery. On the prairie the flower sends a tap root seven to eight feet into the earth. Here that is impossible. How the flower got here and how it survives will probably forever remain a puzzle.

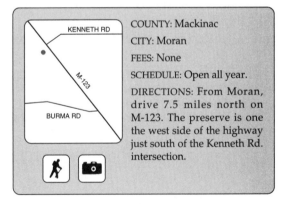

KENNETH RD

M-123

BURMA RD

COUNTY: Mackinac

CITY: Moran

FEES: None

SCHEDULE: Open all year.

DIRECTIONS: From Moran, drive 7.5 miles north on M-123. The preserve is one the west side of the highway just south of the Kenneth Rd. intersection.

196 CUT RIVER BRIDGE

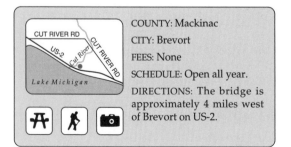

At 55 mph the view from the 641-foot-long Cut River Bridge is beautiful but brief. The cantilevered span, about four miles west of Brevort, carries US-2 over a deep gorge that the appropriately named river has chiseled from a high bluff overlooking Lake Michigan. The highway runs along the edge of the bluff, parallel to and about 100 yards back from the beach, and motorists crossing the bridge have a grandstand view of the lake 159 feet below.

You can get a longer and closer look at the scenery from two roadside parking lots, one at each end of the bridge, plus a trail that descends to the river. At the parking lot at the east end of the bridge, a picturesque, heavily shaded picnic area spreads over a thick, grassy lawn. From the picnic area, a paved footpath hugs the lip of the gorge as it passes just under the bridge's superstructure, then drops to the bottom of the bluff. The steep trail alternates between sharply inclined pavement, manmade stairs, and steps cut right into the hillside. Outstanding examples of mature white pine and red pine line the trail, and labels identify each species.

From the bottom of the bluff, it's only a few yards walk along the river to the lakeshore. The river cuts through pillow-soft sand on its last rush to Lake Michigan, and kids love to play civil engineer by trying to rechannel the water. From the bottom of the bluff, the trail turns inland and leads along the east bank of the river, passes under the bridge, and after about 100 yards, climbs back up to the picnic area.

You can also take in the sights from the middle of the bridge on a pedestrian walkway that crosses the span. The view is thrilling, and so is the feeling of being less than a yard away, separated only by the width of a guardrail, from cars whizzing by at highway speeds. And if you get caught on the bridge when a semi-truck and trailer crosses, the swaying and vibration may be more memorable than the view.

COUNTY: Mackinac

CITY: Brevort

FEES: None

SCHEDULE: Open all year.

DIRECTIONS: The bridge is approximately 4 miles west of Brevort on US-2.

FOX RIVER PATHWAY 197

Ernest Hemingway liked this area so much that he wrote a short story about it. Today, on the little-known and seldom-used Fox River Pathway, experienced backpackers can enjoy beautiful scenery and adventure little-changed from when the famous author visited 75 years ago.

Hemingway made his backpacking, trout-fishing trip to the Fox River in 1919 or 1920, while he recovered from war wounds. The trip provided the inspiration for one of his famous Nick Adams stories, "The Big Two-hearted River." The fact that there is a Two Hearted River not too far from the Fox confused Hemingway fans for awhile, but the author, in a letter to his father in 1925, identified the Fox River trip as the source of his story.

The area had gained some notoriety even before Hemingway's story. During the white-pine boom of the late 1800s, Seney — largely because of a national (and at least partially fabricated) expose of the city's prostitution, white-slavery operations, saloons and shady boom-town characters — became known as "Hell Town U.S.A." The main street of Seney was, in fact, at the time lined with 21 saloons and punctuated at both ends with competing brothels.

Today, the 27.5-mile Fox River Pathway begins near Seney, but backpackers passing through the peaceful village can only try to conjure up a mental image of the Seney of the last century.

The strenuous three- to four-day hike to Kingston Lake State Forest Campground, four miles short of Pictured Rocks National Lakeshore, begins at the Seney Township Campground, on the Fox River just north of town. Twenty-one numbered stops along the route mark out forest-management projects,

remnants of the logging era and other points of interest. Still visible along the Pathway, for example, are the foundations of a lumber camp, an abandoned logging railroad, traces of a winter ice road and ruts left by the big wheels used to move logs during the summer months. Farther up the trail, a turn-of-the-century logging dam still holds back the waters of Stanley Lake. And near the end of the trail on the Kingston Plains, hundreds of white-pine stumps jut from the ground as a memorial to the great trees.

The path never wanders far from the Fox River, which, as Hemingway discovered, is an excellent trout stream. Numerous stands of jack pine — a natural-succession tree left in the wake of lumbering and the almost inevitable forest fires of that era — line the trail. The path also passes by red-pine plantations and, near Stanley Lake, a wild-blueberry management area that is regularly burned to stimulate new growth and improve picking. Camping is permitted at the Fox River State Forest Campground.

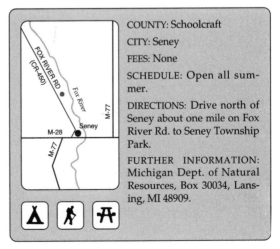

COUNTY: Schoolcraft

CITY: Seney

FEES: None

SCHEDULE: Open all summer.

DIRECTIONS: Drive north of Seney about one mile on Fox River Rd. to Seney Township Park.

FURTHER INFORMATION: Michigan Dept. of Natural Resources, Box 30034, Lansing, MI 48909.

198 SENEY NATIONAL WILDLIFE REFUGE

About 100 years ago, humans began assaulting the vast Upper Peninsula area of marshes, rivers, pools, creeks, sandy ridges and bogs known as the Great Manistique swamp. After nearly 50 years of exploitation, parcel after disfigured parcel was then abandoned. But careful and patient reconstruction and rehabilitation by state and federal agencies brought the area back to life, then returned it to nature's grand design as the Seney Wildlife Refuge.

And life has been more than just restored at Seney — it thrives there. Over 200 species of birds, for example, have been spotted in the 95,000-acre refuge, and it is now recognized as one of the best birding spots in the Upper Peninsula. Mallards, Black Ducks, Ring-necked Ducks, Common and Hooded mergansers, Blue-winged Teal and Wood Ducks nest in the area, and snipe regularly feed along the pool edges. Pileated Woodpeckers, warblers, sparrows, Kingfishers and several species of grouse also help fill the bird checklist available at the Visitor's Center. And beaver, black bear, otter, muskrat, fox, mink coyote and the rare Eastern timber wolf are among 50 species of mammals that call the refuge home.

In short, Seney today is much like it was for centuries before lumbermen invaded the area in the late 19th century and nearly clear-cut

the magnificent stands of white pine. Deliberate and accidental fires razed the timber barons' slashings, and a development company later drained the land and sold it to farmers. But nothing grew in the poor soil, so parcel by parcel, as discouraged farmers failed to pay their taxes and left, the land reverted to the state.

In 1935, at the urging of the Michigan Conservation Department, the federal government took over the land and created the Seney National Wildlife Refuge. Crews from the Civilian Conservation Corps and other Depression-era agencies moved in to begin the extensive restoration work. They constructed roads, drainage ditches, dikes and an elaborate water-control system, all of which in turn created 7,000 acres of open water in 21 major pools to attract and shelter waterfowl.

A captive flock of Canadian Geese were released, and the goslings born to them were allowed to migrate south in the fall. The next spring, they returned. In 1936, for the first time in decades, geese had come back to Seney, and they have done so each spring since. By 1944 a firmly established flock thrived in the refuge, and today their descendants — adults and goslings, all looking for handouts — act as unofficial hosts at the Visitors Center parking lot.

Man did not perform restorative surgery on the entire parcel, however, and 25,000 acres have remained untouched since the logging era. Within this wilderness area, low, sandy dunes created by prehistoric glaciers have been formed by the wind into long ribbon-like ridges. Lines of these brush- and tree-covered ridges run like parallel islands through the sections of the wilderness but particularly at 9,500 acres known as Strangmoor Bog, which because of its unique character has been designated a Registered National Landmark.

Plan to spend two hours to a full day here. A good place to start is on the Marshland Wildlife Drive, a seven-mile auto tour that begins near the Visitors Center, then winds through the eastern edge of the refuge on one-way roads past panoramic views of the marshland and manmade pools. Feel free to park your car anywhere along the drive where there is room to pull off. And you may want to do it often, as excellent views of Great Blue Herons, Sandhill Cranes and many other shorebirds and waterfowl seem to come at every turn. Bald Eagles, too, nest in the refuge, and during the drive you normally can spot the one of at least two nests that is usually active. Plan to spend at least an hour on the drive.

You can get more intimate views of the refuge from the 1.4-mile Pine Ridge Nature Trail, which starts to the right of the Visitors Center, circles one of the smaller pools, passes through a wooded area, then skirts a larger pool before returning to the parking lot.

Exhibits and displays at the Visitors Center (almost worth a trip in itself) illustrate and explain the history of northern forests and the refuge as well as the principles and purposes of wildlife management at Seney.

Each year 50,000 people — many of whom go out of their way — visit this fascinating living attraction created by man and nature.

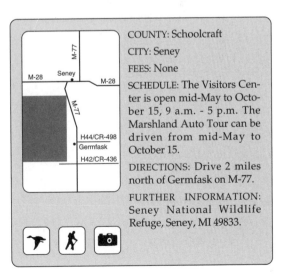

COUNTY: Schoolcraft

CITY: Seney

FEES: None

SCHEDULE: The Visitors Center is open mid-May to October 15, 9 a.m. - 5 p.m. The Marshland Auto Tour can be driven from mid-May to October 15.

DIRECTIONS: Drive 2 miles north of Germfask on M-77.

FURTHER INFORMATION: Seney National Wildlife Refuge, Seney, MI 49833.

199 SCOTT'S POINT

Out of the way but not hard to get to, Scott's Point is the answer to a lazy man's wish for a deserted island. Even though you can drive right up to the beach on two-lane blacktop, when you take your first step out onto the almost untouched shore, it's not hard to imagine you've been marooned. Adding to the illusion is the sight of green humps of land 10 miles to the south. They're the Beaver Island Archipelago, and this is the closest view of the islands across Lake Michigan from anywhere on either peninsula.

Anyone who loves to wade, play in the sand, sunbathe and beachcomb in splendid seclusion will find this the perfect spot for a day's outing. The wide, sandy beach ever so gently tips into the lake, and at some places the water is only ankle-deep 20 yards out from shore. In fact, the shoreline here is so tentative about where water should end and land begin that sometimes the actual shore is indistinct. In some spots along the beach, the water covers the sand no deeper than coffee poured into a saucer to cool. It's a great area for wading, and the hardpacked beach is a sandcastle builder's dream come true.

Occasional areas of rocky cobblestone interrupt the flat expanse of sand. In places, wind and wave action has created long points of stone and bric-a-brac that reach well out into the shallows. You can walk 20 to 30 yards out into the lake on these miniature capes — the tops of which are barely three or four inches out of the water — and view the shoreline from a perspective that normally would involve getting at least your feet wet. Several swift-moving and icy-cold creeks cut channels through the beach on their way to Lake Michigan, and they not only add another touch of beauty to the surroundings, but also have a magnetic pull on kids of all ages who try to build Hoover Dams out of sand.

Back from the seemingly endless beach, interdunal ponds separate the sand from where the forest begins. The shallow ponds, shoreline and forest attract and shelter a wide variety of wildlife, including terns, Piping Plovers and Great Blue Herons. Dwarf lake iris and Lake Huron tansy, two threatened Michigan plants, also find sanctuary here.

The only concession to humans at Scott's Point, other than the road leading to it, is a small picnic grounds set back from the beach in a sparse stand of cedar. The few tables are old and worn and the grills are rusty, which, all in all, seems more appropriate than if they were new and shiny.

COUNTY: Mackinac

CITY: Gould

FEES: None

SCHEDULE: Open all year.

DIRECTIONS: From US-2 at Gould City, turn south onto Gould City Rd. and drive 9 miles to the park, at the road's end.

US-2

Gould City

GOULD CITY RD

LAKE MICHIGAN

BIG ISLAND LAKE 200
WILDERNESS AREA

This rugged area in the Hiawatha National Forest is not for everyone. If you're willing to accept the challenge of making your own way through a near-trackless wilderness while living out of your backpack, or if you are a canoeist looking for an extensive system of lakes to explore or fish, then Big Island Lake Wilderness Area is a place you ought to visit. but if you just want a pleasant stroll along easily walked and well-established trails, turn to any of a hundred or so other pages in this book.

Although this area has felt and still exhibits the imprint of man's presence, it is wild, rugged and uncompromising. From county roads 437 on the south and 445 on the west, faint two-tracks penetrate the area, which is closed to motorized vehicles. but other than posted canoe portages that link many of the 23 small lakes in the region, there are no marked trails. A compass, a topographical map from the District Ranger Office (see *Further Information*), and your orientation skills are all that's available to negotiate the land that's home to Pine Martins, bobcats, raccoons, porcupines, black bear, loons, beaver, ducks, Sandhill Cranes, and an occasional Bald Eagle.

The area was heavily lumbered between the 1890s and the 1930s, when first the pine and later the hardwoods were cut. Countless stumps stand in mute testimony to the lumberman's ax, and old logging roads, railroad grades and four abandoned logging camps add a ghostly eeriness to the area. In the hundred years since the lumberjacks' passing, maple, white birch, beech and quaking aspen have reclaimed the rolling hills, while hemlock, spruce and balsam inhabit the lowland areas and border the many streams and lakes.

You can backcountry camp throughout the wilderness area. Low-impact practices are encouraged, and you must carry out all refuse that you can't burn.

An average of 160 inches of snowfall here each winter, which makes for excellent opportunities for snowshoers and cross country skiers. As with hikers, only those with extensive outdoor experience should make solo trips.

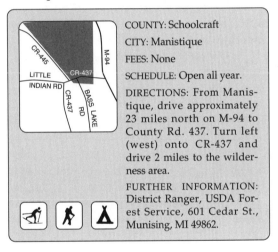

COUNTY: Schoolcraft

CITY: Manistique

FEES: None

SCHEDULE: Open all year.

DIRECTIONS: From Manistique, drive approximately 23 miles north on M-94 to County Rd. 437. Turn left (west) onto CR-437 and drive 2 miles to the wilderness area.

FURTHER INFORMATION: District Ranger, USDA Forest Service, 601 Cedar St., Munising, MI 49862.

201 RIVERBANK SANCTUARY

For nearly 40 years, this relatively small Michigan Audubon Society preserve lay hidden away in the Upper Peninsula, unknown to even most of the organization's members. Though the society acquired the property in 1947, they didn't place signs there until 1986, the same year the local Audubon chapter discovered the sanctuary's existence. Today, the 23-acre parcel — which is surrounded by other natural attractions, including Indian Lake, magnificent Lake Michigan shoreline, and Palms Book State Park — remains a little-used gem of natural beauty.

The preserve, which lies along the south bank of the picturesque Indian River, shelters a startling array of Michigan flora and fauna, and the profusion of plant and animal life almost requires that you bring a small library of nature guides. The terrain alternates between low, wet bogs and sandy, wooded ridges. Tamarack, black spruce, white cedar, yellow and paper birch, balsam fir, aspen, red and white pine, sugar maple and white oak create a many-shaded green canopy, with a wide variety of shrubs and ferns standing in the trees' shadows. Even closer to the ground, fragile mosses and delicate wildflowers add color to the landscape. Wild strawberries, Indian pipes, star flowers, Canada mayflowers, wild roses, Jack-in-the-pulpits, marsh marigolds, and forget-me-nots only hint at the profusion of seasonal blooms scattered within the preserve.

A host of wildlife also resides here or occasionally passes through, including three species of squirrels, snowshoe hares, skunks, beaver, deer and black bear. Common Loons, Bald Eagles, Pileated Woodpeckers, Wood Ducks, Ovenbirds and Evening Grosbeaks are only a few of the birds you might see.

COUNTY: Schoolcraft

CITY: Manistique

FEES: None

SCHEDULE: Open all year.

DIRECTIONS: From the intersection of M-94 and County Rd. 440 on the northwest side of Manistique, drive approximately 1.5 miles west on CR-440.

FURTHER INFORMATION: Michigan Audubon Society, 6011 W. St. Joseph, Lansing, MI 48917.

NINGA AKI PATHWAY 202

How Native Americans used sphagnum moss as America's first disposable diaper, made tea from white-pine needles to cure sore throats, and splinted broken bones with birch bark are only a few of the fascinating bits of Indian lore you'll learn along the Ninga Aki Pathway.

Located on the aptly named Garden Peninsula, the interpretive trail takes you through a quiet, picturesque section of the Lake Superior State Forest and also back in time to when Native Americans depended entirely on nature for food, clothing, medicine and building materials. Ninga Aki means "Mother Earth" in the Ojibwa tongue, and at 15 numbered stops along the trail, you'll discover just how important the forest resources were to every aspect of the Indians' daily lives. They used ground juniper berries, thimbleberries, balsam fir, aspen seeds, brackens, the inner bark from dogwood, and numerous other plants for everything from reducing a fever to making bread dough to lashing together a wigwam.

The short, easily walked trail begins at the 18-site Portage Bay State Forest Campground, which hugs the bay and looks out over the vast expanse of Lake Michigan. In addition to hiking, campers here can also swim from a fine beach that fronts the campsites or fish for bass, perch, bluegill and pike in the bay's sheltered waters. The campground also serves as a great base for exploring the unspoiled beauty of the Garden Peninsula. The out-of-the-way finger of land has miles of beautiful shoreline, lonely and picturesque backcountry roads, and a quaint fishing village near its tip.

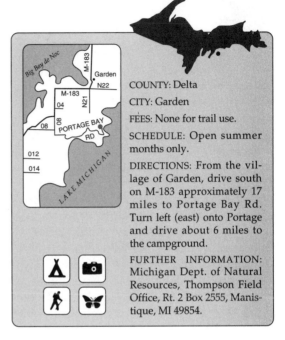

COUNTY: Delta

CITY: Garden

FEES: None for trail use.

SCHEDULE: Open summer months only.

DIRECTIONS: From the village of Garden, drive south on M-183 approximately 17 miles to Portage Bay Rd. Turn left (east) onto Portage and drive about 6 miles to the campground.

FURTHER INFORMATION: Michigan Dept. of Natural Resources, Thompson Field Office, Rt. 2 Box 2555, Manistique, MI 49854.

203 STURGEON RIVER

In its last 17-mile serpentine march to Lake Michigan, the Sturgeon River passes through a section of the Hiawatha National Forest notable for its untamed beauty and ease of access. Because of its pristine condition and the beautiful landscape — vast pine and hardwood forests, huge cedar swamps and black-spruce bogs — it winds through before emptying into Big Bay De Noc, the Sturgeon has been nominated under the Michigan Natural Rivers Act for designation as a Wild-Scenic River. It's easy, both literally and figuratively, to see why. If you catch even a glimpse of the swiftly flowing stream as it disappears around one of its ever-present bends, it will stay fixed in your mind. And you don't have to drive miles out of your way over two-tracks or hike through rough country to experience its grandeur.

From US-2, heading southeast from Nahma Junction, County Road 497 borders the west bank of the river for five miles to the head of Big Bay De Noc. The paved road is more patches than original blacktop, which is no problem because it helps you take your time and enjoy the sights. Though rarely far from the road, the river weaves in and out of view because it is usually screened by the lush pine and hardwood forest. You can get closer looks from several pulloffs where you can park and explore on foot.

Wildlife abounds in the area, and it would be rare not to spot a grouse, skunk, raccoon, porcupine or other animal crossing the road.

At Nahma, where the Sturgeon slides into Lake Michigan, County Road 497 junctions with County Road 499. You can head back to US-2 by turning west onto 499, and if you do, you will take in entirely different scenery. On its seven-mile loop back, the old blacktop edges the shallow, grassy shoreline of Lake Michigan. This is not the dramatic meeting of land and water we've come to expect along the lake, but rather an almost indistinct merging of the two elements. On the water side of the low dunes, the barely sloping sand makes a long run to meet Lake Michigan. Beach grasses cover much of the area and reach out into the lake, which gives the impression that a vast wetlands is slowly rising from the water. You can pull over at several turnouts along the road and explore the miles of fascinating shoreline on foot.

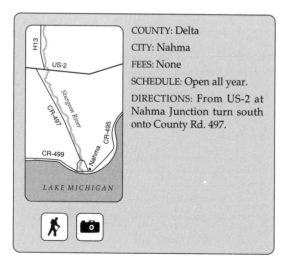

COUNTY: Delta

CITY: Nahma

FEES: None

SCHEDULE: Open all year.

DIRECTIONS: From US-2 at Nahma Junction turn south onto County Rd. 497.

BAY DE NOC — GRAND ISLAND TRAIL 204

The Bay De Noc— Grand Island Trail follows an old Chippewa Indian portage that connected Lake Superior to Lake Michigan. Indians and early explorers used this trail to transport canoes, supplies and trade-goods between the two lakes.

The trail, which begins just east of Rapid River near the head of Little Bay De Noc, follows the valley of the Whitefish River for most of its 36-mile length and never strays far from County Road 509. The trail meanders through stands of jack and red pine in the southern half of its south-to-north route. In the northern half, it zig-zags across CR-509 and winds over maple- and birch-covered hills before ending at M-94 approximately 10 miles short of Munising and Lake Superior.

There are three trailheads with wells at each: at the south end (CR-509), at the north end (M-94 at Ackerman Lake), and near the middle on CR-509 at the county line.

Backcountry camping is permitted anywhere along the trail, and 17-site Haymeadow Creek National Forest Campground, with pit toilets, is about seven miles north of the trailhead just after crossing Haymeadow Creek.

Bay De Noc—Grand Island trail is open in the winter for cross country skiing and is also popular with mushers.

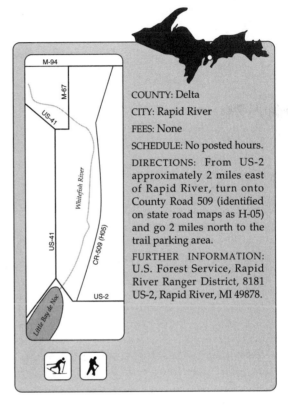

COUNTY: Delta

CITY: Rapid River

FEES: None

SCHEDULE: No posted hours.

DIRECTIONS: From US-2 approximately 2 miles east of Rapid River, turn onto County Road 509 (identified on state road maps as H-05) and go 2 miles north to the trail parking area.

FURTHER INFORMATION: U.S. Forest Service, Rapid River Ranger District, 8181 US-2, Rapid River, MI 49878.

205 PENINSULA POINT LIGHTHOUSE PARK

In a state made up of so many peninsulas, the finger of land that juts out into Lake Michigan to separate Big and Little Bays De Noc is often forgotten or ignored. Except for a private campground, the seldom-visited peninsula is nearly devoid of commercial tourist attractions. But the 18-mile drive from US-2 to its tip, called Peninsula Point, is well worth the time and gas for anyone who treasures little-visited, out-of-the-way scenery or an unusual picnic spot.

A pleasant, grass-covered picnic grounds surrounds the remains of an old lighthouse at land's end. From the open, sunny meadow, you get great views of Lake Michigan in three directions. Visible five miles across Little Bay De Noc (but 35 miles away by car) is the city of Escanaba. And south from the tip of the peninsula, you look right down the throat of Green Bay. Only the foundation of the lightkeeper's house remains, but the light tower is still standing and you can climb to its top on an iron corkscrew stairway to a sweeping view of the green shores that trace the distant edge of the vast expanse of water.

The shoreline — flat slabs of bedrock that reach out into the lake — isn't good for swimming. But beachcombers will delight in poking around in the ankle-deep water, examining driftwood captured by the point, and turning over an occasional odd rock.

On the western side of the peninsula, a short nature-hiking trail heads north along the shore, then turns inland. For the first few hundred yards, as it cuts through a thick woods fringing Big Bay De Noc, the path is rarely out of sight and sound of the wave-lapped shore. When the trail curls inland, it crosses a quiet cedar swamp, where you slip over wet areas on a boardwalk. The last quarter mile of the trail turns back south and joins the narrow one-lane road leading to the tip of the point.

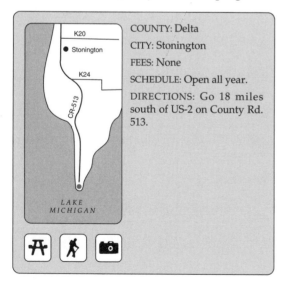

COUNTY: Delta

CITY: Stonington

FEES: None

SCHEDULE: Open all year.

DIRECTIONS: Go 18 miles south of US-2 on County Rd. 513.

SQUAW CREEK OLD GROWTH AREA 206

A walk through the Squaw Creek Old Growth Area is a journey back in time. Take just a few steps off County Road 513, and you can't help but feel what the state's great forests must have looked like before the lumbering era.

The 65-acre preserve doesn't contain a stand of virgin timber, because several thinnings occurred prior to 1940, when the area was added to the Hiawatha National Forest. But when loggers worked this area in the late 1800s, a significant number of large trees were left untouched, and they have grown into magnificent specimens. Today, you can hike beneath towering white pine, hemlocks, huge hardwoods and red pine, the smallest of which are telephone-pole size.

Old Squaw Creek, which cuts across the southern half of the old-growth area, adds its own special charm to the scenery. The fast-moving, red tinged creek flows between high banks that twist and turn through the woods like a partially uncoiled spring. Huge trees grow along the banks and in many places tilt toward each other from opposite shores to form a green tent over the cool water.

There are no marked trails, but old two-tracks and narrow, overgrown roads — closed to all but foot traffic — penetrate to every corner of the hushed, pine-scented woods. Walking is easy over the needle-soft trails, and the lack of a dense understory in many places invites you to wander at will among trees that will dwarf you. If you plan to hike to the far reaches of the tract or if you like to blaze your own trail through the woods, be sure to take a compass.

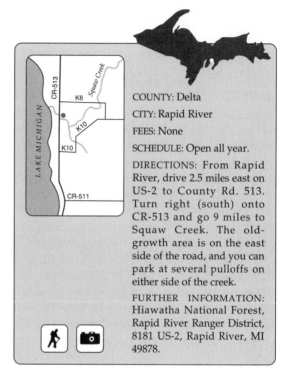

COUNTY: Delta

CITY: Rapid River

FEES: None

SCHEDULE: Open all year.

DIRECTIONS: From Rapid River, drive 2.5 miles east on US-2 to County Rd. 513. Turn right (south) onto CR-513 and go 9 miles to Squaw Creek. The old-growth area is on the east side of the road, and you can park at several pulloffs on either side of the creek.

FURTHER INFORMATION: Hiawatha National Forest, Rapid River Ranger District, 8181 US-2, Rapid River, MI 49878.

207 PIERS GORGE SCENIC AREA

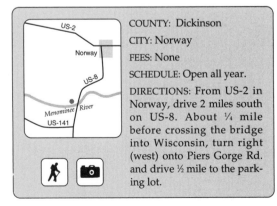

The Menominee River's tortuous run through Piers Gorge — just south of Norway, Michigan — marks the most magically beautiful point along the entire Michigan/Wisconsin border. The Menominee forms the longest river boundary in Michigan and makes up nearly a third of the state line on the western end of the Upper Peninsula. The rust-colored, swiftly moving river is beautiful anywhere along its length, but the scenery is simply spectacular at Piers Gorge, where the water is dramatically funneled through steep-sided rock walls and forced over a succession of stony shelves.

The gorge's walls, which rise as high as 70 feet above the river, twist and turn like an amusement-park water slide. In places, only bare bedrock guards the penned-in water, but more often, trees cling to the near-vertical walls and soften the view. Four separate waterfalls, each with its own distinct character, send the river into tumultuous descents. They are cheated of some of their glamour by the almost continuous rapids that kick up white water and create a roar throughout the river's journey through the gorge.

You can take in memorable views of all four falls and the rapids from a trail — first used by Indians to portage their canoes around the falls — that follows the top of the gorge. The level, easily walked path begins at a parking lot at the end of Piers Gorge Road and crosses a small cedar swamp before slipping through a mature northern forest of hardwoods and pine. Offshoots from the trail snake out to the edge of the gorge, and others creep down the steep slope to the very edge of the churning water. A three-mile round trip along the top of the gorge to all the falls can take more than an hour and several rolls of film.

COUNTY: Dickinson

CITY: Norway

FEES: None

SCHEDULE: Open all year.

DIRECTIONS: From US-2 in Norway, drive 2 miles south on US-8. About ¼ mile before crossing the bridge into Wisconsin, turn right (west) onto Piers Gorge Rd. and drive ½ mile to the parking lot.

STATELINE NATIONAL 208
RECREATION TRAIL

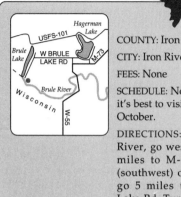

This short, pleasant and scenic Ottawa National Forest trail marks the starting point of the only state boundary line in the Upper Peninsula that isn't water. The trail begins at a small picnic grounds at the south end of Brule Lake. From near there, at the headwaters of the Brule River, the boundary between Wisconsin and Michigan heads overland northwest almost 70 miles to the Montreal River, south of Ironwood. An interpretive sign at the start of the pathway explains the significance of the area and the work of the surveyors in laying out the boundary.

From the interpretive sign, the trail runs south along the edge of the Brule River a third of a mile through a picturesque hardwood forest to the Mile Post Zero survey monument, which marks the exact starting point of the overland boundary line. Another third of a mile downriver, the trail ends at the Treaty Tree Site. There, an interpretive sign and the time-weathered stump of the treaty tree sit on the spot where two pacts were signed with area Indians in order to safeguard the surveyors as they ran the boundary line.

Facilities at the small picnic area at the trailhead include five tables and grills, a well, pit toilets, and a boat launching ramp onto Brule Lake.

COUNTY: Iron

CITY: Iron River

FEES: None

SCHEDULE: None posted, but it's best to visit May through October.

DIRECTIONS: From Iron River, go west on US-2 2.5 miles to M-73. Turn left (southwest) onto M-73 and go 5 miles to Hagerman Lake Rd. Turn right (north) onto Hagerman and drive 2 miles to West Brule Lake Rd. Turn left (west) onto W. Brule and go 2 miles to a north-south road junction. Turn hard left (south) and drive one mile to the picnic area.

FURTHER INFORMATION: Ottawa National Forest, Iron River Ranger District, 801 Adams, Iron River, MI 49935.

209 LAKE OTTAWA RECREATION AREA

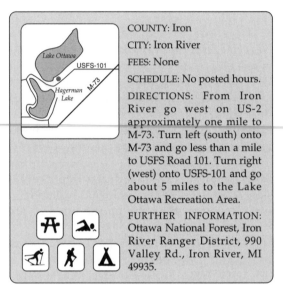

More than 14 miles of hiking trails are the main draw to this parcel of Ottawa National Forest land. Birdwatchers, wildflower enthusiasts, photographers and other outdoor lovers will all find something to hold their interest on the varied routes that wind over steep hills, through hardwood forests and across gently rolling countryside with many panoramic views from the higher elevations.

The trail mileage is divided almost equally between two systems. The Ge-Che Trail System's six loops web the south shore of Lake Ottawa. Connected to the Ge-Che system on its west end is another series of loops, the Hagerman-Brule Lake Trail System, which probes the land west of Hagerman Lake. Parts of both trails are open in the winter for cross country skiing.

Facilities and activities at Lake Ottawa include a 32-site lakeshore campground, a short interpretive trail, boat access, swimming, fishing and a large picnic area.

COUNTY: Iron

CITY: Iron River

FEES: None

SCHEDULE: No posted hours.

DIRECTIONS: From Iron River go west on US-2 approximately one mile to M-73. Turn left (south) onto M-73 and go less than a mile to USFS Road 101. Turn right (west) onto USFS-101 and go about 5 miles to the Lake Ottawa Recreation Area.

FURTHER INFORMATION: Ottawa National Forest, Iron River Ranger District, 990 Valley Rd., Iron River, MI 49935.

SYLVANIA WILDERNESS AND RECREATION AREA

If you find sublime joy in getting off the beaten track and surrounding yourself with pristine wilderness, the 18,000-acre Sylvania Wilderness and adjacent 3,000-acre Recreation Area may be as close to nivana as you can come in Michigan. Located in the Ottawa National Forest in the western Upper Peninsula, this vast track of woods and water beckons to anyone who yearns to camp, fish, hike, canoe, or ski in relative solitude amid breathtaking natural beauty.

Canoers and hikers can make scenic day trips or extended overnight outings within the Wilderness. Twenty-six miles of trails crease the area, and most of the 30 crystal-clear lakes are connected by unmarked portages. Motorized traffic on land is strictly prohibited and boats with motors are only allowed on two lakes. Sixty lakeside wilderness campsites are scattered throughout the pristine old-growth forest, and each has a wilderness latrine and cast-iron fire ring. Permits are required for overnight campers as well as day-use visitors and party size is limited to lessen the impact on the area. There is no fee for wilderness camping, but from May 15 through September 30 you must register at the entrance. You can self-register the rest of the year.

Trails are open for cross country skiing in the winter but are groomed only by use.

The Recreation Area adjoining the Sylvania Wilderness holds a 48-unit tent-trailer campground for those who wish to taste the wilderness from a more comfortable base. The campsites have picnic tables, fire rings and nearby flush toilets. West of the campground is a swimming beach, picnic area and day-use building with hot showers and flush toilets.

Whether you choose to experience the area as a backcountry wilderness camper or by short day trips from the campground, the scenery will impress. Maple, birch , hemlock, spruce and fir — much of it virgin timber — cover the area, and fall color here is spectacular. Deer, coyote, fox, mink, porcupine and bear are commonly seen, and two relatively rare birds in Michigan, the Bald Eagle and the Loon, nest in the area.

A trip here should begin with a stop at the visitors center on the corner of US-45 and US-2 in Watersmeet. Exhibits, slide shows and summer evening nature programs are offered along with a variety of interpretive materials. A self-guided, paved nature trail winds through some of the Center's 25 acres. The building is open from 9 a.m. to 5 p.m., mid-May through mid-October, and contains information on the entire Ottawa National Forest.

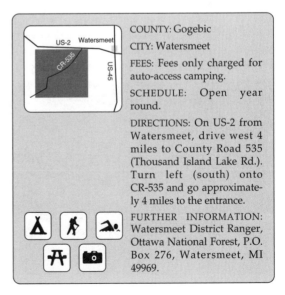

COUNTY: Gogebic

CITY: Watersmeet

FEES: Fees only charged for auto-access camping.

SCHEDULE: Open year round.

DIRECTIONS: On US-2 from Watersmeet, drive west 4 miles to County Road 535 (Thousand Island Lake Rd.). Turn left (south) onto CR-535 and go approximately 4 miles to the entrance.

FURTHER INFORMATION: Watersmeet District Ranger, Ottawa National Forest, P.O. Box 276, Watersmeet, MI 49969.

211 BLACK RIVER HARBOR AREA

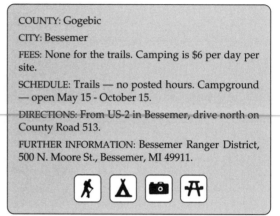

Seven breathtaking waterfalls along one of Michigan's finest whitewater rivers is the main draw to this picturesque harbor area tucked away in the extreme western Upper Peninsula. In just one 10-mile stretch of County Road 513 — which follows the Black River valley for 15 miles from Bessemer north to Black River Harbor on Lake Superior — short ¼- to 1.5-mile trails through hardwood and hemlock forests lead to splendid views of six of the falls: Algonquin, Great Conglomerate, Gorge, Potawatomi, Sandstone, and Rainbow. Because of their unique design, including a series of stairways and observation platforms, the trails to Gorge and Potawatomi falls are exceptionally beautiful.

In this section of the Ottawa National Forest, you can also hike alongside the last 10 miles of the Black River to where it empties into Lake Superior. A 30-mile segment of the yet-to-be-completed North Country Trail — a National Scenic Trail that will eventually link the east-coast Appalachian Trail to the Lewis and Clark Trail in North Dakota — begins near the Copper Peak Ski Flying Hill on CR-513, parallels the river, and passes all

COUNTY: Gogebic

CITY: Bessemer

FEES: None for the trails. Camping is $6 per day per site.

SCHEDULE: Trails — no posted hours. Campground — open May 15 - October 15.

DIRECTIONS: From US-2 in Bessemer, drive north on County Road 513.

FURTHER INFORMATION: Bessemer Ranger District, 500 N. Moore St., Bessemer, MI 49911.

seven major falls before turning east at Rainbow Falls and heading toward Porcupine Mountains State Park.

Facilities at a 40-site campground at Black River Harbor include flush toilets, a trailer dump station, a picnic area and a children's playground.

GOGEBIC RIDGE

(continued from p. 221)

on FR-400 about a mile to a short, well-marked trail that leads to Picturesque Cascade Falls is well worth the effort. The North Country trail continues from FR-400 another 3.3 miles to Forest Road 630 then another 3 miles to Norwich Road. The final 5-mile stretch between Norwich Road and Victoria Road follows the historic Norwich Mine area cliffs, with many viewpoints to the Ontonagon River.

The Gogebic Ridge Trail is open in the winter for cross country skiing but is not groomed or maintained.

GARY W. BARFKNECHT

GOGEBIC RIDGE HIKING TRAIL 212 and NORTH COUNTRY TRAIL (Bergland Segment)

One completed Michigan portion of the North Country Trail, which will eventually link the Appalachian Trail in Maine to the Lewis and Clark Trail in North Dakota, connects Porcupine Mountains State Park to Norwich. Called the Bergland Segment, this 37-mile stretch holds the potential for a true wilderness experience, including some of the most rugged, remote and scenic hiking in the state. Backcountry camping is permitted anywhere along the route, most streams and rivers are unbridged, contact with other people is rare, and for most of its length, the trail is several miles from the nearest road. Hikers embarking on this section, then, should be in good physical condition and should carry a map available from Ottawa National Forest headquarters or the Bergland Ranger Station.

Neatly intersecting the Bergland Segment at almost its halfway point is the Gogebic Ridge Trail, a relatively new 8.7-mile route through cedar swamps and along ridge lines in the Ottawa National Forest. This trail, built by the Youth Conservation Corps in 1976, begins on road FR-250 one mile north of Merriweather. The path heads east along the north and east shore of Weary Lake, then rises to a beautiful scenic overlook of Lake Gogebic. From there, the trail turns north and crosses rough and rugged country until it intersects with M-64 three miles north of Bergland and eight miles south of White Pine. The trail crosses M-64, then ends a half mile east of old M-64 at the Bergland Segment of the North Country Trail.

From the junction of the two trails, hikers have three choices. One: They can retrace their steps back to FR-250.

Two: They can head west on a potential 18-mile backpacking venture to Porcupine Mountains Wilderness State Park. From the North Country/Gogebic Ridge intersection, the trail turns north, crosses M-64, old M-64 and the main branch of the Big Iron River before crossing the west branch of the Big Iron River and meandering westerly along the river valley until ending at the South Boundary Road at Porcupine Mountains. Shallow depressions and old foundations along the way are the only reminders of the area's rich lumbering and copper mining history.

Three: Hikers can turn east and walk approximately 19 miles to the North Country Trail's end, at Victoria Road just beyond Norwich. This section intermittently follows several escarpments offering scenic views of the surrounding area and dips into lowlands to cross several creeks. Approximately 7.5 miles east of the Gogebic/North Country intersection, the North Country Trail crosses Forest Road 400. From that point, a side trip south

(Continued on p. 220)

COUNTY: Ontonagon

CITY: Merriweather

FEES: None

SCHEDULE: Open year round.

DIRECTIONS: From M-28 at Merriweather, turn north onto FR-789 and go one mile to the trailhead.

FURTHER INFORMATION: District Ranger, Ottawa National Forest, Bergland, MI 49910.

213 BROCKWAY MOUNTAIN DRIVE

The highest above-sea-level roadway anywhere between the Alleghanies and the Rockies is right here in Michigan. It's called Brockway Mountain Drive, and spectacular views come like stop-action movie frames as the pavement twists and turns for 9.5 miles along the edge of precipitous cliffs in the northern Keweenaw Peninsula. An added plus for nature lovers: Two Michigan Nature Association sanctuaries plus some great birdwatching sites are located along the drive.

The volcanic bedrock of Brockway Mountain, which runs like a spine along the northern edge of the peninsula, slopes gently toward Lake Superior to the north, dips below the waters, then thrusts up again miles out in the lake to form Isle Royale. But the south side of the mountain ends abruptly at the edge of a cliff that in many places appears to rise almost vertically from the valley floor 300 feet below. It is along this cliff that Depression-era public-works laborers constructed the road an average of 700 feet above Lake Superior and 1,300 feet above sea level.

At the eastern end, just before the road turns back on itself as it snakes off the mountain, a beautiful panoramic view of Copper Harbor, Lake Superior and Lake Fanny Hooe comes from a scenic overlook with parking facilities. About three miles farther west, spectacular views of the semi-alpine habitat of the surrounding countryside comes from Brockway Mountain Lookout, at 1,337 feet above sea level, the highest point on the drive.

Many of the plants found here are also found on threatened or endangered lists, and Brockway Mountain is the only place in Michigan where a few of those rare species grow. Forty-seven species of trees and shrubs — including shadbush, red-berried elder, buffaloberry, arrowwood, snowberry, and the popular thimbleberry that makes great jams and jellies — grow on the mountain. The list of more than 700 flowers identified here includes trillium, Indian pipe, buttercups, wild strawberry and several kinds of orchids.

To help ensure the preservation of the area's plant life, the Michigan Nature Association, in 1979, acquired the James H. Klipfel Memorial Nature Sanctuary — 160 acres within a half mile of the drive's highest point — and the Brockway Mountain Nature Sanctuary, a 78-acre parcel adjacent to the east end. Parking areas at both are good places to leave your car and enjoy some unforgettable scenic vistas plus close-up looks at the flora by walking along the roadway. You can also explore the sanctuaries, but you shouldn't venture into the woods without a compass.

The entire Keweenaw Peninsula is a major spring hawk migration route. At Brockway Mountain the drafts created by the cliffs attract numerous hawks that ride the rising air as they effortlessly soar northeast to the end of the peninsula where they strike out across Lake Superior. Since many of the

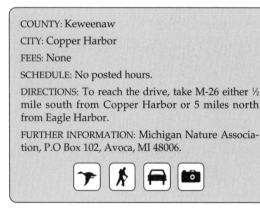

COUNTY: Keweenaw

CITY: Copper Harbor

FEES: None

SCHEDULE: No posted hours.

DIRECTIONS: To reach the drive, take M-26 either ½ mile south from Copper Harbor or 5 miles north from Eagle Harbor.

FURTHER INFORMATION: Michigan Nature Association, P.O Box 102, Avoca, MI 48006.

GARY W. BARFKNECHT

hawks, while using the updrafts, are below the cliff top, observers have the unique opportunity to look down on them. The Klipfel Sanctuary and the adjacent Brockway Mountain Lookout are both excellent locations to watch the spring hawk migration, which reaches its peak in mid-April. At the lookout on one 1976 day, for example, a pair of experienced hawk spotters counted 1,033 birds of prey. Sharp-shinned and Broad-winged hawks were the most plentiful, but also numbered among the day's sightings were Snowy Owls and Bald and Golden eagles.

214 M-26

The slender ribbon of asphalt that hugs the rock-bound northern coastline of the Keweenaw Peninsula between Copper Harbor and Eagle River ranks as one of the most beautiful scenic drives in the Great Lakes.

For most of the 14-mile distance between the two small villages, M-26 dips and turns like a miniature roller coaster along shoreline that seems totally out of place in Michigan. Only yards from the shoulder of the road, huge slabs of darkly colored bedrock — sculpted by wind and waves into long, bony fingers that parallel the highway — tilt into the sparkling water of Lake Superior. At other spots the canted, aging rock rears into the air before plunging into the lake.

Scattered along the drive are four stops you shouldn't miss — two Michigan Nature Association preserves (identified by small "protected area" signs), a waterfall, and a roadside park.

At an MNA preserve 4.5 miles south of Copper Harbor, you can park on the highway's wide shoulder and explore the unique rock formations that dip into Lake Superior. When you climb over the rugged shoreline, you may be astounded to find life struggling for existence in the extraordinary environment. Beautiful flowers sprout from small cracks in the rock; many-colored lichen appears wedded to the stone; and gnarled, stunted trees — natural bonsai that have been shaped by the elements — cling precariously to the rock.

About four miles farther south, another MNA preserve and an adjacent roadside park present two strikingly different vistas. At the roadside park, several picnic tables are sheltered behind a huge, craggy rock dome that compels you to climb to its top for a sweeping view of Lake Superior. Just west, the MNA preserve borders both sides of the road, but it's the landward side that calls for attention. There, a faint but posted hiking trail slips into an enchanted forest, where trees drip with lichen and nearly every rock and downed tree is covered by a deep cushion of moss.

Another mile or so south, M-26 crosses the Silver River. Practically from the exact point where the road bridges the stream, the water plunges toward the lake in a series of drops called Silver River Falls. You can't see the falls from your car, but it's a short, easy climb from a parking lot beside the bridge down the slope for a great view.

From Silver River it's 4.5 miles to Eagle River, and along that stretch of the road, Lake Superior is seldom seen as M-26 tunnels through a pristine forest and borders a picturesque inland lake.

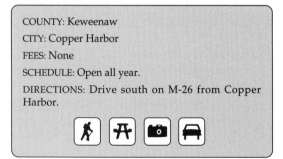

COUNTY: Keweenaw

CITY: Copper Harbor

FEES: None

SCHEDULE: Open all year.

DIRECTIONS: Drive south on M-26 from Copper Harbor.

Amid the hustle and bustle of the major natural, historical and commercial attractions at Copper Harbor is a short hiking trail that you shouldn't miss. The half-hour walk, which includes some unique views of this northern Michigan outpost, ends at one of the most dramatically beautiful beaches in the Keweenaw Peninsula, if not the state.

From the trailhead, at the west side of the Copper Harbor Marina, you slip into a primal northern forest as the path moves around the western end of the harbor. The trail is never far from the water as it cuts through the dense forest of coniferous trees, stunted by both the harsh northern winters and their exposed position near the lake. The trees are laden with moss and lichen, and in places the forest floor is thick with ferns. Turn your back to the forest, and you'll take in picturesque views of the little village across the bay.

After about three quarters of a mile, the trail forks. The right-hand path continues along the bay side of a long peninsula — which has sheltered Great Lakes shipping since the first schooner dropped anchor in 1843 — and eventually ends at its tip, Hunter's Point.

The other path cuts across the narrow peninsula to Agate Beach, which absolutely wows first-time visitors. Huge chunks of bedrock — some of the world's oldest exposed rock — lie scattered across the beach. Conifers of all shapes and sizes line the edge of rock outcroppings that overlook the beach, and in some places the trees seem to have sprung whole from the living rock. Other smaller craggy outcroppings lie half buried in a vast cushion of small stones and pebbles that cover the shore. Look closely at the bedrock and you'll see delicately colored lichens plastered to it. More obvious is the

array of wildflowers that grow out of pockets and fissures. Hidden among the millions of stones and pebbles that line the beach are prized Lake Superior agates, and the entire area is a treasure trove for beachcombers and rockhounds.

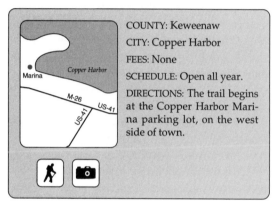

COUNTY: Keweenaw

CITY: Copper Harbor

FEES: None

SCHEDULE: Open all year.

DIRECTIONS: The trail begins at the Copper Harbor Marina parking lot, on the west side of town.

216 ESTIVANT PINES SANCTUARY

On Michigan's northernmost piece of real estate in 1970, loggers who couldn't see beyond a quick profit were quickly cutting down 500 acres of virgin white pine, the Upper Peninsula's last stand and one of only three or four stands remaining in the entire state. But the Michigan Nature Association stepped in and, with the help of contributions from people throughout the state (but especially the Keweenaw Peninsula), created the Estivant Pines Sanctuary to save a few remaining specimens of Michigan's official state tree.

One of the trees now protected in this 200-acre preserve is the Leaning Giant, at 23 feet in circumference and 120 feet tall, Michigan's largest white pine. This awe-inspiring, alarmingly canted pine, as a matter of fact, is the only one left uncut in a 20-acre parcel on the southern edge of the sanctuary across the Montreal River.

A grove of magnificent cathedral pines located in the center of this quiet, remote land is also impressive and inspiring. Red oak, spruce, tamarack and balsam surround the white pine here, and the sanctuary also shelters several kinds of orchids, rare ferns, beaver, deer, bear and coyote.

A well-marked trail from Burma Road winds through the preserve for a half mile to the cathedral grove and past a beaver pond, then, after another half mile, reaches the Leaning Giant. Several other trails crisscross the area. But because the sanctuary embraces a wild and rugged terrain marked by cliffs, rock outcroppings, abandoned copper mines, dense forest, marshes and swamps, you shouldn't leave the main trail without a compass and topographical map.

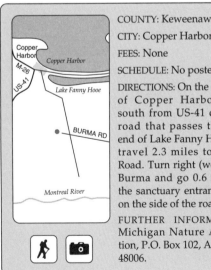

COUNTY: Keweenaw

CITY: Copper Harbor

FEES: None

SCHEDULE: No posted hours.

DIRECTIONS: On the east side of Copper Harbor, turn south from US-41 onto the road that passes the west end of Lake Fanny Hooe and travel 2.3 miles to Burma Road. Turn right (west) onto Burma and go 0.6 miles to the sanctuary entrance. Park on the side of the road.

FURTHER INFORMATION: Michigan Nature Association, P.O. Box 102, Avoca, MI 48006.

KEWEENAW BAY SHORELINE DRIVE 217

Visitors to the uniquely scenic Keweenaw Peninsula are mesmerized by the beauty of its northern shoreline. the county's only major roads, US-41 and M-26, parallel the north side of the peninsula, and there's so much to see and do along those two highways that most tourists never think to explore Keweenaw's south side. They should. The neglected 20-mile-long blacktop road that runs between Gay and Lac La Belle along the edge of Lake Superior holds half a day's worth of beautiful and unusual scenery, all of which you can enjoy without leaving your car.

Beginning at Gay, on the south end of the drive, the road slips through the forest that borders the big lake, and you get only intermittent views of the water. Just when you begin to get frustrated with the peek-a-boo glimpses of Superior, the road reaches Burnette Bay Park, about seven miles north of Gay.

At that roadside park, a sandy swimming beach dips into the chilly waters of the great lake, and a few scattered picnic tables line the beach. But it's the magnificent view of Superior that demands your immediate attention. To the east, the deep blue-green water stretches to the horizon, and 30 miles across the water to the south rise the outlines of the Huron Mountains. You can take in the entire scene without leaving your vehicle, but the sandy shoreline has an almost irresistible pull and most travelers walk the shore and even wade in the bracingly cool water.

Continuing on the drive north from the roadside park, more-frequent views of the lake and Huron Mountains will keep your head turned to the right. Just before the road veers away from the shoreline and cuts cross country to Lac La Belle, a breathtaking view of Bete Grise Bay and the eastern tip of the Keweenaw Peninsula pulls drivers to the side of the road for a final and memorable look.

From there the road cuts west, away from the shoreline, through a dense northern forest before reaching Lac La Belle. On the outskirts of the tiny village is a final reward — a lovely roadside park with a picture-perfect waterfall and picnic area. You can easily see Haven Falls from the road, but you really shouldn't pass up the opportunity to park, and more closely explore the curtain of water pouring over a near-20-foot-tall, sheer wall of rock. The small picnic area is deeply shaded, and the falls takes center stage at this natural version of a dinner theater.

COUNTY: Keweenaw

CITY: Gay

FEES: None

SCHEDULE: Open all year.

DIRECTIONS: Drive north from Gay.

218 STURGEON RIVER SLOUGHS WATERFOWL AREA

The Sturgeon River Sloughs Waterfowl Area catches many Keweenaw Peninsula visitors off guard. Most of us expect dramatic or at least clearly defined meetings of land and water in the remote, rugged area. So when driving US-41 south of Houghton, it can come as a surprise when the highway passes a vast wetlands created by the Sturgeon River as it flows into Portage Lake.

The waterfowl area encompasses a huge diked flood plain and vast marsh, most of which can be seen from the top of an observation deck just off US-41 at the back of a gravel parking lot. When you climb the nearly two-story tower, you'll be convinced you are seeing the flattest stretch of real estate in the entire peninsula. Drainage ditches etch the fields close at hand, but in the distance the only evidence of the ditches are slight folds in the marsh's grand expanse of waving grass. Binoculars are a must if you want to search out distant Great Blue Herons or catch a glimpse of a Sandhill Crane.

Adjacent to the observation deck, the three-mile Bert DeVriendt Nature Trail slips through a gate in a fence and then follows the top of the dikes that circle the waterfowl area. The woodchip-covered trail passes the brushy fringes of channels alongside the dikes, reed-choked marshes, and open fields, all of which offer good birding opportunities nearly any time of the year. Beaver, mink, muskrat and raccoon also inhabit the area, and interpretive signs along the path tell of the history of the natural area and the flora and fauna usually found on the hike.

COUNTY: Houghton
CITY: Chassel
FEES: None
SCHEDULE: Open all year.
DIRECTIONS: From Houghton drive 7 miles south on US-41.

STURGEON RIVER GORGE 219 WILDERNESS AREA

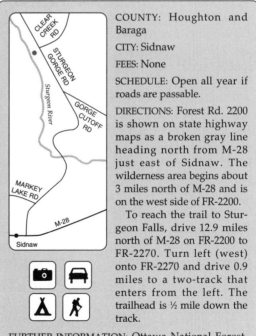

The heart of this spectacular wilderness area in the Ottawa National Forest is, as the Forest Service describes it, "the deepest readily accessible gorge east of the Mississippi." Michigan's "Grand Canyon" is a 250- to 300-foot-deep, one-half- to one-mile-wide trench carved out of the Upper Peninsula's high, rolling landscape by the swift-moving Sturgeon River. But "readily accessible" must be qualified. The gorge is surrounded by 14,139 acres of wilderness, and to get the most-stunning views, you have to drive nearly 10 miles on a narrow forest road, then do some strenuous hiking. But it's worth the side trip and the exercise, because the gorge is a one-of-a-kind experience in the Midwest.

For day-trippers the most popular destination (and by popular I'm not talking Disneyland crowds, but maybe one or two other people a day) is the hike down into the forest-shrouded gorge to see Sturgeon Falls. Depending on road conditions, it's anywhere from a half-mile to a mile hike down an old two-track. The road falls over the side of the gorge, then parallels the river high above the water. The scenery is fantastic as the trail slowly descends to just above a long series of falls, the last of which, Sturgeon, is a 40-foot drop through a narrow chute.

From Forest Road 2200, which borders the east side of the gorge and wilderness area, you get occasional panoramic views of the green-clad canyon. The road descends into the valley about five miles north of M-28, and as it crosses a one-lane bridge, you get a marvelous view of the roiling water. On the north side of the river, the road climbs the steep valley wall and then borders the gorge for several miles. Turnoffs, old two-tracks closed to vehicles, and foot trails break off from the road and head toward the gorge.

There are few marked or formal trails and no campgrounds within the wilderness area, but you are free to wander throughout the rugged, heavily wooded terrain. Be sure to take a compass and write for a map if you plan an extended outing. Motorized and mechanized quipment are not allowed in the area, designated a National Forest Wilderness in 1987. You can backcountry camp throughout the area or also set up at a small, picturesque national forest campground just outside the wilderness area at the point where FR-2200 crosses the river. But please leave no trace of your visit.

COUNTY: Houghton and Baraga

CITY: Sidnaw

FEES: None

SCHEDULE: Open all year if roads are passable.

DIRECTIONS: Forest Rd. 2200 is shown on state highway maps as a broken gray line heading north from M-28 just east of Sidnaw. The wilderness area begins about 3 miles north of M-28 and is on the west side of FR-2200.

To reach the trail to Sturgeon Falls, drive 12.9 miles north of M-28 on FR-2200 to FR-2270. Turn left (west) onto FR-2270 and drive 0.9 miles to a two-track that enters from the left. The trailhead is ½ mile down the track.

FURTHER INFORMATION: Ottawa National Forest, Kenton Ranger District, Kenton, MI 49943.

220 ABRAMSON ROADSIDE PARK

The grand expanse of Upper Peninsula wilderness can sometimes be too overpowering to fully take in or experience. It's the old saying of not being able to see the forest for the trees. But within an easy hundred-yard stroll at this postage-stamp-size roadside park, you get a wonderful slice of western U.P. beauty that's easy to digest and appreciate.

COUNTY: Baraga

CITY: Three Lakes

FEES: None

SCHEDULE: None

DIRECTIONS: From the junction of US-141, US-41 and M-28, go 6.5 miles east on US-41/M-28.

The park nestles in a bend of Tioga Creek, right next to highway M-28. Picnic tables and grills lie scattered across a grassy meadow on the inside of the creek's loop and only a few feet from a small waterfall whose copper-colored water tumbles over a series of small, rocky ledges and boulders. The low, rhythmic rumble of the falls adds background music to any roadside repast. Just below the roiling water, you get good views of the falls and creek from a footbridge that leads to a few more picnic tables on the outside of the creek's bend.

From the larger picnic area, a woodchip-covered trail follows the creek upstream through a narrow, forested valley to a second, slightly larger falls. Several towering old-growth white pines, which somehow escaped the lumbermen's axes, line the trail and cast their shadows over the strikingly beautiful valley and swift-moving water. At the end of the trail, the second waterfall pours over a bedrock outcropping into a quiet pool. Most visitors make the brief walk to the falls, take in the scene, then leave without realizing that just above the falls and visible from the end of the well-worn path is a beaver dam.

Faint trails wind through the woods around the falls to a memorable view of the quiet pond that's backed by deep-green pines and necklaced with silent wetlands and dead trees killed by the flooding. You can creep to within a few feet of the beaver dam and also walk along barely discernible trails that head off along the edge of the pond.

McCORMICK WILDERNESS

(continued from p. 231)

Ranger Office for detailed maps, camping techniques and local road conditions. Mechanized and motorized vehicles or equipment are not allowed. Cross country skiers are welcome, but winters here can be brutal, with fast-changing weather and road conditions. Go prepared and don't go alone.

McCORMICK WILDERNESS 221

Even a quick glance at a state highway map suggests the remoteness of this 27-square-mile area of National Forest wilderness. Go on, get out the map, look at the Upper Peninsula and trace US-41 from Marquette west to L'Anse. About halfway between those two towns, and the width of a thumb north of Lake Michigamme, sits the rugged, isolated and scenic McCormick Wilderness. As the map indicates, this area is nearly smack dab in the middle of one of the state's largest expanse of wilderness.

The property served as a vacation retreat for the Cyrus McCormick family, of reaping machine fame, until the 1967 death of Gordon McCormick, who willed the estate to the National Forest Service. The McCormick family kept much of the land from being lumbered, and as a result, impressive stands of white pine grow on many areas of the property. Other sections of the Wilderness haven't been logged for more than 70 years, and a lush second-growth forest covers the once-cut-over land.

Don't let the fact that this place was once the playground of the rich and famous mislead you into thinking it's user-friendly. This is not Cannes or Vail. This is a wilderness of high hills, deep forests, rambunctious rivers, rocky cliffs, primeval lakes, rough bedrock outcroppings, and vast muskegs, all devoid of any but the faintest trails. The land is so remote and little-visited that two waterfalls — East Falls and North Falls, which drops 140 feet in an eighth of a mile — not generally listed in even the most-comprehensive guides to Michigan waterfalls, hide in the area.

"Easy" can hardly if ever be used to describe the hiking conditions here. Foot trails and paths at one time webbed the tract, but those old routes, used by the long-ago McCormicks, have become overgrown and most have all but disappeared. Except for a three-mile-long foot trail that connects County Road 607 to White Deer Lake, where the family estate once stood, hikers have to find their own way into the wilderness. The U.S. Forest Service recommends that you take a U.S. Geological Survey Quadrangle Map (available from the address below), a compass, and a survival kit for even a day trip here. It's rough going and not for the novice, but the exertion and hardship pay off in equal rewards — the chance to enjoy waterfalls few people even know exist; a rugged, unspoiled wilderness; more solitude than most hermits experience; spectacular views of the Huron Mountains to the north; and possible spottings of moose, Pine Martin and beaver.

You can backcountry camp throughout the area, but leave no trace of your passing. And before camping here, write or visit the Kenton

(Continued on p. 230)

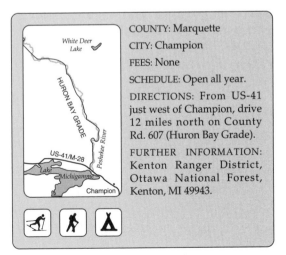

COUNTY: Marquette

CITY: Champion

FEES: None

SCHEDULE: Open all year.

DIRECTIONS: From US-41 just west of Champion, drive 12 miles north on County Rd. 607 (Huron Bay Grade).

FURTHER INFORMATION: Kenton Ranger District, Ottawa National Forest, Kenton, MI 49943.

222 ANDERSON LAKE PATHWAY

On Anderson Lake Pathway's four loops, hikers and cross country skiers can tour the heart of the Escanaba River State Forest. Ranging in length from 2 to 4.3 miles, the loops cross rolling to hilly terrain covered with beautiful stands of hardwoods and pines. Three small lakes, marshes, and scattered interpretive signs, which point out the area's natural features and history, add interest and variety to any trek.

The pathway begins at a 19-site state forest campground, which is strung out along the west shore of Anderson Lake. The quiet, secluded campground makes an excellent base from which to explore both the trail system and the few forest roads that pierce the remote and scenic state forest land. The sandy swimming beach next to the campground is a good spot to cool off weary feet, or more if you like. And there's a boat launch onto the lake, which holds out possibilities for good catches of bass, perch, pike and bluegills.

Three of the pathway's four loops are suitable for cross country skiing and progress in difficulty from beginner through advanced. Trails are groomed, and there is a plowed parking lot at the trailhead.

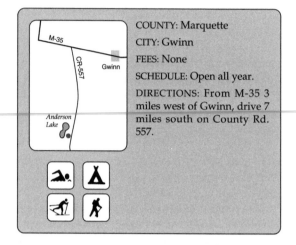

COUNTY: Marquette

CITY: Gwinn

FEES: None

SCHEDULE: Open all year.

DIRECTIONS: From M-35 3 miles west of Gwinn, drive 7 miles south on County Rd. 557.

SUGAR LOAF MOUNTAIN PATHWAY 223

From the peak of Sugar Loaf Mountain, you can take in the most spectacular and memorable view of the Lake Superior coastline to be had between the Pictured Rocks and the Keweenaw Peninsula. But you'll probably be tired when you do.

It doesn't seem like it should be much of a climb. From its starting point to the top of the mountain, Sugar Loaf Mountain Pathway gains only 315 feet in elevation. That's barely more than a football field turned on end. But to the seriously out of shape and those who generally forego stairs in favor of elevators, legs will be quivering and lungs bursting by the end of the hike.

The trail starts gradually from the parking lot, ascending through a beautiful birch and mixed evergreen forest. But just when it lulls you into thinking, "Gee, this is an easy walk," the trail hits a seemingly endless series of staircases. Sixteen separate flights of stairs, to be exact, that circle around or climb right up the face of huge rock outcroppings. Moss and ferns cover the aging bedrock, and gnarled, old trees cling for life to it.

The final flight of stairs takes you to the top of the nearly bald dome of rock and panoramic views from three separate observation plat-forms. Marquette Harbor, to the east, looks like a model train layout; the green humps to the west make it easy to imagine you're in the Appalachian Mountains; and to the north stretches the great expanse of the world's largest freshwater sea.

You can get even more exercise and stunning beauty by following the trail that heads north along the shoreline from the top of the mountain. A one-mile hike will take you to Wetmore Landing, and 1.6 miles farther, the trail ends at Little Presque Isle. The terrain is rough and hilly, and you will climb and descend many more flights of stairs.

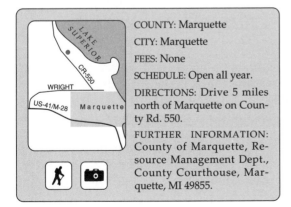

COUNTY: Marquette

CITY: Marquette

FEES: None

SCHEDULE: Open all year.

DIRECTIONS: Drive 5 miles north of Marquette on County Rd. 550.

FURTHER INFORMATION: County of Marquette, Resource Management Dept., County Courthouse, Marquette, MI 49855.

224 PRESQUE ISLE PARK

Presque Isle Park offers the most striking scenery of any city park in the Upper Peninsula, and maybe the state. From the 328-acre peninsula, which curls out into Lake Superior on the northwest side of Marquette, you get knockout views of the great lake, Marquette Harbor, and rugged shoreline at every turn of your head.

A narrow, one-way blacktop road that circles the peninsula alternates between slipping through a dense northern forest and edging the coastline, where panoramic views of the lake slow motorists to a crawl. At several turnouts you can stop and admire the scenery or leave your car for walks on numerous short trails that lead to overlooks of the peninsula's towering cliffs, sand beaches and ancient rock outcroppings. In the evening the most popular spot in the park is Sunset Point, at the north end of the peninsula, where the sun's descent into the lake rarely fails to beguile.

If you'd prefer to explore the park on foot, nature and hiking trails also eventually arrive at all points of interest, including some that motorists can't reach.

White-tail deer, former residents at a now-closed zoo, freely roam the area and can be fed by hand.

You can picnic at two different areas. One grassy site, just inside the park entrance, covers the southern tip of the peninsula and overlooks Lake Superior and the busy harbor. Tables and grills at another picnic grounds line the west shore of the park where a wide, sandy beach will have sand castle builders breaking out shovels, trowels and buckets. Don't be tempted to swim, however, because conditions are hazardous. If you want to get wet, you can jump into a swimming pool,

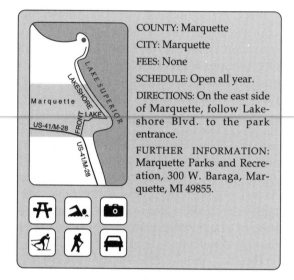

COUNTY: Marquette

CITY: Marquette

FEES: None

SCHEDULE: Open all year.

DIRECTIONS: On the east side of Marquette, follow Lakeshore Blvd. to the park entrance.

FURTHER INFORMATION: Marquette Parks and Recreation, 300 W. Baraga, Marquette, MI 49855.

Michigan's largest, a quarter mile away near the park entrance.

Other facilities here include tennis courts, a 160-foot water slide, a park store, and in the winter, extensive cross country ski trails.

Also, from a public viewing area near the giant Lake Superior and Ishpeming Railroad Ore Dock, just outside the park entrance, you can get close-up looks at huge ore boats being loaded with taconite.

ROCK RIVER CANYON WILDERNESS
(continued from p. 235)

southern edge of the preserve. The shallow, secluded lake rests in the bottom of Rock River Canyon, and sandstone walls rise sharply from the water's edge. Fishermen with the tenacity and stamina to scramble down to the water can test their skill and luck against the rainbow trout, brook trout, brown trout, coho salmon and northern pike that inhabit the picturesque lake.

Two canyons, cut more than 150 feet deep into the Upper Peninsula's sandstone bedrock, are the highlight at this remote corner of the Hiawatha National Forest.

The wilderness area surrounding the canyons was extensively logged between the late 1800s and 1930, and a second-growth forest of northern hardwoods now covers the plateau through which the Rock River and Silver Creek have sculpted deep, parallel grooves that look like they could be ruts from the giant wagon pulled by Paul Bunyan's blue ox, Babe.

The canyons themselves have remained relatively undisturbed by humans. Their floors are wet and dense with vegetation, and their walls are interrupted by caves and a beautiful waterfall. At the canyons' edges, water and weather have worked at the sandstone outcropping and fashioned openings 10 to 40 feet deep in the soft rock. In the winter, water seeps over the canyon walls, freezes, and forms spectacular ice curtains that hang in front of the caves. Waterfall lovers will want to add Rock River Falls — described as one of the most beautiful and remote in Alger County — to the list of those they have seen and photographed. The Rock River takes a 20-foot leap off a sandstone ledge and dives into a dark, quiet pool.

Getting down into the canyons over their rough walls is, at best, difficult. But an unmatched sense of personal solitude and a chance to explore the unique scenery and terrain are the payoffs for the strenuous climb.

Hiking in the rest of the wilderness area is easier, since most of the 5,343-acre preserve is relatively flat and easily walked. Old logging roads, skid trails, and two abandoned railroad grades provide access, but there are no marked trails. If you plan an extended hike or overnight backpacking trip here, you should write for a detailed topographical map, available for $3 from the Hiawatha National Forest, address below.

The area is bounded on the east and west by Forest roads 2279, 2276 and 2293, and several jumping-off places are scattered along those narrow roads. For a good taste of the area and the shortest route to an overlook of Rock River Canyon and Falls, take Rock River Road north out of Chatham and drive approximately 4 miles to USFS- 2276. Turn left (west) onto 2276 and drive approximately 3.8 miles to USFS-2293. Turn left (south) and go approximately ¾ mile to a small, marked parking area on the left side of the road. A ¾-mile-long trail leads downhill from the parking lot to the falls and canyon.

Also worth seeing is Ginpole Lake, near the

(Continued on p. 234)

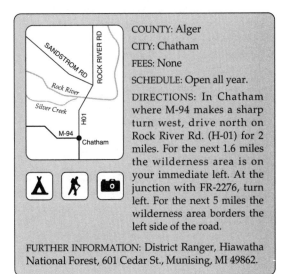

COUNTY: Alger

CITY: Chatham

FEES: None

SCHEDULE: Open all year.

DIRECTIONS: In Chatham where M-94 makes a sharp turn west, drive north on Rock River Rd. (H-01) for 2 miles. For the next 1.6 miles the wilderness area is on your immediate left. At the junction with FR-2276, turn left. For the next 5 miles the wilderness area borders the left side of the road.

FURTHER INFORMATION: District Ranger, Hiawatha National Forest, 601 Cedar St., Munising, MI 49862.

235

226 GRAND ISLAND

In 1657 Pierre Radisson, the first European to visually embrace the odd-shaped chunk of land plopped into Lake Superior just a half mile from the shoreline near present-day Munising, called Grand Island a "terrestrial paradise." Since then no one has argued with his description, and most visitors come away from a trip to the eight-mile-long, three-mile-wide island agreeing that nature has created one of the most beautiful spots in the world.

The trouble was that, until recently, few people had a chance to enjoy the second-largest of the Lake Superior islands that lie in American waters. The Cleveland Cliffs Iron Company bought the island in 1901 and used it as a private hunting preserve and corporate retreat for the next 89 years. That all changed in 1990, when the federal government purchased Grand Island for 3.4 million dollars and designated it as a National Recreation Area.

Plans for future use and the number and kinds of facilities will probably remain unclear until the next century, but you shouldn't wait to visit. Right now, you have free run of almost the entire island, and it's not going to get any prettier. The country's westernmost stand of virgin beech trees plus white pine the equal of or even larger than those at Hartwick Pines State Park grow here. One-mile-long Echo Lake, near the center of the island, is the largest beaver pond in the world. Caves and waterfalls not listed in even the best of guidebooks dot the island, and bears, coyotes, beaver, grouse, loons and an occasional eagle grace the land, water and sky.

But it's the island's spectacular 35-mile-long shoreline that will leave you with the most lasting impressions and will convince you of the rightness of the island's name. Sheer 200-foot sandstone walls have been sculpted by wind and battered by waves and ice into a scenic marvel that rivals the world-renowned Pictured Rocks National Lakeshore, just across Munising Bay. The park service is currently developing a lakeshore trail, that will allow full exploration of the unusual scenery, and other footpaths already lace the island's interior.

You can camp anywhere on public land (18 summer cottages and two lighthouse remain in private hands), but be warned that in May and June black flies can make life miserable.

Grand Island's history is as fascinating as its scenery. The island stumps geologists. They can explain the formation and existence of all the world's islands except this one. Maybe the Indian legend is right. Chippewas who lived here believed that the Great Spirit,

COUNTY: Alger

CITY: Munising

FEES: Fare for a Pictured Rocks Cruises boat trip to and from the island is $7 round trip.

SCHEDULE: The island is open all year. Pictured Rocks Cruises makes two trips to the island daily in the summer. Call or write for a current schedule. Also, it may be possible to reach the island during the winter by snowmobile or possibly skis.

DIRECTIONS: To get to Pictured Rocks Cruises, in Munising from where M-28 makes a 90-degree turn, go west on M-28 ¼ mile to Elm St. Turn right, onto Elm, and go 2 blocks.

FURTHER INFORMATION: Hiawatha National Forest, Munising Ranger District, 400 E. Munising Ave., Munising, MI 49862.

Pictured Rocks Cruises, P.O. Box 355, Munising, MI 49862; (906) 387-2379.

BRUNO'S RUN HIKING TRAIL 227

Winding through a maze of picturesque lakes scattered across the heart of Hiawatha National Forest, the 7.5-mile-long Bruno's Run Hiking Trial offers hikers and backpackers anywhere from a challenging one-day hike to a leisurely two- or three-day trek amid striking landscape.

Though it can be done, most hikers have trouble maintaining a fast enough pace to close the circle in a single day. It's not that the walking is difficult, but rather there is just too much natural beauty to hurry past. The pathway touches nine different lakes and crosses several sparkling streams, and its southern section runs over low foothills dotted with scenic overlooks. Between Fish and Moccasin lakes, the trail follows an old logging grade and penetrates a stand of mature hemlocks so imposing they bear the name Hemlock Cathedral. And if you stay alert and move with a minimum of noise, you have excellent chances of spotting the area's abundant wildlife.

The trail passes two national forest campgrounds. Hiking clockwise from the main trailhead at Moccasin Lake, the campground at Pete's Lake is 1.3 miles down the trail. The sites at Widewater Campground are about a mile walk counterclockwise from the same trailhead. Backcountry camping is also allowed anywhere along the route.

A map, available from the National Forest's Munising Ranger District, shows the length of each stage of the trail and also the location of several access points. The easiest-reached trailhead is on the north end of the loop at Moccasin Lake next to a small picnic grounds.

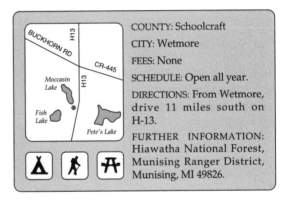

COUNTY: Schoolcraft

CITY: Wetmore

FEES: None

SCHEDULE: Open all year.

DIRECTIONS: From Wetmore, drive 11 miles south on H-13.

FURTHER INFORMATION: Hiawatha National Forest, Munising Ranger District, Munising, MI 49826.

having nothing else to do, began creating giants. But the Spirit lost interest and, instead of giving the giants life, threw one into Lake Superior. Grand Island is that giant's body, and two smaller islands to the west, Williams and Wood, are the giant's hands. The Great Spirit threw the other giants onto the mainland, where they became the hills of Munising.

The Chippewas lived on the island well into the 19th century, and Europeans had settled here by the 1840s. The first two houses built by Europeans still stand, as do two picturesque lighthouses erected in 1867. Both lighthouses are privately owned and not open to the public.

228 WHITEFISH POINT

Jutting out into Lake Superior and pointing to Canadian bluffs, Whitefish Point and its adjacent waters during spring migration is one of Michigan's best birdwatching sites. Birdwatchers from at least 14 states and four countries have recorded sightings of 230 species including Golden and Bald eagles, plus unusual birds such as the Arctic Tern, Iceland Gull, Arctic Loon, Parasitic Jaeger, Willet, Black Scoter and Surf Scoter. And Whitefish Point is undoubtedly the best place in Michigan to spot migrating birds of prey. More than 10,000 hawks, for example, are among the 15,000-20,000 birds of prey that pass through the area each spring.

Why here? Most birds do not like to cross large bodies of water on their long migration flights and will follow shorelines until land runs out and they are forced over open water. So Whitefish Point, the northernmost piece of land in the eastern Upper Peninsula, acts like a giant funnel, channeling birds to the tip, then across Whitefish Bay.

In April, winter finches and hawks lead the migrating hordes, which build steadily through May, then taper off and end in mid-June. April is the best month to spot birds of prey; loons, grebes and ducks arrive in late April and May; and songbirds make their appearance throughout May and in early June.

Since 1978 the Whitefish Point Bird Observatory, an independent non-profit group supported by the Michigan Audubon Society and other organizations, has studied the great flights of birds that have passed through here. Those studies include annual spring bird-banding projects. In 1984, for example, trained banders using mist nets captured, tagged and released 3,069 birds, including 36 Great Horned Owls, 38 Barred Owls, 11 Great Gray Owls, 25 Long-eared Owls, 1,293 Sharp-shinned Hawks and 13 Red-tailed Hawks. If you happen to be there during banding activities, you may, with permission, take pho-

tographs. The Observatory also requests that all birdwatchers at Whitefish Point turn in their sighting information to help in the group's studies.

Whitefish Point has not only sheltered birds, but also ships plying the waters of the world's largest freshwater lake. Offering protection from the great storms that sweep across Superior, the point has long been one of the lake's most important landmarks for sailors. A beacon has shown them the way since 1849.

But because countless craft have not quite made it into Whitefish Bay's sheltered waters, it is also known as the "Graveyard of the Great Lakes." The earliest known wreck is that of the schooner *Invincible*, which sank in 1816. The most recent: the legendary *Edmund Fitzgerald*, which went down in 1975 just 15 miles northwest of the point with all 29 hands aboard. A unique "iron pile" lighthouse — constructed in 1861 to replace the original beacon and now listed in the National Register of Historic Places — is the centerpiece of a museum dedicated by the Great Lakes Shipwreck Historical Society to the memory of all Great Lakes sailors.

Beachcombers and rock hounds will like the long sand-, pebble-, rock- and driftwood-strewn beach.

COUNTY: Chippewa

CITY: Paradise

FEES: None

SCHEDULE: No posted hours.

DIRECTIONS: Go 11 miles north of Paradise on Wire Rd.

FURTHER INFORMATION: Whitefish Point Bird Observatory, c/o Michigan Audubon Society, 6011 W. St. Joseph, Lansing, MI 48917 or Great Lakes Shipwreck Historical Society, Route 2, Box 279A, Sault Ste. Marie, MI 49783.

Alphabetical Listing of Areas

THE AUTHOR

Tom Powers is the Supervisor of Services to Adults and Outreach at the Flint Public Library. He has authored four previous books: the original *Natural Michigan, Michigan State and National Parks: A Complete Guide, More Natural Michigan,* and *Michigan In Quotes.*

When not at the library or researching and writing about the Great Lakes area, Tom can usually be found dividing his time among reading, birdwatching, traveling and cooking.

Barbara, his wife of 30 years; his two children and their spouses; and his three grandchildren bring constant joy to his life.